T0199536

A Moving Subject

Focus Animation

Series Editor:

Giannalberto Bendazzi

The **Focus Animation Series** aims to provide unique, accessible content that may not otherwise be published. We allow researchers, academics, and professionals the ability to quickly publish high impact, current literature in the field of animation for a global audience.

This series is a fine complement to the existing, robust animation titles available through CRC Press/Focal Press.

Series Editor Giannalberto Bendazzi, currently an independent scholar, is a former Visiting Professor of History of Animation at the Nanyang Technological University in Singapore and a former professor at the Università degli Studi di Milano. We welcome any submissions to help grow the wonderful content we are striving to provide to the animation community: giannalbertobendazzi@gmail.com.

A Moving Subject

Giannalberto Bendazzi

CRC Press
Taylor & Francis Group
Boca Raton London New York

CRC Press is an imprint of the
Taylor & Francis Group, an **informa** business

First edition published 2021
by CRC Press
6000 Broken Sound Parkway NW, Suite 300, Boca Raton, FL 33487-2742

and by CRC Press
2 Park Square, Milton Park, Abingdon, Oxon, OX14 4RN

© 2021 Taylor & Francis Group, LLC

CRC Press is an imprint of Taylor & Francis Group, LLC

ISBN: 978-0-367-56185-7 (hbk)
ISBN: 978-0-367-56689-0 (pbk)
ISBN: 978-1-003-09897-3 (ebk)

For Ilaria

Contents

Author

A FORMER PROFESSOR AT THE Nanyang Technological University of Singapore and the Università degli Studi of Milan, Italian-born Giannalberto Bendazzi has thoroughly investigated the history of animation for more than forty years. A founding member of the Society for Animation Studies, he has authored or edited various classics in various languages and has lectured extensively on every continent. He received an honorary doctorate from Lisbon University in 2019. He is the editor of the Focus Animation series of books for CRC Press. He also is the author of the three-volume set *Animation - A World History* (CRC Press 2016).

Introduction

THE READER WILL FIND diverse essays collected in this book, and I am confident that they will not view them as disparate. The same standpoint and the same love are actually at the base of historical research like the one on the first abstract colour experiments, of a theoretical effort at defining the medium, of a reasoning on early African animated films, and so on, from 1972 to today. In my long career in animation I have contributed a world history, a monograph on pioneer Quirino Cristiani, and an anthological monograph on master Alexandre Alexeieff. It seemed fair to me not to deprive the collected essays (otherwise unobtainable) to readers who value my work.

Introduction

CHAPTER 1

The Italians Who Invented the Drawn-on-Film Technique*

THE BROTHERS ARNALDO GINANNI Corradini (1890–1982) and Bruno Ginanni Corradini (1892–1976) were born in Ravenna, Italy, into an aristocratic (they were earls) and educated family. At a very early age, they started cultivating poetry, writing, and painting. They also took an active role in the debate between "Tradition" and "Modernism" that agitated the realms of literature, art, and music in Italy, from the turn of the century until the outbreak of World War I. Arnaldo mainly involved himself with painting, while Bruno focused more on literature.

After 1914, the brothers joined the Futurist movement, where they used pseudonyms, Arnaldo Ginna and Bruno Corra, to

---

* Originally published in *Animation Journal*, Tustin, California, Spring 1996. Updated version.

distinguish their separate identities. For convenience we will refer to them by their pseudonyms in this chapter, even though some statements were actually published under their true names.

Fascinated by the possible correspondence between sound and colour, in about 1909 the brothers created a "chromatic piano" whose keys corresponded to a parallel number of coloured light bulbs. Subsequently they carried out several experiments with what we now call direct painting on film, abstract cinema, or coloured abstract animation.

At first, they made a number of tests, including removing the projection shutter and projecting alternating frames of different colours to get an optical mixture of another colour. They then composed four films by painting directly on the surface of clear film strips to explore four different aspects of synaesthesia or correspondences between the arts. Lacking exact titles, the films can be called a "Thematic Development of a Harmony of Colours" based on a divisionist painting by Segantini (it was eighty metres long, or ten minutes running time); a "Study of Effects between Four Colours, Two Complementary Pairs"; a "Translation and Adaptation of Mendelssohn's Spring Song Intertwined with a Theme from a Chopin Waltz"; and a "Translation of Mallarmé's Poem 'Flowers' into Colours".[1] The longest of these films was more than 200 metres – around twelve minutes in projection. They subsequently "sketched" three more experiments on film strips (it is not clear whether they fully completed the films in a rough form or just made sample frames like a storyboard).

These three works explored abstract visual phenomena. One begins with a pure green screen, then a tiny red star appears in the middle, grows until the screen is all red, and then green spots burst out and reclaim the whole screen, making it all green again "for a whole minute". The second work develops a white and a yellow line moving over a solid blue background. The third shows seven cubes, each a colour of the rainbow, moving, layering, and warping against a black background. The last two films, again about eleven minutes in length, bear formal titles. *The Rainbow* is a "symphony" in which the spectrum of colours "throb", "bubble", "drown", and "explode" against a grey background. In *The Dance*, the dominant colours crimson, violet, and yellow continuously separate, unite, and "whirl upwards as the most agile pirouettes of spinning tops".

Scholars have often doubted the existence of these six (or maybe nine) films, especially because up to the present (and very likely forever) actual prints of the films have never been found. The only original source we can relate to is a chapter in a volume called *L'esilio di D'Annunzio e il "San Sebastiano"* (D'Annunzio's Exile and the "Saint Sebastian") edited by Bruno Corra and Emilio Settimelli and published in 1912 in Bologna by Libreria L. Beltrami. I will try to prove that this source is totally reliable, and thus that these films really existed, with all the theoretical and historical ramifications that this implies.

D'Annunzio's Exile and the "Saint Sebastian" is a peculiar volume, and its description is necessary to understand the significance and the assumptions of the particular chapter we will scrutinise. In fact, it is not a book in the strictest sense, but rather a "monograph" in a magazine, which Corra and Settimelli published after their literary weekly *A Defense of Art*, published in Florence for the two previous years, had failed. Their intention was to proceed, through this new format, with their line of thought that had been interrupted.

They also wanted to start a series of volumes/magazines with the collaboration of the members of their original artistic coterie (see the introduction "What Is This Publication?" pp. 7–9).[2] The language employed in the volume is journalistic, colloquial, and, at times, like that of an open letter. Corra and Settimelli are not compiling closed essays, but rather passionately pursuing a dialogue with an ideal reader that they feel close to and involved with. In Bruno Corra's chapter, "Chromatic Music", he describes in minute detail the experiments that he carried out together with his brother Arnaldo. He offers a vast array of technical details, describing both successes and failures of the various tests. At the end, he also addresses himself directly to anyone interested in these experiments, inviting them to write to him, offering him the chance to give more details.

Is this source reliable?

If it is reliable, what exactly are the correct dates for the films that it mentions?

The answer to the first question must be positive. Corra's essay presents the tone and language of a recent discovery, which he announces to friends and colleagues, inviting them all to follow this new and certain path. At one point in the essay, Corra even says where he keeps the films: in the drawer of the desk where he is writing. Furthermore, the text is supported by a variety of "technical" details that would be unknown except through direct, practical experience. Finally, he calls for other people to join in and share his experience – a call that no imposter would make, since they would run the risk of a competitor coming to inspect his studio and find out the truth – something particularly dangerous in the climate of personal and ideological conflicts such as existed at that time in Italy. Therefore, since Corra's text appears reliable, the films must have existed.

We can only deduce from reasoning when the films were made. Bruno Corra literally tells us that the first four films were painted "From last June to October". He then adds that the subsequent films were "done during the last few months". The book bears the date of 1912, without mentioning the month of publication. Does Corra refer, then, to the summer/autumn/winter of 1911 (with the book being published in the first three months of 1912)? Or does he mean the summer/autumn of 1912, with the book being published in December 1912?

Other passages from different chapters let us know that the two authors finished writing and assembling their texts during a winter; e.g., on page 14 Corra says "it has been snowing for two days" and on page 26 Corra refers to "one of my love affairs of two months ago – it was warmer then, it was autumn".

At least a few weeks would have been necessary for publication in that era. Each lead line would have been "composed" (picked up with tweezers and placed into a form), the pages would have been printed once for proofs (which had to be corrected), and eventually the pages would have been printed, folded, sewn, and bound – all by hand. It seems unlikely, then, that all this work could have been accomplished in the last days of December 1912 (which also contain family Christmas festivities). Even stronger evidence appears in the chapter "The Future Great Writer" (pp. 125–156). In the chapter, Settimelli reviews books by "young" writers, recently published, 126 titles "listed from October 1910 to December 1911, according to the *Bulletin of the National Library in Florence*" (p. 127). Since these reviews were openly biased, pertaining to the current ideological debate, it seems reasonable to assume that the author would want to express his opinion about the latest titles, so that his arguments would be relevant and up to date. Therefore, *L'esilio di D'Annunzio e il "San Sebastiano"* must have been published soon after December 1911. Otherwise, had it been December 1912, Settimelli would have selected books from summer and autumn 1912.

A final clinching piece of evidence for an early 1912 publication date comes from the chapter on Gabriele D'Annunzio, in which Corra refers to "Song for Tripoli" as something very recent (p. 36). These ten poems, inspired by the Italian–Turkish war for the conquest of Libya, were published in the leading daily newspaper *Corriere della Sera* between October 1911 and January 1912.

Thus, it seems most likely that Arnaldo Ginna and Bruno Corra produced their first four films ("Segantini", "Complementary Colours", "Mendelssohn", "Mallarmé") between June and October 1911, and their last two films, *The Rainbow* and *The Dance*, would have been finished a few months later. The brothers painted all these films directly on celluloid film strips (after the emulsion had been removed) using a special ink/paint used to tint photographs and slides.

The most important ramifications to arise from our study of Corra's text come from the dating of the films of Ginna and Corra.

We now know that an abstract cinema was born at almost the same time as abstract painting, since Wassily Kandinsky's first experiments with abstracting landscapes began in his water-colours around 1910. Therefore, we must overturn what has been considered common knowledge: that abstract cinema had started (around 1921) as an imitation and derivation of abstract painting – that painting, the "higher" form of art, had opened the way and inspired the "lower" art of cinema. In fact, abstract cinema was born from its own roots independent of painting. It pursued and accomplished the aspiration for a synaesthesia between sound and colour that had been prefigured in the eighteenth century by the French scientist Father Louis-Bertrand Castel (who built an ocular harpsichord) and carried on by various artists and scholars in the nineteenth and early twentieth centuries – perhaps the most famous example being the Russian composer Aleksandr Skriabin, whose "Prometheus" symphony, with colour projections written into the score, dates from 1910, the same year as Ginna and Corra's experiments with the chromatic piano and probably their first film tests.[3]

It is also important to remark that in Ginna and Corra's films we are dealing precisely with animation cinema, the same type that decades later would be produced by Len Lye and Norman McLaren. Corra tells us that he and his brother understood that the results could have been satisfying only if the film was divided into "bars", that is, by considering and painting the effect of the movement frame by frame. Finally, it is worth quoting the passage in which Corra tells us that he has tried to

> introduce into the sonata of colours something that could correspond to the accompaniment, which is so distinct in classical music. We prepared seven bulbs, each with one colour of the spectrum. By lighting one or

the other according to piano, while the symphony was playing on the screen, we should have had the creation of *colour environments.* [italics in original Italian]

While this experiment failed on technological grounds, in that the ambient colours bled and mixed with the colours projected on the screen, this experiment still anticipates various genres of modern-day performances, beginning with Jordan Belson's Vortex Concerts in the 1950s, and including "expanded cinema" and "light shows".

In terms of the concrete history of cinema, or rather of animation, the experiments of Ginna and Corra had no genuine influence. Screenings of their films seem to have remained confined to their home, and perhaps the only spectators were the filmmakers themselves. Nor is there any evidence that later filmmakers such as Ruttmann, Lye, or McLaren knew about Corra's article "Chromatic Music". Therefore, it is still fair to say, once again, that the filmmaker who actually inaugurated the "genre" of film-directly- painted-on-filmstock was the New Zealand artist Len Lye, whose *A Colour Box* (1935) has been widely viewed, debated, and imitated (especially by Norman McLaren, to whom we owe the vast diffusion of this technique, still present and vibrating to this day). But we still must not underestimate the almost prophetic importance held by the experiments of the Ginanni Corradini brothers, as well as the technical and theoretical remarks expressed by Bruno Corra in his writings.

For closer study, the text of Corra's 1912 chapter "Chromatic Music" is published in this book (see Chapter 2). It is interesting to note that in 1916 Ginna shot and edited the live-action experimental film *Vita Futurista* (Futurist Life), the only official film of the Futurist Movement. The "Chromatic Music" films were not his only cinematic achievement; however, *Vita Futurista* also seems lost, except for several still photos. The footnotes contain a number of books that are useful for further consideration of

these two artists, concerning their participation in Futurism and
their subsequent painting and literary careers.

NOTES

1. The canvas by the Lombard painter Giovanni Segantini (1858–1899) is probably
"Ebbrezza di sole" (Intoxicated by the sun), a girl lying in a field, painted several
times around 1885, with dazzling spangles of colour in the meadow flowers – though
it might also have been "Ragazza che fa la calza al sole" (Girl knitting in the sun-
light, 1888), in which the girl sits in a field with farm animals, a fence and buildings
behind her.

The moody, atmospheric Symbolist poem of Stéphane Mallarmé (1842–1898), in
elegant rhymed French verse, gives many colour and action cues:

THE FLOWERS

From golden showers of the ancient skies,
On the first day, and the eternal snow of stars,
You once unfastened giant calyxes
For the young earth still innocent of scars:
Young gladioli with the necks of swans,
Laurels divine, of exiled souls the dream,
Vermilion as the modesty of dawns
Trod by the footsteps of the seraphim;
The hyacinth, the myrtle gleaming bright,
And, like the flesh of woman, the cruel rose,
Hérodiade blooming in the garden light,
She that from wild and radiant blood arose!
And made the sobbing whiteness of the lily
That skims a sea of sighs, and as it wends
Through the blue incense of horizons, palely
Toward the weeping moon in dreams ascends!
Hosanna on the lute and in the censers,
Lady, and of our purgatorial groves!
Through heavenly evenings let the echoes answer,
Sparkling haloes, glances of rapturous love!
Mother, who in your strong and righteous bosom,
Formed calyxes balancing the future flask,
Capacious flowers with the deadly balsam
For the weary poet withering on the husk.

(TRANSLATION BY HENRY WEINFIELD)

2. The Table of Contents includes: (1) "La dedica al … Silenzio" (Dedication to …
Silence), anonymous, but by both authors; (2) "Che cosa è questa pubblicazione"
(What Is This Publication?), anonymous, but by both authors; (3) "Il pastore,
il gregge e la zampogna" (The Shepherd, the Flock and the Bagpipe), by Bruno

Ginanni Corradini; (4) "L'esilio di D'Annunzio e il *San Sebastiano*" (The Exile of Gabriele D'Annunzio and *Saint Sebastian*), by Emilio Settimelli; (5) "*La Difesa dell'Arte* e il suo cenacolo" (*The Defense of Art* and its coterie), by Emilio Settimelli; (6) "*Chantecler*-interpretazione lirica" (Chanticleer-Lyrical Interpretation), by Bruno Ginanni Corradini; "Il futuro grande scrittore" (The Future Great Writer), by Emilio Settimelli; "Musica cromatica" (Chromatic Music), by Bruno Ginanni Corradini; (9) "Per un giudizio della *Difesa dell'Arte*" (For a Judgement of *In Defense of Art*), anonymous, but by both authors. These are, in part, literary controversies: in favour of Carducci, against D'Annunzio and the cultural establishment, while, on the other hand, espousing a radical modernist renewal with calls for proposals and new texts. The themes continue to be those that were typical of the literary magazines at the beginning of the twentieth century in Italy, promoted by very young elites of intellectuals: criticisms and praises, battles between cultural coteries, attacks against the "Old", aggressive displays of new proposals.

3. On the origins of Ginna and Corra's colour experimentation in ideal, mystical philosophy, Giovanni Lista wrote:

> The cultural choices of romantic symbolism dominate these experiments. The poetry that is applied in painting follows the method enunciated by Rudolf Steiner, who proposes that the weakness of sensory data be overcome in order to directly reach the screen of the consciousness' condensation ... The so-called Occult [hidden] Sciences (theosophy, spiritualism, metaphysics, etc.) constitute the prime component in the cultural background of Ginna ... The second component is to be found in the Wagnerian and proto-expressionist culture. The abstract short films confirm in this sense what I wrote a few years back in reference to Ricciotto Canudo: All the early theoreticians and experimenters of cinema as an art have been Wagnerians, for they identified within the filmic image the fluidity and immateriality of music. ("Ginna e il Cinema Futurista" [Ginna and Futurist Cinema], *Il Lettore di Provincia* [Longo, Ravenna, September 1987], 17–28)

There is no evidence that the abstract films of Ginna and Corra were ever shown in public, not even during the many Futurist manifestations of the following years when the brothers became active members of the movement. Indeed, their kind of experiment with pure abstraction clashed with the official Futurist ideology advocated and rigidly applied, especially by Umberto Boccioni, who wanted the Futurist artists to represent motion but only through static tableaux. The *Manifesto Tecnico della Pittura Futurista* (Technical Manifesto of Futurist Painting), signed by Boccioni, Carrà, Russolo, Balla, and Severini, published 11 April 1910, says, "We want the dynamic sensation manifested as such ... Because of the persistence of images on the retina, things in motion multiply, deform chasing one another as vibrations in space they cross. So, a running horse does not have four legs: it has 20 legs".

CHAPTER 2

Chromatic Music by Bruno Ginanni Corradini (1912)*†

I ONLY WANT TO SET forth some facts. Nothing else. So, don't expect any attempt at elegance in my writing.

Should I succeed in making myself clearly understood, then I shall have achieved my purpose. I am writing this essay only to prepare the audience that will devote itself to fully appreciating and calmly judging the symphonies of colour which we will perform, I hope quite soon, before crowds in theatres. I wrote "we", meaning my brother and me, for it is only thanks to my brother, who is an accomplished painter, that the practical translation of this art vision (to which I can only offer my theoretical and intuitive contribution) can be made possible.

---

* Originally published in *Animation Journal*, Tustin, California, Spring 1995. Updated version.
† First published in Italian as "Musica cromatica", a segment of *L'esilio di D'Annunzio e il "San Sebastiano"*, Bologna, Italy: Beltrami, 1912.

At the moment, the art of colours that is being practised can only be explained through an analogy with painting. The painting is a "medley" of colours that are situated in such reciprocal patterns as to represent an idea. (Please note that I have defined the art of painting as an art of colours; I am not taking into consideration the other lineage that derives from another art form, for I do not want to digress excessively.)

It is possible to create a new and more rudimentary painting art form, by applying to the canvas masses of colours arranged in a harmonious pattern one with another, so as to please the eye without them having to represent a specific image. This would correspond to what we call "harmony" in music, so we can call this "chromatic harmony". These two art forms, chromatic harmony and painting, are spatial. Yet music tells us that something completely different exists, i.e., the medley of sounds that follow one another in time, the motif, the theme. So, by analogy, the Art of Colours can create a temporal form of art that will be a medley of chromatic tones offered successively to the eye, a motif of colours, a chromatic theme.

Some examples will surely help: a flower bed, a children's kaleidoscope, women's fashionable dresses, the stained-glass windows of a church – these are all chromatic harmonies. The moiré patterns on an iridescent shot silk, some types of fireworks, meadows blowing in the wind, a kaleidoscope rotating continually and gradually, the sea – all these provide examples of chromatic motifs.

In his novel *Le Lys dans la vallée* (*Lily of the Valley*, 1835), Honoré de Balzac has described extensively the art of gathering flowers. The beauty of nature is made up of motifs and harmonies; just glance around and you will see a harmony, walk and you will witness a symphony.

Almost always, in nature, harmonies and symphonies are combined in colour and shape – for example, those storms that offer frightening and powerful symphonies of clouds. Walking through a crowd means plunging into a beautiful symphony of colours, shapes, sounds, of tactile and muscular feelings, of balances, etc.

The taste for colour, which appeared strongly for the first time in the paintings of the Venetian artists (Giorgione, Titian, Tintoretto, Veronese, Tiepolo) has gloriously established itself in all European paintings of these past years. This tendency to give the art elements – colours, forms, lines, sounds, words – an expressive meaning rather than a representative one, is seen not only in the domain of painting (through Expressionism and the taste for landscapes – forms that aim at the music of colours), but it is also to be found in literature (through Symbolism), in music (through the innovations of Strauss, Debussy, Dukas, Ravel), and in architecture (through the Art Nouveau, with its indefinite, undulating, misty styles). The chromatic harmony is most suitable when the artist is trying to create an environment, especially in decorative painting. Recall the latest decorative endeavours of Klimt. [Corradini discusses written theoretical sources and musical forms for two more pages, omitted here.] So, two years ago, after having established the theory of Chromatic Music in all its details, we decided to make a serious attempt at producing a music of colours. We started thinking about the equipment that probably did not exist and would have to be designed by us in order to perform our ideas. We tried new paths, mainly guided by our intuition, although the fear of making mistakes always brought us to rely on the physics of light and sound, through the works of Tyndall and many others. Naturally, we applied the laws of parallelism between the arts, which we had already determined. For two months, we each studied separately without telling each other our results. Then we compared, discussed and combined our observations together. We agreed on the idea (which we had already formed before our studies of the laws of physics) to stick with music, and to transpose the tempered musical scale precisely onto the field of colours.

On the other hand, we knew that the chromatic scale has only one octave, and that the eye, unlike the ear, does not possess a *resolving power* (although, as I think about it now, I have some reservations about that). Thus, it became clear to us that it was necessary to apply a subdivision of the solar spectrum, even though this would be artificial and arbitrary, since the effect derives mainly from the *relationship* among the colours that make an impression on the retina. So, for each colour, we chose four gradations at equal distances within their spectrum – four reds, four greens, four violets, etc. In this way we managed to lay out the seven colours in four octaves: the final violet of the first octave was followed by the first red of the second octave, and so forth. In order to translate all this into practical terms, naturally, we used a set of twenty-eight coloured electric bulbs that corresponded to the twenty-eight keys on our keyboard. Each bulb was surrounded by a conical reflector-shade. In our first experiments, we tried using the light directly, but later on, we placed a pane of frosted glass in front of each light. The keyboard was just like a regular piano keyboard (except three octaves shorter). If you played an octave, for instance, two colours blended, just as two simultaneous sounds blend on the piano.

When we tested this chromatic piano, the results were so good that we thought, at first, we had finally solved the problem. We played with chromatic combinations of all sorts, composed some sonatinas in colours – nocturnes in violet and mattinatas in green – and we "translated", with some necessary modifications, a Venetian Barcarole by Mendelssohn, a Rondo by Chopin, and a Sonata by Mozart. But eventually, after three months of experiments, we had to admit that with the limited means of this chromatic piano, no further progress was possible. We could obtain pleasing effects that nevertheless failed to totally capture and hold one's attention. We had only twenty-eight tones available, and the blending did not work well. The sources of light were not strong enough; if we used more powerful lights, then the intense heat would cause them to lose colour within a few days, and then we had to colour them again with the exact shade – an enormous waste of time. It was clear to us that in order to obtain those impressive orchestral effects that can convince crowds, we would have to use an amazingly intense light – that would be the only way to leave the restricted field of scientific experimentation and enter directly the realm of performance practice.

We thought about the movie camera since. With slight changes, this instrument would be capable of offering excellent results. As a source of high-intensity light, it gave the best we could want. Furthermore, it also allowed us to resolve the other problem with blending colours, since instead of needing hundreds of separate colours, we could take advantage of the persistence of vision process to mix several quick colours into any particular hue on the retina. All we needed was to have the component colours pass in front of the lens in less than one tenth of a second. In this way, with a simple cinematic apparatus, with small equipment, we could obtain the numerous and powerful effects of the great musical orchestras, the true chromatic symphony.

But this was all on a theoretical level. In reality, we bought a camera and several hundred metres of film. We then removed the emulsion from the film and painted on the clear film strip, trying out a few tests. As is often the case, what we planned to do partially worked out and partially failed. In order to obtain a harmonious, gradual and uniform pattern of chromatic themes, we removed the rotating shutter and the claw action, but unfortunately this caused the experiment to fail: instead of obtaining the wonderful harmony of blended colours that we expected, the result on screen was an incomprehensible chaos of colours. Only later did we understand why. Then we put back in place everything we had removed, and we decided to consider the film that was to be painted as being divided into bars. Each bar was of the same length as the space covered by four sprocket holes, which, at least on Pathé film, corresponds to one complete rotation of the shutter, one projected image. We painted another piece of film accordingly and tested it out in projection. The blending of colours (which was our primary concern) was very successful, but the overall effect was less satisfying. We had, however, already understood that not much could be expected in this sense until we could develop the skill – which can only come with years of experience – of mentally picturing the whole gradual development of a motif as it will be projected on the screen, even while it is being slowly laid down with a brush on the celluloid. Such skill involves the ability to mentally blend several colours into one, and, at the same time, break down one colour into its components.

At this point, when we felt our experiments were progressing positively and stably, we found it necessary to pause and concentrate on all possible improvements to the equipment.

The projector basically remained the same, except that instead of the arc lamp that we had used up until then, we installed another arc lamp with three times as much power. We then tried different types of screens: a simple white cloth, a white cloth drenched with glycerine, an aluminium foil surface, a cloth covered with a paste which gave almost phosphorescent reflections, an almost cubic tent of very thin gauze through which the beam of light could penetrate and should have produced the effect of a swarm of white smoke. But eventually we went back to the cloth which we simply stretched on a wall. We removed all the furniture, covered the whole room in white – walls, floors, and ceiling – and during all the performances we wore white clothes. Up to the present day, we have never obtained better results, and we have continued working in our white room, which turned out to be very functional.

The results of this period of experiments, which ran from last June to October, consists of four little reels of film, of which only one is longer than 200 metres; they are right here in my drawer, packed in their boxes, *labelled*, ready for the future museum (please forgive what may sound like arrogance, but is only a father's love for these dear children, which please me so much with their little mugs dirty from the rainbow, and with their little air of mystery). The first reel contains the thematic development of a harmony of colours, taken from one of Segantini's paintings – the one in which we see houses in the background and in the foreground a woman lying down in a meadow. The grass of the meadow, all intermixed with little flowers, is rendered through the pointillist technique with a bustling explosion of varied colours; the grass is alive, everything vibrates, seems covered with a breath of harmony, you can see the creative power of Spring materialise in the lively spurts of lights – this chromatic harmony so impressed us that we developed it thoroughly in 180 metres of film. The second reel is a study of the effects between four colours, two pairs of complementary ones: red/green and blue/yellow. The third reel is a translation and arrangement of Mendelssohn's "Spring Song" intertwined with a theme taken from a waltz by Chopin. The fourth reel, perhaps the most interesting, is a translation into colours of the famous, marvellous poem of Stéphane Mallarmé, "Flowers".

Meanwhile, our artistic tools were improved, but, as every artist knows, these tools still often betrayed us. Obviously, we could not paint with oils the way you can on canvas. At first, we tried alcohol-based paints that were easy to apply and would dry almost immediately – but they also lost their colour quickly.

Then we tried the liquid colours sold by Lafranc, which are used for tinting slides, and we obtained good results from them. We also tried aniline solutions, tested new formulas from a wide range of books, and attempted mixing together different kinds of colours. Still to this day, the best effects have been obtained by simply modifying and revising the colours meant for tinting slides; we are still researching in this direction, hoping to develop a colour that, compared to the existing ones, offers more intensity and transparency. We have not yet, for example, succeeded in obtaining quite intense and transparent gold and silver colours, which should produce very powerful sensations.

We wanted to introduce into the sonata of colours something that would correspond to the accompaniment, which is so distinct in classical music. We prepared seven bulbs, each with one colour of the spectrum, mounted on a base that could be carried around the room. By lighting one or the other according to plan, while the symphony was playing on the screen, we should have had the creation of *colour environments,* which, in order to accompany the general tuning of the themes that were developing, would in some way lead the spectator into a proximity of feeling. When we first tried it, however, the light from the bulbs dispersed with similar tones to the film projection, causing a change in the effect of the symphony, making it excessively uniform, and only occasionally creating some pleasantly bizarre chromatic medley. Now, I will repeat, we are preparing to carry out this experiment again under new conditions which, we hope, will allow us not only to solve this problem but also to gain new insight and thus allow us to obtain a wider variety of effect and more space to freely move about.

I have nothing else to say on this topic. We still have not found more powerful means of execution. It goes without saying, though, that we have no intention of stopping at this point. Before performing in front of an audience, however, we will need to attain a higher degree of formal refinement.

All that remains to be said concerns the work we have done these last months, during which we have slightly neglected the music of colours because we were waiting for a type of clear film that we had long sought in vain, but now the Lumiere company had promised to give us some. We also both focused some on our respective art forms of painting and literature.

Before describing the latest successful symphonies of colours (since, for the moment, nothing more can be done), I will try to give the reader an idea, albeit a vague one, of the effects of a medley of colours extended in time: I will show the reader a few sketches (that are right here in front of me) from a film we have been planning for a long time, one that will precede our public performances, and will be accompanied by suitable explanations. It will contain approximately fifteen extremely simple chromatic motifs, lasting about one minute each, each one separate from the next. These will help the audience see the legitimacy of chromatic music, understand how it works, and, eventually, put the spectator in a position to appreciate the symphonies of colour that will at first be simple and then become gradually more complex. I am now looking at three chromatic themes sketched on celluloid strips: the first is as simple as you can imagine, with only two complementary colours, red and green; at first the whole screen is green, then a little red star with six points appears in the middle, rotating and vibrating its points like tentacles; then the star enlarges, enlarges, enlarges until it occupies the whole screen, the whole screen is red; then unexpectedly across the whole illuminated surface appears a nervous outbreak of green points that enlarge, enlarge, enlarge until they devour all the red, until finally the whole screen is green, which lasts one minute. The second chromatic theme is in three colours: sky blue, white, and yellow. On a blue field, two lines, one yellow and the other white, move and bend toward each other; they separate, curl up, then approach each other undulating until they intertwine with each other. This is an example of a linear theme as well as a theme of colours. The third theme involves all seven colours of the solar spectrum in the shape of small cubes, which at the beginning are arranged in a horizontal line on the lower part of the screen, against a black background; they move in jerky little spasms, they unite in groups, they crash against each other, break to pieces that quickly fly back together again, they shrink and expand, they arrange themselves in horizontal rows and vertical columns, they enter inside each other, they warp, etc.

And now all that remains for me is to bring the reader up to date with our latest experiments. These are two films of about 200 metres. The first is *The Rainbow,* and the colours of the rainbow constitute the dominant theme, which appears from time to time in different forms, and always more intensely until eventually it explodes with dazzling violence. At the beginning the screen is grey, then bit by bit on this grey background manifests, like the lightest of agitations, iridescent throbbing that seems to climb from the depth of the grey, like bubbles in a spring that rise to the surface, burst and disappear. The whole symphony is based upon this contrasting effect between the cloudy grey of the background and the rainbow, clashing one against the other: the fight escalates, the colour spectrum drowning in ever blacker tornados which whirl from the back towards the foreground; the rainbow struggles, manages to wriggle free, gleams, then disappears again and returns more violently to attack the edges of the screen, until in an unexpected dusty collapse all the grey crumbles, and the rainbow triumphs in a whirl of pinwheels, which in their turn finally disappear, buried under an avalanche of colours.

The second film is *The Dance*. The dominant colours, crimson, violet, and yellow, continually reunite with each other, separate and whirl upwards as the most agile pirouettes of spinning tops.

I have finished. There is no need for me to continue writing, for I can only offer a very remote idea of the actual effects of the colours. Each person has to imagine it for himself.

All that can be done is to open the way, and I think I have accomplished this a little.

Is there anybody in Italy who wants to be seriously involved in these things? If so, please write to me, and I will be extremely glad to tell you everything (and it is a lot) I did not have a chance to write here – and that could make your own work easier.

CHAPTER 3

The First Italian Animated Feature Film and Its Producer*

H ISTORIANS OF ITALIAN CINEMA have always ignored *La rosa di Bagdad* (1949), despite its many important claims. This original production is the first animated feature made in Italy. It can also be noted to be the first Italian colour feature-length film, appearing three years before the live-action feature *Totò a colori* (directed by Steno, using the Ferraniacolor process), which is generally cited by scholars in this regard.[1] Additionally, the film represents a significant transition between a very rudimentary protohistory of Italy's animated cinema and its true artistic and industrial birth.

---

* Originally published in *Animation Journal*, Tustin, California, Spring 1995. Updated version.

La rosa was directed by Anton Gino Domeneghini (Darfo, Brescia, 30 April 1897–Milan, 6 November 1966) – journalist, writer, entrepreneur, advertising agent. It is especially fitting to highlight the work of Domeneghini because he was probably the one and only producer-entrepreneur in the world of Italian animation: a man who could have been the right catalyst, the "Italian Disney" for the whole industry, had he had more luck.

The film's first public screening was at the Venice Film Festival in the summer of 1949, where it won the Grand Prix in the "Films for Youth" class. On the same occasion, the animated *I fratelli Dinamite* (*Dynamite Brothers*, 1949), by Nino Pagot, was shown in the "Fiction Film" category. It was then that the dispute began (never to end) over which should be considered the first animated feature – and the first colour feature (live action *or* animated) – made in Italy.[2] This essay addresses many of these issues. It is based on interviews and documents provided to the author by the following people: the late Angelo Bioletto, *La rosa*'s character designer; the late Libico Maraja, the film's background artist; the late Raffaella Domizio Domeneghini, the producer's widow; the late Fiorella Domeneghini, the producer's daughter; the late Guido Zamperoni, the film's chief animator; the late Gianfranco Barenghi and the late Luigi Landenna, two of the film's animators; and the late Walter Alberti, director of the Cineteca Italiana of Milan.

As a young man, after having fought with the rank of artillery lieutenant during World War I, Domeneghini took part in the Fiume enterprise, by the side of Gabriele D'Annunzio, the famous poet and adventurer, and returned with a permanently disabled leg and a medal of valour. Politically speaking, Domeneghini was a supporter of the Nationalist Association, which merged with the Fascist party in March 1923 (five months after the "March to Rome", which brought Benito Mussolini to power).[3]

Domeneghini was a loyal Fascist and also held some political appointment but, with characteristic contradiction, he used his position in the right-wing party for helping the poor. His contradictions went much further: he was also a Mason, which was not allowed of Fascists, and a faithful Catholic, which was not allowed of Masons.

Early in his career, Domeneghini was employed in the field of publishing. For three years, he was the chief editor of the daily *La provincia di Brescia* (*The Province of Brescia*). He then founded and edited the monthly *La rinascita* (*The Rebirth*) and the weekly *Il giornale del Garda* (*The Journal of Garda Lake Area*). For many years, he was also the Vittoriale press office chief, again under D'Annunzio's orders. In this position, through the Sonzogno publishing house, he published the *Italians' Vittoriale* volume.

In the advertising world, Domeneghini made his debut in 1927, by collaborating with the American agency Erwin Wasey & Co. In 1929, he founded IMA (an acronym for Idea – Method – Art), an advertising organisation that was of great importance between the 1930s and the 1960s, until its breakup after Domeneghini's death. To give some idea of IMA's importance, in Italy the company launched Coca-Cola, Christian Dior products, Coty perfumes, Bosch refrigerators, BP petrol, Gillette razor blades, Bulova watches, and Hoechst colours.

When World War II started (for Italy, it was on 10 June 1940), advertising in the country became virtually nonexistent.

Domeneghini wanted to keep his staff of artists and collaborators together, so he embarked – more or less on impulse – on the production of a feature film: *La rosa di Bagdad*. The film was based on his own story idea, which he constantly modified with the help of scriptwriters Ernesto D'Angelo and Lucio De Caro. The crew literally began from nothing, due to the fact that none of them had experience in the field; still, they threw themselves, body and soul, into the enterprise.

For the production, Domeneghini hired the stage designers of the Teatro alla Scala, Nicola Benois (who very soon retired) and Mario Zampini; the musician Riccardo Pick Mangiagalli; the animator Gustavo Petronio (one of the few working in Italy at the time);[4] the executive producer Federico Pedrocchi;[5] the caricaturist Angelo Bioletto; and the illustrator Libico Maraja. At its largest, his staff numbered forty-seven animators and assistant animators, twenty-five in-betweeners, forty-four inkers and painters, and five background artists, in addition to technicians, general workers, and administrative assistants.

In Italy, cinema was at that time a small but strong industrial force. In the year 1940, eighty-three (live-action) feature films were produced, and the output continued at about the same pace during the war, with the exception of 1944, when the country itself was a theatre of combat and film production decreased considerably. By 1949, when Domeneghini's film was eventually released, the industry's output was just a bit larger, consisting of ninety feature films.

Animation, on the other hand, was still in its infancy when Domeneghini undertook the production of *La rosa*. Many people had tried to make cartoon films, but generally the results were amateurish, and the filmmakers gave up after one or two unsuccessful shorts. The only lasting work was done by Luigi Liberio Pensuti, who had made a number of educational films in Rome since 1928; however, technically and stylistically, his work was of little importance.

It is worth noting that, in this era of dictatorship, cinema was not actually used as a means of propaganda: the openly "Fascist" films were three or four in twenty years. Italian films for children (actually, there were few of them; children's true heroes were America's Mickey Mouse, and Laurel and Hardy) and children's literature were less influenced by true Fascist values than by the rhetoric of contemporary education: love the country, love the family, be obedient, be a good student, and be a good Catholic. This was in its own way oppressive propaganda, but it was also the same kind of education that every other European nation was giving to its young citizens.

Due to the 1943 bombings over Milan, Domeneghini and his staff (together with their families) had to move to the little village of Bornato, near Brescia. Here the production went on in two big villas, nonstop until the group broke up at the end of the war. At that time, Domeneghini was arrested by the partisans because of his Fascist past, but after a few months he was declared innocent and released. After this incident, he began working again and eventually rebuilt IMA into one of the most important advertising agencies in Italy, as it once had been.

La rosa was almost finished during the war, except that it became necessary to reshoot the entire film in Great Britain. Two cameramen by the names of Pellizzari and Manerba were sent to Anson Dyer's Stratford Abbey Films at Stroud to shoot all the scenes with Technicolor equipment, which was not available in Italy at that time. The film had already been shot with the German Agfacolor process, which was easily available even during wartime to a country allied with Germany, but a disturbing green shade had ruined the whole work. The final dubbing was done in Rome in 1949.

The plot of the film is as follows: caliph Oman, a debonair and good-natured man, reigns over Bagdad. His ministers, Zirko, Tonko, and Zizzibè, are everywhere esteemed for their knowledge (though, in fact, they are often simple and funny creatures). An ongoing problem is finding a husband for the caliph's beautiful adolescent granddaughter, Zeila. This young beauty has a crystal-clear soprano voice, which she uses to gladden her grandfather and others, accompanied by a teenage musician, Amin. A messenger is sent to call together all the princes who may seek Zeila's hand in marriage, but the wicked sheik Giafar, helped by the diabolic wizard Burk, plots to be the only suitor. Against him fight the musician Amin, backed up by the magpie Kalinà and the three ministers; unfortunately, the latter very soon are forced to give up, since drinking from the fountain of youth turns them into babies. Amin manages to escape from Burk and to find, with the help of a good fairy, the lamp of Aladdin, whose genie defeats the wicked. At the end, goodness is rewarded, and Amin marries Zeila. The film respects the rules of fairy tale, with the struggle of Amin corresponding to a "rite of passage", in which the adolescent matures, grows and therefore can become first a husband and then a king.

Although based on *One Thousand and One Arabian Nights*, the setting of *La rosa* is in a Bagdad of pure fantasy. So pure is the fantasy that one can easily detect an Italian Roman Catholic point of view in the film's "message" and in the philosophy of its characters, even if everything is set in a country full of minarets and lead by a clearly Islamic caliph. The Roman Catholic religion is evident even iconically: Amin's mother has the features of a Madonna and the old beggar looks like a protecting saint.

The pacing of the action is uneven, and, because *La rosa* was dubbed after its footage was shot, the finished picture looks a bit technically outdated. Nonetheless, it has good qualities as far as the development of the plot, the quality of the drawings, and the skilfulness of the animation. Some sequences are memorable: the dance of the charmed snakes by Amin's flute, his air battle with Burk, Zeila singing at sunset in front of an applauding crowd (a scene reflecting the influence of Italian opera), and the final fireworks. The three sages have too much in common with the Seven Dwarfs of Disney or the *Turandot* ministers Ping, Pang, and Pong; and Zeila is psychologically even weaker than Snow White. The Magpie is however a nice character with great audience appeal, and Burk is among the most wicked of the "heavies" in animation history. His personality is minimalistically delineated through his appearance as a black spot.

Domeneghini's wish was to create a moral tale, in which children could find delight as well as a lesson about good behaviour. This goal he shared with the pedagogy of his time. Domeneghini preferred sentimental scenes rather than comedy and often disagreed with his artistically strongest collaborator, Bioletto, who had an excellent comic mind. The combination of their forces causes the film to become a strange (but pleasant) cocktail of dramatic action and comic entr'actes, merged with a third element: the very beautiful sceneries of Libico Maraja, who established the story's atmosphere both psychological and narrative.[6]

It is obvious that the strongest influence on the film came from Disney's *Snow White and the Seven Dwarfs* (1937), a print of which had admittedly been studied frame by frame at the editing machine. Princess Zeila is a stand-in for the Princess Snow White, and the Three Ministers have the same comic function as the Seven Dwarfs. There is also some influence by the Fleischer brothers, given the "rubbery" animation of some of the characters. It would nevertheless be a mistake to undermine the influence of the Italian popular theatre of glove marionettes and, above all, the Italian opera.

The influence of the latter is evident in the music provided by Riccardo Pick Mangiagalli,[7] a rival of Pietro Mascagni and Umberto Giordano; even the psychology of a character is often described in music, in the purest operatic tradition. It is also evident in the actions of the characters. *La rosa* is, without a doubt, a film of drawn actors, rather than drawings in movement (something Domeneghini and his crew had learned quickly from the Disney lesson); but the performance of these characters is not like that of the cinema or stage performance. Actions are "exaggerated", "openly expressed", even "delivered", exactly as tenors and sopranos do in the opera.

According to rooted rumours, the results of the film at the box office were mediocre, and in years to come the film was always labelled a flop. The blame was laid upon bad distribution by United Artists. In actuality, though the film's distribution may have been underdeveloped, the actual box office figures show the film was not a flop at all. In the 1949–1950 season, *La rosa* earned L. 247,500 (equivalent to 2019 US$142,177, using a 2019 exchange rate), much less than the highest earner of the year, the legendary (in Italy) *Catene* (*Chains*), directed by Raffaello Matarazzo and starring Amedeo Nazzari and Yvonne Sanson, which brought in L. 1,470,000 (US$844,449). On the other hand, *La rosa*'s earnings do compare to a number of other popular films, such as *Miss Italia*, with Gina Lollobrigida and Constance Dowling (L. 189,000 or US$108,572), and *La bellezza del diavolo* (*The Devil's*

Beauty), directed by René Clair and starring Gérard Philipe and Michel Simon (L. 178,200 or US$102,368). Keep in mind that the average price of a movie ticket in Italy at the time of La rosa's release was about L. 95 or US$1.35.

As this evidence shows, La rosa actually was a good performer at the box office. What then caused the film to acquire such a bad reputation? Almost certainly, it was a miscalculation of profit and loss. During the war, production costs were high and Domeneghini had to ask for loans from friends and former customers of IMA (one of the most generous was Maurizio Heim Esquenas of Calze Fama, a stocking manufacturer). In return, Domeneghini promised to double the investor's money or even – characteristic of his flamboyant style – to triple it. Actually, the film failed to meet its economic potential and the investment balanced its costs without yielding the promised big profits.

Part of the problem was associated with international versions. La rosa was triumphantly released in London (its songs dubbed by a young Julie Andrews); it was also successfully distributed in Belgium and France; and in the Netherlands it even inspired the creation of a line of chocolates called Rosa di Bagdad. Still, dishonesty and unkept promises prevented the film from becoming truly profitable abroad.

Domeneghini's experience with filmmaking left an impression on him. In later years, he abandoned animated features, giving up on the idea of a religious animated feature with a realist style (as he preferred), Il Presepe (The Crib) or È nato Gesù (Jesus Is Born). Instead, he concentrated his efforts on his work as an advertising agent. Apart from some commercials, the only animation produced by Domeneghini in the following years was a short film, La passeggiata (The Walk), based on the poem of the same title by Gabriele D'Annunzio and the inventive sets of the painter Gerardo Carpanetti. Toward the end of his life, Domeneghini made plans for a new feature film, L'isola felice (The Happy Island), which was supposed to use the combined techniques of live action and animation, but these plans never coalesced.

The estrangement of Domeneghini from animation is witnessed (as it often happens) more by what he did not do than by what he did. It seems significant that he did not take part in the booming market for animated television commercials, which occurred when Italian television was opened up for advertising in 1957. Production in this field flourished during the last nine years of Domeneghini's life: a period during which he remained a powerful media man, still strong and full of plans, and always in a position to gather his former staff members together in a film-producing structure. His absence from this lucrative market seems to reflect an unfortunate, self-imposed distancing from the field of animation.

In the final analysis, it is true that *La rosa* had very little effect on the future of Italian animation; in fact, it seems that a great amount of potential was lost following its production. Two of the film's most talented contributors, Bioletto and Maraja, left the field, soon followed by other members of the crew who went on to work in graphics, comic strips, and illustration. In the years to come, publicist Gianfranco Barenghi was about the only member of the production team listed on the film's credits to continue working in the animation industry.

Stylistically, the film also seems to have had little impact, since no other animated features based on fairy tales were made in Italy.

Certainly, *La rosa* did not draw the attention of critics, even if the press reported quite a lot about Domeneghini's project. Discussions of the film generally consisted of banalities about the abstract concept of its tale, the abstract idea of films for youth, and the daring plan of a Italian man to compete with Disney. The highbrow critics (mainly essayists) did not take part in this discussion at all. They had no interest in animated films, works for children and teenagers, or anything outside the central political-aesthetic debate at that time, which centred on Neorealism and its possible end.

The presence of an authentic entrepreneur like Domeneghini could have been crucial in the development of the Italian animation industry. Instead, its development was controlled by filmmakers who became producers (such as Nino Pagot, Bruno Bozzetto, and Roberto Gavioli) or shrewd opportunists of the market (such as Ezio Gagliardo, for his Rome-based Corona Cinematografica). One cannot find the presence of authentic entrepreneurs who dared to embark on a risky enterprise, starting from nothing, and without giving up in the face of great difficulty. Domeneghini had been clever enough to understand that one had to profit from the war to carry on production. He also managed to turn on the machine of marketing, at that time practically unknown in Italy, turning *La rosa di Bagdad* into a book (published by Baldini & Castoldi, Milan; then by Mondadori, Milan), a line of children's composition books, and a comic book. What he lacked, compared with a figure like Walt Disney, was that uncommon craze for his own enterprise and the egocentrism: he coordinated a bunch of artists he liked and respected, holding them only loosely to his own ideas, while the "Wizard of Burbank" selected and company-trained a crew of artists who would conform to his own vision of art and storytelling.

Furthermore, he was disadvantaged by having a studio in Milan, since the whole of the Italian film industry was based in Rome, where the political power stayed. The structure of the Italian cinema industry, tied to government intervention, automatically marginalised any non-Roman productions.

As far as the history of Italian animated film is concerned, it seems that Domeneghini was the right man at the wrong time.

Both Domeneghini and the Pagot brothers were outsiders, and yet they were agile enough to precede the heavy industrial machine of the Italian cinema in the rush to colour – though theirs were one-shot exploits. Too few were their followers for the establishment of a real animation industry, too little was the market until television advertising boomed in the late 1950s.

Thus, apart from the films of Disney in America, the animated feature remained a rarity. Of course, there were the silhouettes of Lotte Reiniger (*Die Abenteuer des Prinzen Achmed* [*The Adventures of Prince Achmed*], 1926) and some puppet films (e.g., the Soviet *Novy Gulliver*, by Aleksandr Ptuško, 1935), but very few had preceded the Italians with cel- and colour-animated features: the Barcelonese with *Garbancito de la Mancha* (1945, directed by Arturo Moreno) and *Alegres Vacaciones* (*Merry Holidays*, 1948, directed by Moreno); the Danes with *Fyrtøjet* (*The Magic Lighter*, 1946, directed by Svend Methling,)); the Soviets with *The Humpbacked Colt* (1947, directed by Aleksandra Snezhko-Blotskaya and Ivan Ivanov-Vano); and a few more. Countries with a solid cinematographic tradition and strong resources, like France, Great Britain, and Germany, would begin creating animated features in later years. In Italy, one must wait until 1965 to see a film like that: *West and Soda*, directed by Bruno Bozzetto. In the meantime, many things had changed.

BACKGROUND: LIBICO MARAJA

Libico Maraja (Bellinzona, Switzerland, 15 April 1912–Montorfano, Como, 30 December 1983) was highly appreciated for his painting, drawing, and, above all, illustrating. His experience as a background artist for *La rosa di Bagdad* was his only foray into film, but it was nonetheless a distinguished and very important venture: as a matter of fact, one could say that with this work he became the forerunner of a group of artists (Giovanni Mulazzani, Giancarlo Cereda, and Antonio Dall'Osso, to name only a few) who were destined to provide benchmarks in the Italian animated film industry.

A good colourist, with an incisive line, Maraja gave bis best to *La rosa*. He was equally skillful in portraying fantastic as well as naturalistic environments, and created soft, elaborate settings of landscapes and palaces in an imaginary East, influenced by an amalgam of colonial postcards, the architecture of Eclecticism, Hollywood movies, and the legendary *Arabian Nights*.

Maraja also illustrated the book version of *La rosa,* which Domeneghini adapted from the film. In the book, one finds unusually volumetric illustrations of the environment and figures, as well as a great gestural expressiveness of characters, underlined by a distortion that (perhaps unexpectedly) arises from Maraja's experience working frame by frame in animation.

In fact, when he first worked at IMA, as an animator, he revealed himself to be among the most sensitive to the Disney philosophy of "personality animation". In her *History of Italian Illustration* (Bologna: Zanichelli, 1988), Paola Pallottino defines Maraja's work as a combination of "fantasy-humor" and "grotesque elements".

Most of the artist's energies were devoted to book illustration, working for publishers such as Baldini, Carroccio, D'Anna, Fabbri, Mondadori, and Rizzoli, to illustrate the works of such authors as Andersen, Carroll, Cervantes, Collodi, De Amicis, Dickens, Dumas, Grimm, La Fontaine, London, Manzoni, Homer, Perrault, Salgari, Shakespeare, Swift, Twain, Verne, and Wilde.

Maraja's paintings were featured in an exhibition at the Broletto Palace in Como, 1–14 October 1982. In the exhibition's catalogue (Bologna: Zanichelli, 1988), Alberto Longatti writes:

> I have a feeling Maraja has always been, at all levels of his work, fundamentally an illustrator, in the literal sense of the word. That he has constantly "illustrated" one might say, a foreign entity, something outside himself; and therefore, that he consciously or not has avoided throwing himself directly onto the canvas. From this comes the particular configuration, and the original sense of mixing, in alternate periods, of realism and a gentle kind of expressionism, along with abstraction. In any case, what is more important for him is to paint: you can see that in the precision of execution and the refined completeness of the visual field, even in the most modest

pictures published in the illustrated volumes of novels for teenagers.

BACKGROUND: ANGELO BIOLETTO

Angelo Bioletto (Turin, 30 September 1906–Milan, 25 December 1986) worked at IMA between 1942 and 1944, the three most decisive years in the creation of *La rosa di Bagdad*. Almost all the film's characters were created by Bioletto, and all accounts indicate that, after Domeneghini, he left the clearest and longest-lasting mark on the film. He taught his associates the need to "animate" – that is, to make the figures "play" and not just "move"; it was thanks to his constant perfectionism and drive that a multitude of novices working on the film acquired a professionalism and, in some cases, an authentic skill in the field of animation.

The artistic dyarchy of Domeneghini and Bioletto is itself probably responsible for the cohabitation of styles and plans that makes *La rosa* almost two films in one.

On the one hand, the producer/screenwriter/director (Domeneghini) intended to transpose on the screen a story with all the characteristics of a fairy tale: love, adventure, emotion; good against evil; and a final moral message based on the triumph of hope. His narrative grew out of assimilated traditions of storytelling as well as his own personal view of the world, which motivated Domeneghini's own behaviours at work and in society.

On the other hand, the artistic director (Bioletto) drew his great inspiration from journalistic caricature, the traditions of satire, the great comedy heritage of variety shows, and the cinema, to create a daring and merry film about the world of the intellectual (and quite extra-moral) laugh.

While it could be argued that both Domeneghini and Bioletto followed Disney's example, it is also true that one saw his Snow White side, while the other saw his Donald Duck side.

Bioletto was born into a wealthy family in Turin, shortly before his father went bankrupt, left the family and moved to South America. A self-taught caricaturist and graphic artist, Bioletto was already using his skills to earn a living when he was in his teens. For more than seven years, he drew a series of humorous cartoon columns (among them "Bioletto has seen" based on everyday life in town) for the daily newspaper *La Stampa*.

Bioletto became a national celebrity because of the radio program "The Four Musketeers", written by the humourists Angelo Nizza and Riccardo Morbelli. The program began on 18 October 1934, aired on Thursdays at 1:05 p.m., but soon was switched to Sundays, where it remained until 28 March 1937.

It has been said that the program was responsible for the sale of many radios; during its three years, ownership increased from 535,000 to more than 900,000. One day, Bioletto met Nizza at the entrance of the *La Stampa* headquarters (at the time, Nizza worked there as a reporter) and proposed to illustrate the program's characters for a competition hosted by its sponsor, the food manufacturer Perugina-Buitoni.

And so, the most popular picture-cards in Italy were born. One hundred were produced and enclosed into packages of chocolate and pasta. A person had to stick the cards into a picture-card album and, when 150 such books were collected, he or she won a Topolino car (which, at that time, cost L. 9,750 – ten times the annual salary of a good office worker). With fewer picture-card albums, a person could win many other prizes. Picture-card fever spread and the hunting of card number twenty, the elusive "Ferocious Saladin", became a true national pastime.

Eventually, the competition ended, World War II began, and Bioletto's contributions to *La Stampa* were stopped due to heavy interference by censors, who did not like the difficulties of the time to be printed so clearly in black and white. But the artist's fame and skill were very attractive to Domeneghini, who was always hunting for the best available persons on the market; Bioletto was offered a job immediately.

After his experience with *La rosa,* the Piedmontese artist no longer worked in animation. Instead, he tried his hand at comic strips a few times, then devoted himself completely to illustration for thirty years (until his death), creating plates for educational publishers.

NOTES

1. It is worth also mentioning *Mater Dei* (1950) by Emilio Cordero, a barely distributed, barely known religious production.
2. Though they were launched at the same time, during the Venice Film Festival in 1949, the two films have different registration dates recorded in the Public Cinematographic Register by SIAE (Società italiana autori e editori). *I fratelli dinamite* was registered in 1947 with the number 672, while *La Rosa* was registered in 1949 with the number 799; however, SIAE's officials maintained that a given registration date does not imply that a film had been finished and ready to screen. For that reason, the 1949 date (of the first public screening) should be considered effective for both films.
3. The town of Fiume, in the Istria region (today Rijeka, Croatia) , was inhabited by Italians but, before the war, was the possession of the Austro-Hungarian Empire. The Versailles peace agreements did not award the town to Italy, and this outraged the public. D'Annunzio, at the head of a group of armed patriots, occupied the town, claiming it for Italy. This "coup de main" caused quite a heroic stir among nationalists. In the big and complicated mosaic that was later to be Italian Fascism, the Nationalist sector always had the "heroic" role and looked at D'Annunzio as an inspiration. D'Annunzio never completely accepted Mussolini's dictatorship nor his plebeian style and secluded himself in a rich internal exile in his Garda lake villa, named "Il Vittoriale degli Italiani" ("The Monument to Italians' Victory").
4. According to the book *L'Italia di Cartone,* by Piero Zanotto and Fiorello Zangrando (Padova: Liviana, 1972; a scarcely reliable source), Petronio was born in Trieste in 1889; in that case, he would have been fifty-three years old while preparing the movie. But, according to testimonies, he looked old at that time. He had heart disease and had to give up the production due to poor health.
5. Federico Pedrocchi (Buenos Aires, 1 May 1907–Milan, 20 January 1945), a scriptwriter and drawing artist, was one of the founders of the Italian comic strip industry. He was an editorial manager at Mondadori's in 1938, fought in the war between 1941 and 1943, and then – after working at IMA – became the editor of the Il Carroccio publishing house.
6. The animator, comic strip artist, and painter Guido Zamperoni, a key figure on Domeneghini's staff, revealed an odd detail during a conversation with this writer in January 1993: "I had a dear friend, former fellow boy scout, Nino Pagot, a good drawer. Domeneghini and I both thought to appeal to him, since he already had some experience with a cartoon movie and knew the basics of the business. But Pagot was not willing to join IMA, as he loved his professional independence". Pagot actually directed the animated feature *I fratelli Dinamite.*

CHAPTER 4

Defining Animation*

A Proposal

"ART IS EVERYTHING THAT Mankind calls art", wrote Dino Formaggio in the introduction of *L'arte come idea e come esperienza*,[1] "this is not – as some might think – a simple opening line, but rather, it might possibly be the only acceptable and verifiable definition of the concept of art". I will begin by anticipating the conclusions of this brief study to suggest that the definition of animation[2] be formulated by paraphrasing the approach of the Milanese academic, and maybe with an ulterior accent on the time element to which he dedicated the paragraphs following this affirmation. (He analysed visual art thoroughly and therefore it is understood that, if one wants to categorise, animation is a subfamily in the larger family of visual art.)

Consequently: "Animation is everything that people have called animation in the different historical periods".

---

* Originally published in Italian as "Definire l'animazione" in *ITINERA – Rivista di Filosofia e di Teoria delle Arti e della Letteratura*, Università degli studi di Milano, May 2004.

I have taken the liberty to update the original language because, as a historian, I find myself particularly aware of the rapid variations in word meanings resulting from changes in mentality and – above all – in technology, which have taken place over the years and which I have witnessed in part.

It is important to note that between about 1895 and 1910 the term *animated* was applied to things that today are called *live action*, which we often group in a distinctly different category. At that time, "animated photography" was the common term, and a little later the equally rudimental phrases *moving picture* or *motion picture* came into use. I prefer this term instead of animated films for reasons that will become clearer later on.

Animated cartoon became official only after the first book on the subject was published. After that,[3] a glance at theatre programs issued from 1925 to 1939 by the London Film Society (one of the first and most prestigious film clubs in the world) is enough to realise that in the first half of the last century the idea of animation did not extend to the abstract films of Ruttmann, Fischinger, or Richter. Their works were instead considered experimental and grouped with others that in our time are known as live-action avant-garde films. Furthermore, the word *animation* did not exist as a noun – it was only used as an adjective with the "cartoon": *animated cartoon* (as used previously).

Later, in 1949, in his influential and very much studied work *Der Film. Werden und Wesen einer neuen Kunst*,[4] the theorist Béla Balász separated the two concepts by writing about "absolute" and "abstract" films in chapter XIV and "animated drawings" along with optical effects in chapter XV.

As far as popular opinion is concerned, most of moviegoers and even some of the cinema scholars continued for decades to think of animated works as a movie "genre", like westerns, space operas, war pictures, and so on. Some still think this way.[5]

The noun *animation* began to be used by French specialists in the 1950s, when an international cultural movement was consolidated between Paris and Cannes that attributed a specific meaning to this form of art.

The movement also objected to the dominant interpretation of the term, both in aesthetic and economical terms, popular due to the works of Walt Disney starting in 1928 (with the short film *Steamboat Willie* starring Mickey Mouse) and even more so in 1937 (with the feature film *Snow White and the Seven Dwarfs*).

In 1960, in the lakefront city of Annecy in Savoy, the world's first "Festival International du film d'animation" was held.

This movement set the stage for the birth in 1962 of the Association international du film d'animation (ASIFA), a sort of United Nations for directors, producers, and researchers in the sector. The preamble of its statute gave the first official definition:

> [While live action cinema] proceeds towards a mechanical analysis, through photography, of occurrences similar to those that shall be presented on the screen, animation cinema creates the occurrences using instruments different from those used for automatic registration. In animated films, the occurrences take place for the first time on the screen.

The second statute was adopted in 1980. After eighteen years of viewing works produced with the most diverse forms of image manipulation, it became understood that the original definition was overly dependent on the traditional concept of animated drawings.

Another definition was selected, using a negative format: "Any cinematographic production that is not a simple recording of real life in 24 photograms per second is defined as animation". At the time of writing, even these words are losing their meaning with the advent of digital techniques that are erasing the very concepts of cinematography, photogram, and filming.

At this point, it is necessary to try to identify some tangible element, without however bringing ourselves to ask whether a *specific animation concept* exists (in the same way that decades ago, during the quest to attribute a notion of art to film making, people began asking if there was a *specific film concept*).

If we took this approach, we would risk turning many theorists' or artists' "poetics" into a categorical "aesthetic". We would have to take sides for everything, wanting to obtain a lowest common denominator of the case histories instead of getting to the theoretical level. Moreover, once again, we would risk exposing the words to the aging process that deteriorates meaning through the passing of time and historical events.

This task needs to be dealt with, though, in order to begin participating in that generalised feeling that leads animators to perceive certain films as *their own*. In other words (in reference to the definition stated at the beginning) we need to begin to understand which elements have caused people in different time periods to call certain things "animation".

First, I'll try to clear the field of the misunderstanding that animation is movie genre. A genre has a reason to exist inside a certain form of expression. For example, in prose literature, there are several genres: legal thrillers, adventure, romance, science fiction, etc. In painting, we have portraits, landscapes, still life, abstract, etc. And live action films can be classified, as already stated, as westerns, soap operas, war pictures, etc.

"Genre" is a difficult concept for many, but in extremely simple terms, it could merely be based on a deal between the manufacturer and the user. On the guarantee for the user, that is, that this specific product will satisfy some of his specific requests.

To clarify, if you want horses, wide open spaces and shootouts, choose a western. If you like to be scared, go for a horror film. Genres are known for being repetitive – and therefore reassuring. Quite the reverse, films by top-name directors are innovative by nature. (However, we should not deny it has happened several times that a creative director with a stronger influence or a stroke of luck made an important film defined within a genre.)

Getting back to the subject, if one loves animated thrillers (a genre) and finds himself watching a classic film, he will probably be disappointed. Those who love Disney musicals like *Beauty and the Beast* have a strong possibility of being confused by an abstract film. Bugs Bunny's pie-in-the-face antics clash with the humour of Eastern Europe of the Communist era.

Therefore, many genres exist within animation. This is a good starting point for introducing it not a genre or macro-genre, but as a separate style of filmmaking, a brother to live-action cinema.[6]

When filmmaking began, in the last two decades of the 1800s, the practical application was based on the principle of bombarding the spectator with a series of still frame slides. Cinematographers and projector technicians knew that when static images are presented in sequence at a velocity of over sixteen to eighteen frames per second, the human eye perceives them as a fluid image. With a series of very rapid stop-and-go techniques, the camera photographed the successive phases of the actions that took place before it. The projector used the same procedure to present the images to the public. That was the system utilised to "write the movement" ("cinematography" = *kinéma* + *graphéin* in Ancient Greek).

The crank on the movie projector was turned by hand, and so the operator had an almost physical relationship with the film and its sequences. It wasn't hard to understand that, once the projection speed became standard, several "effects" became possible in the filming phase. One of these "effects" consisted in taking photograms one by one (stop motion) instead of using continuous movement, and changing the position of the object during the pause that the filmmaker allowed between one frame and the next. During projection, the object seemed to come to life.

This "effect" allowed for the development of a language. Through the single photogram technique, it was possible to invent types of movement that don't exist naturally, and in that way conquer the fourth dimension (time) after the two dimensions of painting and the three of sculpture.

This is what we mean intimately by animation: not so much the attribution of motion but the attribution of a soul (or a personality) to objects, forms, or shapes (even abstract) that are otherwise lifeless.

The language of animation was historically connected to the entertainment industry in a wide sense. It was first channelled into the production/distribution/projection industry for public entertainment businesses (cinemas); then it went into television and then the internet. Of course, it is correct to use the terms animated film, animated cartoon, animated short film, animated feature, animated TV series, or animated genre film (comedy, horror, western, etc.).

A question arises, though. When it becomes possible to attribute a personality to otherwise inert things through the use of technologies different from traditional filmmaking, can those products also be called animation?

A famous example tells us that yes, they can. Between 1892 and 1900, the Frenchman Emile Reynaud showed his *Pantomimes Lumineuses* to a paying audience at the Musée Grévin. The production presented brief comedy skits of drawings that came to life and action thanks to an instrument (not a movie camera) that he had invented, the Théâtre Optique. Specialists in animation have never had any doubts about including Reynaud among the pioneers of their art.

The language of animation shares many characteristics with its close relative, live-action cinema. Let's look at two of these attributes: (1) its ability to give life to works of narrative and non-narrative natures, and (2) its audiovisual characteristics.

1. The psychological component of believability is hazy in animation, while in live action it is fundamental. In live action, the realness of the actors and settings and the public's ability to identify with the scene is crucial to the film's timing. The spectator has no doubts that the action on the screen takes the same amount of time it would in

real life for real events, and his involvement in the personal drama on the screen allows him to not get bored if there are cases of prolonged close-ups, monologues, or dialogues in or out of the field.[7] Narration is favoured. In a way, we could say that live action cinema is comparable to prose in literature.

With animation, the public has to deal with drawn or painted images, models, or digital images. In other words, things that are not real. Emotional identification is more difficult, even though over time it has become easier because younger generations grew up with this form of entertainment and the use of symbols is commonplace in everyday situations. Narration is not excluded, as we can see from the existence of a large number of long films, but it is more difficult because the concept is based on stylised film content that the spectator must accept and interiorise. There are many very short works in which elliptical and symbolic languages are dominant, and so there is a certain liking to poetry – literature in verse – which also includes longer works but is at its best in short form, allusive, full of analogies.

Let's go back to the assumption that the base of animation is the attribution of a soul (or a personality) to objects, forms, or shapes (even abstract) that are otherwise lifeless; in other words, that the base of animation is the creation of movements and the choreography of shapes.

If this was all there is to it, we could say that it is just a specialised section of kinetic fine art.

2. The other half of the question (especially the non-narrative aspect) lies in the soundtrack. It's not painting – it's music. The animation language is exquisitely audiovisual. In the opinion of this specialist operating inside the sector, it is the most audiovisual of audiovisual languages.

Animated forms, figures, and characters have always had a close connection with music and sound in general. Musicians that work with animation have experimented since the thirties with the most revolutionary techniques. Music and noises and voices and sound effects have almost always been included together in the soundtrack, and thought to be of equal importance by musicians, who often made headway in this particular field prior to and better than their counterparts in traditional music.

If there are doubts about the sound/vision synergy, we could try a simple experiment: show any short film from the Golden Age of Hollywood without the soundtrack (for example, an episode of *Tom and Jerry* or Wile E. Coyote and the Roadrunner). We would see that the work would lose its weight and meaning without the sound. If this is the case with mass production and industry, the elite works would be absolutely devastated: for example *Strojenie instrumentòw* (*Tuning the Instruments*, 2000) from the Polish director Jerzy Kucia, a film that intertwines sound and images in an inextricable way.

Given the aforementioned examples, it would be superficial to think that we have touched on all of the numerous nuances and feelings that make up the idea that each person working in this sector attributes to the matter at hand.

The outer margins, in particular, are always in movement. Should we consider (or not) the old adage, "If this scene can be filmed live, it isn't necessary to draw it"? Is time-lapse photography (the technique that allows us to watch a flower bloom in seconds) a category of animation or not? What about virtual reality (used in flight simulators for student pilots)? How should we define the numerous touch-up operations that post-production technology makes it possible to do on images in films like *Titanic* or *Lord of the Rings*? Where it is possible to animate in real time, like it is possible to act in real time, do we have animation or do we have a puppeteering art instead?

In essence, and I apologise for the intellectual gibberish, the conclusion that we have reached is this: we can explore the phenomena of this particular creative branch of art until we touch on a categorical quality, but without actually giving it a precise collocation. Now – to draw conclusions and get to the point – we need to recall the definition made in the opening: "Animation is everything that people have called animation in the different historical periods".

This is not tautological, as it could seem. It isn't because it refers to an element that is outside the realm of pure words. It refers to the attitudes maintained throughout the various time periods by specialists in the sector from all over the world – diverse in culture and political and social conditions, but in agreement in their opinions.

This tells us that a language called animation exists as an autonomous form of art, with its own role and space. This also tells us that animation has its own place in history, just like any other relevant human activity.

In addition, this definition has the virtue of blocking the temptation to do intellectual gymnastics while splitting hairs in hopes of grasping the profound essence of the concept.

Many years' worth of experience in the field, in addition to a lesser amount of time spent in the library, have convinced this author that definitions are necessary and useful, on the condition that they do not spark intricate debates. Pure discussion often hinders the comprehension of life and/or creative works.

This study should be therefore taken as a non-dogmatic preamble to the actual work of the human sciences specialist, which consists exactly in achieving that very comprehension.

CITED FILMS

Steamboat Willie (Walt Disney, 1928).

Snow White and The Seven Dwarfs (David Hand, 1937).

Beauty and the Beast (Gary Trousdale and Kirk Wise, 1991).

Tuning the Instruments (*Strojenie instrumentòw*; Jerzy Kucia, 2000).

Titanic (James Cameron, 1997).

Lord of the Rings trilogy (Peter Jackson, 2001–2003).

NOTES

1. Dino Formaggio, *L'arte come idea e come esperienza*. Milan: Mondadori 1981, p. 11.
2. I prefer this term instead of animated films for reasons that will become clearer later on.
3. E.G. Lutz, *Animated Cartoons: How They are Made, Their Origin and Development*. New York: Scribner's, 1920.
4. Béla Balász, *Der Film. Werden und Wesen einer neuen Kunst*. Wien: Globus, 1949.
5. On 11 September 2003, the American doctoral student Shana Heinricy wrote a message to the internet discussion group of the "Animation Journal List" to ask for clarification. She said that the professors advising her for her PhD (!) thesis were making her call animation a "film genre" and she voiced her doubts in this regard. The scholar Maureen Furniss, coordinator of the group, answered sarcastically that if animation is a genre then so is live-action cinema.
6. Here, in order to once and for all eliminate the clichés, I insist that though there is a rather substantial number of animated production destined for children, it would be a grave error to catalogue animation as an art form for children alone.
7. For an in-depth analysis of this concept, see Midhat Ajanovic, *Animacija i realizam*, Zagreb: Hrvatski filmski savez, 2004.

CHAPTER 5

African Cinema Animation*

I F THE TOPIC IS "African cinema animation", a question will most certainly be asked: What do we really know about it? Does anybody know anything about it? Amongst the forms of expression of the twentieth and twenty-first centuries, cinema animation is unanimously considered to be the most underestimated, the least explored, and the most misunderstood of all. Within this dispiriting framework, African cinema animation suffers the worst-case scenario. Let us have a look at the written sources: apart from some monographs on the film and theatre director William Kentridge (Republic of South Africa), the precious but thin collection of works by the Swiss Bruno Edera,[1] and the equally thin chapter on this topic in my world history of cinema animation,[2] what we non-African people know about this issue comes from a forty-eight-page booklet *Hommage au cinéma d'animation d'Afrique noire.*[3]

---

* Originally published in English in the online journal *EnterText 4.1* in 2008. Translated from Italian by Emilia Ippolito with Paula Burnett.

Here is a significant quotation from Jean-Claude Matumweni Mwakala's essay *Aspects sociologiques du cinéma d'animation africain* (*Sociological Aspects of African Cinema Animation*) included in the aforementioned collection:

> As we all know, you need large investments to produce a film. The countries which have a prosperous and high quality film industry have invested large amounts of money in this sector. Africa has no cinema industry, and the existing investments are based on co-productions. The norm is therefore a lack of financial means; however, there are a couple of observations to make: for example, the waste of funds carried out by public authorities. The Ndaya International Foundation had obtained funds to finance the series *Kimboo* – which cost around twelve million French francs – together with France. It is known that film directors in Arab countries can count on policies of public financial support for their productions: it is the case in Tunisia, whose film productions have been made possible by the Ministry of Culture.

Matumweni Mwakala says that a lack of infrastructure, investment, and entrepreneurship are at the root of the troubles in African cinema animation. Is he right? If the animation films he takes as models are the approximately fifty episodes of the Franco-Ivory Coast series *Kimboo*, I would say yes, he is right.

Here is one more translated quotation, this from Benjamin Benimana's essay *L'esthétique du cinéma d'animation africain* (*The Aesthetics of African Cinema Animation*):

> The question we should ask ourselves is probably as follows: what kind of cartoons does the African audience watch? As you can guess, most African television channels broadcast cheap cartoons made in the Western countries, in India and especially in Japan.

Is he right? He probably is. However, why does he mention the "audience"? Does the "audience" exist only in relation to cartoons? Here is a quotation from Ngwarsungu Chiwengo's essay, *Le film d'animation africain vu de l'Amérique: le cas de Muana Mboka de Kibushi Ndjate Wooto* (*African Film Animation Seen From America: Muana Mboka by Kibushi Ndjate Wooto*):

> *Muana Mboka* (a short film by Jean-Michel Kibushi Ndjate Wooto, Democratic Republic of Congo) is, in many respects, an important product. Since children in Africa and in other "third-world" countries are exposed to Western films which marginalise and erase black people from their environment, African cartoons play an important role in young people's education.

Is he right? He probably is. However, why does he mention "children" and "young people's education" without considering that cartoons can be regarded as for an audience which is not composed only of children?

I could add for the benefit of the viewer who is not up to date on the subject, that some productions existed in the past in Egypt (for example, films featuring the character Mish-Mish Effendi by the Frenkel Brothers; see Figure 5.1), and that a consistent production still exists these days; that the Maghreb region has also contributed to it extensively; and that other works have been produced in the past fifteen years, thanks to the method of co-production, to which Jean-Claude Matumweni Mwakala refers in his essay.

At this stage, however, I have to say that I will not express my opinion on this topic until we have eliminated some prejudices.

First, cinema animation is *not* a cinema for children. It can be and often is, but not in a different way from live-action films for children, pop music for children, and children's literature. Cinema animation is a cinema, twin brother to live action, with a specific history, a specific aesthetic, a specific market, etc.

FIGURE 5.1 Propaganda film made in the 1940s by the Frenkel Brothers. (Copyright Didier Frenkel. Source: Public domain.)

Second, the problem of viewers and television programmes affects not just African cinema animation but the whole world market (more precisely, the globalised market) of mass media. Separating them and analysing such problems as "African" or as typical of cinema animation means making a terrible mistake in the diagnosis.

Third, cinema animation does not necessarily need big investments, big infrastructures, or businesses. The example of Moustapha Alassane, pioneer of African animation and citizen of one of the poorest countries in the world, Niger, is meaningful in this respect. In 1962 the New York intellectual Dwight MacDonald published the book *Against the American Grain* (Random House), which included the essay "Masscult and Midcult". MacDonald was a contradictory and moody man, but he was ingenious. In this essay, which became a classic, he claimed that communication could be divided into three different kinds: mass culture (Masscult), middle-class culture (Midcult), and an elite culture (Highcult). For example, in literature, Masscult are

Barbara Cartland's novels and in animation, Japanese television series; in literature, Midcult are Stephen King's novels and in animation, Walt Disney films; in literature, Highcult is the Nobel Prize–winner Czesław Milosz's poetry, and in animation, the Russian Juri Norstein's short films, which are highly regarded and rewarded (at animation festivals).[4]

Sociologists and economists will not agree, since the state of the play is certainly more complex than this. However, forty years on, the division into three categories still serves for the examination of our topic, and those categories are even more exclusive.

First of all, if we question African cinema animation we need to know what animation we are talking about. The limited production of African animation will help us analyse it in detail. I will start with the Highcult and its pioneer, Moustapha Alassane. His films have been viewed and awarded prizes at various festivals all over the world; he himself has travelled a lot and has been a member of the jury at prestigious festivals (to my knowledge, at least at Annecy and Clermont-Ferrand). In spite of these facts, he can be considered as a *naïf* auteur. In the short 2001 film *Kokoa 2* (a remake of a film from 1985, about a chameleon fighter which changes its colour to red whenever it gets angry with its adversary; see Figure 5.2), he makes the same mistakes as to timing, script, and filming he had made in *Bon Voyage, Sim*, in 1966 – the first film of his I saw.

The fact is, Alassane has never studied animation. He has invented it. He has not adopted the conventions of timing, filming, scriptwriting, and editing established by Californian or Parisian professionals. He sticks to his own rules, which makes him an original animation director. Multi-cinema viewers, addicted to fast food, might not appreciate him.

However, his compatriots appreciate his films (by his own account). A *naïf* is not a particularly gifted troglodyte; it is a creator who does not want or is not able to accept academic codes, copies of reality, and colour theories. As for style, if the communicator has something interesting to say, we will certainly

FIGURE 5.2 *Kokoa 2* (Moustapha Alassane, Niger, 2001). (Courtesy: Copyright Moustapha Alassane.)

pay attention to him, even though he does not apply our rules. Moustapha Alassane presents us with his vision of Africa, expressed through very simple and cheap technical means, such as animated puppets, direct drawing on the film, and a few others; they are scarcely less simple or more expensive than sculpture and painting, traditional and popular arts which have existed for millennia. Every day animals are represented exactly the way they are (not in caricature): I'm thinking of the funny chameleon in *Kokoa*, or of the inflatable frogs which look like pompous and useless human heads of state in *Bon Voyage, Sim.*

A *naïf* is not a *Muna Mboka*, by the already-mentioned Jean-Michel Kibushi Ndjate Wooto, presents a similar case. The plot is almost negligible: a street boy, like many others in African cities, who lives by misdemeanours and theft, saves a minister's life (ironically, the Minister of Public Works), and is rewarded by him and envied by other people. A realistic (or, better, neo-realistic) film, a tough one, it denounces the African urban reality. Its colours are vivid and violent, its soundtrack noisy and "live", its characters paper-cut; this film is certainly not expensive. Kibushi Ndjate Wooto, unlike Alassane, is not a self-made director. He has studied cinema in Europe and knows the rules of cinema professionals; however, he often ignores them and uses a very personal timing, and clumsy frames and movements, aware that the topic is more important than the time he would need in order to mould the form.

Alassane and Kibushi express themselves through direct means (I repeat this word); they do not use filters. What are "filters"? Filters are big investments which may potentially generate even bigger profits; the large studios have to pay big salaries and be provided with good equipment and software; marketing and dumping strategies enable distributors to export television series cheaply: in a word, the industry. Moreover, the idea of entertainment meant only for children, or else political, ethnic, or educational propaganda – these are non-material filters but no less influential.

People who accept these filters also accept all their consequences. They will make films or television series which will be filtered, harmless, pre-digested, all the same, reassuring: films which will be based on universal stereotypes of movement, mimesis, narrative, characterisation, special effects (like the "Disney Dust", the sparkling stars which accompany any metamorphosis, noticeably in the series *Samba et Leuk*, directed in 1996 by France's Jean-Louis Bonpoint). At this stage, it is meaningless to complain against discrimination, conflicts between the world's North and South, whites versus blacks, colonisers versus colonised.

I do not agree with Benjamin Benimana when he comments on the aesthetics of African cinema animation (I am still translating from the aforementioned booklet):

We need to remember three factors. The first is the "cultural virus" – the infiltration of Western cultural products into Africa. This situation does not help the development of local products. What is worse: mass culture, independently of its origins and its producers' identity, is an industry of standardisation of expression and the emotional modes which carry its products along. Generally lacking specific moral values, this situation subtly destroys very ancient traditions, some of which have existed for millennia, filling them with superficial emotional cliches. The second factor is the major Disneyan aesthetic which has invaded schools and production in Europe and, at a later stage, in Africa. Uniformity has attacked originality and now it is essential to get rid of this artistic monolith. The third factor is that modern cinema animation has developed, and fortunately still is developing, a multiplicity of expressions linked to different artistic traditions, some of which show similar characteristics to the national schools. We think that a study of African cinema animation [...] should be based not on a search for aesthetic similarities with other products, but rather on meaningful differences, which can be used as evaluation criteria.

I disagree, since a few lines earlier he had consented to speak exclusively of "television viewers".

There are numerous examples of this production. *Kimboo* is a series of five-minute episodes in French, directed by Gilles Gay. The already-mentioned *Samba et Leuk* (1996) is a series of twenty-six-minute episodes in French, directed by Jean-Louis Bonpoint. In February 1998, Pierre Sauvalle – originally from Senegal, who studied at the Gobelins school in Paris – founded with Aida N'Diaye a company called Pictoons.

They acquired high technology, trained a lot of young professionals, and started producing television advertisements and soundtracks. Pictoons is the most important example of African animation meant for a global market, in open competition with European, American, and Asian productions. The first series,

Kabongo le Griot (*griot* means "storyteller"; it is a typical persona of African culture, which is based on storytelling), came out in 2000–2002. Its characters are a mix of international standard animation and, in the graphics, Fang or Dogon masks, typical of local cultural tradition (see Figure 5.3). There is also the mixed-techniques series (3D computer animation plus live action) *Grands Masques et les Junglos*, directed by Didier M. Aufort. This series is also in French. I do not know whether these series have been successful, but I must admit that they did not particularly impress me, as a viewer, with their aesthetic outcome.

Norman McLaren, great artist and friend of oppressed peoples, dreamed of animation as the language of developing countries. McLaren spent several years in China and India, teaching the basics of animation techniques to people who had only the most basic means at their disposal. We, the younger ones, also shared this dream with him.

FIGURE 5.3   Image from *Kabongo le Griot* series. (Copyright Pictoon Sarl. Courtesy: Pierre Sauvalle.)

Animation can in fact be quite cheap and technologically simple. In order to safeguard their personal inspiration and national cultural traditions, people from Angola, Liberia, Paraguay, Haiti, Bali, and Nepal can paint or draw their sketches on film and pay for it with their own savings, the same way they would create an oil or watercolour painting. If well done, their film will stay in the viewers' memory and cinema history books along with *Titanic* or *The Lord of the Rings*. It was a dream and it has not come true. However, never say never.

Since we are speaking about colonisers and colonised, please forgive this digression. In different contingent circumstances, I have witnessed two examples of colonisation during my life: Western colonisation of the West (the Franco-American, then only American, colonisation of Italy during the fifties and sixties) and Western-English colonisation of Australia.

The colonisation of my homeland has these days become homology. Italian cinema made by Italians for Italians (I mean "live" cinema, because of the inconsistency of animation products) has been limited to a few television comedians acting for the big screen.

The situation of the Aborigines was and still is different. They have been dispossessed of everything for centuries, and now the authorities offer them a sort of cultural compensation. I have witnessed a project of cultural re-enactment based on animation in Bourke, New South Wales. The aboriginal community, always tending towards visual means of expression, rapidly appropriated simple technological tools and started producing films. These films – this is the most important factor – refused to be "folk", and to propose traditional stereotypes. These films spoke of the Aborigines, their life, and their desires. A few years earlier, an institution called Aboriginal Nations had produced short films in which they tried to "set in motion" traditional aboriginal paintings and tell in this way some legends of the dreamtime. Easy exotics. It was a failure.

Going back to Africa, let me mention a talented white African animation director, Michel Ocelot, born in France and now living in Paris. He has avoided folk and exotic elements in his film animation *Kirikou et la sorcière* (*Kirikou and the Witch*).

In particular two big francophone countries, France and Canada, have invested time and money on animation co-productions, which are the best documented. Probably it is precisely these co-productions I am least interested in: they are not mulatto; they are half black, half white; indecisive as to whether they should be north or south of the Mediterranean, east or west of the Atlantic. *La femme mariée à trois hommes* (*The Wife of Three Men*) by Cilia Sawadogo, for example, is based on beautiful paper drawing and sombre colours. The story is derived from popular tradition in the Congo. However, in terms of style, you can find forty years of the National Film Board of Canada in it – it is a compromise. One more example could be *Succession* by Vincent Gles, also produced by the National Film Board of Canada: wonderful puppets, beautiful lights, great set design, and an African popular story. However, the author has accurately studied and applied the lesson of Jiri Trnka and the Czech school. One more compromise on the aesthetic level.

We should also discuss works produced by schools and universities, such as exercise or diploma films. I have extensive experience of this sort of production: in the last five years I have supervised so many such works. Everywhere, whether the authors were European, North American, Australian, Asian, or Third World students, I have found the same faults: blind trust in software, ignoring the fact that software is only a tool and not a thinking brain; blind and absolute trust in beautiful images, ignoring the fact that in a film, images should be moving; lack of interest in the diegesis (narrative evolution: the evolving plot, which should keep the viewer's attention high); and non-comprehension of the film as an audiovisual product, with a strong tendency to ask a composer friend for a couple of notes of soundtrack as a comment or to fill in the gaps.

I would say that the student-made films I have dealt with all had these faults, to different degrees. I had heard nothing but good about Carlos Spivey, who is in California at UCLA and Loyola Marymount University, but his works disappointed me. *Mama Seed Tree*, which means to communicate the idea of the continuation of life in the mother's womb as in Mother Earth's womb, has weak images and the soundtrack is inadequate. *Whisper* (fixed images opened up by software) and *The World Is a Drum* are equally confusing.

So far we have spoken about black Africa. William Kentridge, an anti-racist white South African auteur of about twenty film animations, who refuses to identify his own work with the cartoon as such, is certainly the most important artistic and intellectual figure on the African continent. It is impossible to separate him from the context in which he has operated and is still working at present. Born in Johannesburg in 1955, he has always been politically and socially active, and won international acknowledgment in the mid-nineties when apartheid finally came to an end (1994). It would be wrong to look for overtly political messages in his film and graphic works (based on charcoal and very few colours). Kentridge is a complex and at times cryptic creator, who makes painful reference to the facts of his homeland, often interiorising them like a poet, in other words leaving them to be expressed by his protagonist, who will then become "everyman" on earth. It is not by chance that his latest work is taken from a highly interiorised novel, foreign to him, *La Coscienza di Zeno* (*Zeno's Conscience*), by Italo Svevo (2002).

The first animated feature film from the continent produced in 2003 in Zimbabwe, *The Legend of the Sky Kingdom*, is made by white Africans – designer and producer Phil Cunningham and director Roger Hawkins, both directing a multi-ethnic group of artists. The film is about three children who escape from an underground city where they are slaves, and go on to reach the Sky Kingdom after a perilous and difficult journey. The technique, a variation on animated puppets, has been named "junkmation" since every character and scene was made by recycling old objects, in fact, junk (see Figure 5.4). This was a respectful

FIGURE 5.4 *The Legend of the Sky Kingdom* (Roger Hawkins, Zimbabwe, 2003). (Copyright Sunrise Media/Sunrise Productions. Courtesy: Roger Hawkins.)

and affectionate tribute to this artistic craft typical of southern Africa, which at times reaches high levels of creativity and which was shown in an international exhibition in Bern, Switzerland, in 2000.

Then we have the Afro-Mediterranean cinema animation. Egypt, as we have already highlighted, had gained an international reputation in animation already by the thirties, when the brothers Herschel, Salomon and David Frenkel, directed *Nothing to Do*, with Mish-Mish Effendi as a protagonist; the film was followed by other sequels about the same protagonist. The films were not very well drawn, very badly animated, and with an even worse script design. Their model was not Walt Disney, rather the Fleischers or else Felix the Cat. As for the name Mish-Mish, it means "tomorrow with apricots", and we will translate it as "jam tomorrow": this was the answer given to the Frenkels whenever they asked for funding for their work. However, Mish-Mish and the Frenkels became so popular that they were able to start a successful advertising agency before the tensions between Egypt and Israel pushed them to emigrate to France in the fifties.

Film animation in Egypt saw a renaissance thanks to Ali Muhib and his brother Husam, who gave birth to the Film Animation Department within the national television channel which was inaugurated in 1960. In 1962 Ali Muhib directed *The White Line*, a film animation plus twenty-five-minute live action, which was a cross between a short musical and a documentary film. It was a lively and excellent film, which made fine use of the split-screen technique (unusual at that time), in a style reminiscent of Piet Mondrian. After eight years of work at the department, during which he trained many young colleagues, Ali Muhib successfully switched to advertising. In 1979 he directed the first Arab animation film series, *Mishgias Sawah*, composed of thirty episodes.

Mohammed Hassib (1937–2001) was one of Muhib's pupils; he separated from him in 1964 to devote himself to advertising, educational films, and live-action feature films. One more important person was Noshi Iskandar (Cairo, 1938), a well-known caricaturist. His first film was *One and Five* (1969), followed by the trilogy *Is it True*, *Abd and Al*, and *Question* (1969), inspired by the war between Israel and Palestine. In 1974 he directed *Where?* and *Room Number...*, a satire on bureaucracy; in 1975 he directed *Excellent*, a denunciation of corruption, and in 1980 *Narcissus*. One of his most faithful adherents was Radha Djubran (1945–1997), who authored the short animation films *Story of a Brat* (1985) and *The Lazy Sparrow* (1991).

Abdellaim Zaki (1939) wrote television soundtracks, live-action feature-film titles, and animation commercials for several Arab countries including Sudan, Jordan, Iraq, Kuwait, and Saudi Arabia (over one thousand), as well as didactic films. Ihab Shaker (Cairo, 1933), painter, caricaturist, illustrator, puppet master, was the most famous animation film director beyond the borders of his homeland. In 1968 he directed *The Flower and the Bottle* in Egypt, then moved to France, where he met Paul Grimault. With his help he directed *One, Two, Three* (1973), a surrealist film with a taste for anecdote, whose characters resemble amoebas. In 1993 he directed *Love Dance*.

Amongst the many Egyptian animation directors are two women. Mona Abou El Nasr has a very personal graphic style. Her *Survival* (1988), made during her stay at the Cal Art school in California, was very successful, along with the television series *Once Upon a Time* (1992). The second woman is Zeinab Zamzam, artist, musicologist, and psychologist, who directed *A Terra-cotta Dream* (1997), a combination of real images and plasticine animation sequences, and the excellent *Open Your Eyes* (2000), also based on the plasticine technique. Both are very refined pieces of work and make Zeinab Zamzam one of the most interesting artists of film animation in Mediterranean Africa.

In conclusion we can say that Egypt is the leading country in film animation in the Maghreb and Arab region at the beginning of the third millennium, and that its artists, technicians, and tools – both financially and technically – promise a great future. However, this country still remains, at present, prisoner of a self-imposed limitation: its products are destined only for Arab countries, and Egyptian directors at international festivals, the place where inspirational experiences are exchanged, are very rare.

I particularly appreciate the work of the Tunisian puppet animator Zouhaier Mahjoub, whose *The Guerbagies* was presented at the Annecy Festival a few decades ago. The government still supports its animation cinema – hopefully Zouhaier Mahjoub and his colleagues will be able to preserve a national culture in the right way.

The first Algerian animation film, *La fête de l'arbre (The Tree Party)* (1963), was produced by Mohamed Aram (Hussein Dey, 1934), only one year after the country became independent. Aram learnt animation techniques on his own; he trained his team and directed films in his spare time – he was mainly a scriptwriter. His first works were educational productions in black and white. *La fête de l'arbre* was an invitation to regrow the vegetation destroyed by napalm. *Ah, s'il savait lire* (*Ah, If Only He Could Read*) (1963) was intended to fight illiteracy, and *Microbes des poubelles* (*Litter Bugs*) (1964) deals with health problems caused by urban life. The large number of productions, over twenty between 1963 and 1999, did not help him solve his problems – a consequence of the lack of support from the cinema authorities in his country. Two of his helpers were Mohamed "Mad" Mazari and Menouar "Slim" Merabtene, directors and comic-strip designers. Mazari directed *Mariage* (*Wedding*) (1966), and Merabtene *Le Magicien* (*The Magician*), (1965). One more Algerian worth mentioning is Mohamed Toufik Lebcir, author of *Branches* (1991), based on the *Thousand and One Nights*, and *Atakor* (1993), the pilot episode of an eponymous series.

Now let us try and change our point of view. Let us completely abandon the notion of quality and consider the financial aspect only. Only rarely does history follow the rules of predictability, therefore I cannot see why African animation history should be any different. Here is a good example. South Korea was, until fifteen years ago, only a cheap-labour country. People who wanted to do film animation organised the creative phase and then left it to be made by the disciplined and cheap Koreans. These days, South Korea has become the third country in the world for producing television series, and short and long films, after the United States and Japan, and above France.

What will happen in fifteen years' time to the powerful Senegal, Egypt, and Republic of South Africa, where production companies aimed at television series are developing these days, or to the Ivory Coast and Zimbabwe? Will they have developed, as Jean-Claude Matumweni Mwakala says, "a prosperous and high quality cinematography, investing in this sector"? Will they have a well-structured, aggressive, and competitive cinema animation industry on the globalised scene, like the South Korean one at present? And if the answer is positive, how will they behave towards the Masscult and Midcult (in MacDonaldian terms)? My answer, though with limited interest – I must admit that I believe more in auteurs than in series – is that only then will we be able to answer the frequent and indispensable question: What is typically African in African cinema animation?

A cowboy in the nineteenth or twentieth century, or else these days, was as exotic in Boston or Manhattan as in Berlin or Manila; however, the Western genre is "typically" American. A giant robot can be found only in toyshops in Tokyo; however, the space-work animation of Goldrake is "typically" Japanese. The mentality and behaviour of the district of Trastevere in Rome is not comprehensible to Italians from Udine and Cagliari; however, Alberto Sordi's or Nino Manfredi's comedy is "typically" Italian.

I mean that cinema and television naturally depend neither on folklore, nor on old or new national or local traditions; for example, nobody in Italy has ever been able to make a good film on the very Italian character of Pinocchio. Cinema and television create their own mythologies (they are autotrophic, in this respect). These mythologies become national brands.

We can therefore say that Highcult auteurs' film animation represents the African soul, but as it has been rewritten by those auteurs. It in fact represents only those auteurs. The only "typically" African feature in their films is the soundtrack, taken from an eternal music, everlasting languages, French and English accents which never had to be invented.

On the contrary, a commercial product which is supposed to challenge, on the global market, other homologous commercial products, this will be the banner of the entire continent or at least of the producing country. In order to achieve this goal, it will have to invent an unprecedented style, an unprecedented narrative, an unprecedented life vision, and stronger tools than its competitors to be appreciated by the viewers. That is what the Japanese have been doing since the sixties with their series. Such a benchmark will become one more commonplace, one of many, waiting for history to follow one of the many rules of unpredictability.

NOTES

1. Bruno Edera, *A la découverte d'un cinéma méconnu: Le cinéma d'animation africain*, Annecy: Festival International du Cinema d'Animation, 1993.

2. Giannalberto Bendazzi, *Cartoons: One Hundred Years of Cinema Animation*, London and Bloomington: John Libbey/Indiana University Press, 1994, 1995, 1999.

3. *Homage to Black African Cinema Animation*, edited by Lomomba Emongo, Strasbourg: Studio Malembe Maa ASBL, a co-production with the Cine-Club de Wissembourg, 2001.

4. Please note that all this is about production and consumption of cultural products, not their *aesthetic value*. There are numerous horrible films made by the elite for the elite, and numerous pleasant television series made by American, Japanese, or Korean chain productions.

CHAPTER 6

Alexandre Alexeieff*

Poems of Light and Shadow

ALEXANDRE ALEXEIEFF (ALEKSANDR ALEKSANDROVICH
Alekseev) was born on 18 April 1901 in Kazan, in Czarist
Russia. He was the third and last child of Maria Polidorova, a
headmistress, and Aleksandr Alekseev, an officer in the imperial
navy. Aleksandr's brothers' names were Nikolay and Vladimir.
One year later, Aleksandr Alekseev Sr. accepted the post of naval
attaché at the Russian embassy in Constantinople (at that time
capital of the Ottoman Empire and now known as Istanbul),
and his family moved with him to the shores of the Bosphorus.
Constantinople was a happy time for the boy, as he enjoyed
the best emotional and material conditions that anyone could
wish for. It came to a tragic end in 1906, when his father died
in strange circumstances, in all likelihood murdered, in Baden
Baden (Germany) while on a diplomatic mission. The family had
to return to Russia and cope with a difficult existence in Saint
Petersburg.

---

* Originally published in Catalonian, Castilian, and English as *Alexandre Alexeieff –
Poemes de llum i ombra*, catalogue of the Sitges 03 festival, Sitges (Spain), 2003.

Though this initial chapter of the artist's life might seem a mere simple melodramatic anecdote, it is of decisive importance in understanding his future inspiration. That interrupted bliss gave rise to a perennial *forma mentis,* sowing in him the need to cling to the moment, to conserve the taste of every joy experienced, and cemented a nostalgic character.

In those days, Saint Petersburg was brimming with writers, painters, musicians, scientists, and thinkers; its theatre scene was buzzing, its elegant life shone. However, Alexandre Alexeieff barely got a whiff of what his new city had to offer. His time was given over to reading and to studying, to training, and to drawing in the Cadet Academy where his position as an officer's son entitled him to a place. Once again, an event in the early years of his life was to leave an indelible mark on the artist's career: his drawing master at the cadet school influenced him categorically by letting pupils explore their potential for fantasy, far beyond the constraints of traditional academic copies from nature. From now on, Alexeieff would never use models except on one occasion, when he turned to his wife Claire for help, using her face to illustrate Malraux's *La condition humaine.*

In 1914, Russia, allied with France and Great Britain, went to war with Germany and the Austro-Hungarian Empire. It was the beginning of World War I, in which the Russian soldiers, facing a German army that was well equipped, well trained, and well officered, fell apart disastrously. The 1917 Revolution put an end to Czarism and set off a civil war that was to last for three years.

In the most chaotic situation imaginable, those 16-year-old cadets were caught between the orders from their superiors and their desire to conduct themselves like self-sufficient adults, between the dizzying hopes of a radical reconstruction of society and humanity; and the daily horrors of the killings, the robberies, the violence.

One group of them was sent deep into Russia to await orders. Alexeieff was holed up in the town of Ufa, near to his mother's brother, Anatoly Polidorov, a socialist lawyer who successfully defended peasants and workers against the arrogance of the rich and powerful. His uncle asked him about his plans for the future, and Alexeieff replied that he wanted to be an engineer. "I thought you wanted to be an artist", quipped his uncle. Alexeieff, fired with revolutionary ideas, said that the country needed engineers to build a society that was new, prosperous, and advanced. "You disappoint me", concluded Anatoly Polidorov. Alexeieff reconsidered his future and took art classes for the rest of the time he was stationed in Ufa. Later he learned that his uncle had been killed by the Bolsheviks, who were somewhat less than accommodating when it came to rival ideas on the left. From that point on, Alexeieff steered well clear of ideologies and all that lurked behind them.

Three freezing months later, the cadets – those who were able to – reached Vladivostok, the furthermost tip of Eastern Siberia. They left on board a warship, but it was several months before they were told that the civil war was over. After a year of aimless drifting, Alexeieff chose France (whose language he had already mastered) as his new home. He still had a letter of introduction that the world-famous painter and illustrator Ivan Bilibin had given in Vladivostok. He landed at Cassis, near Marseilles, and settled in Paris in 1921.

LES ANNÉES DE BOHÈME (THE BOHÈMIAN YEARS)

The set designer Serge Soudeikine (Sergey Sudeikin) read Bilibin's recommendation, and felt also impressed with favour by the novice's personality. In spite of Sudeikin's generous help and advice, the young artist's first year in the intellectual capital of the world was pretty hand to mouth, managing as he did to get only occasional work as a set designer. Things got better over time, and his new friends introduced him into Parisian circles. It was then and there that he met an actress with Georges Pitoëff's company, Alexandra Grinevsky, who he married in 1923 and with whom he had a daughter, Svetlana.

Closest among his new friends were the young surrealist poets, with whom Alexeieff shared a certain understanding about artistic creation: a maximum of spontaneity and a minimum of intellectual control over one's inspiration, to unblock the illogical and often unexplainable mind of the artist. It was one of these leading lights of surrealism, Philippe Soupault (1897–1990), who pointed the Russian immigrant in the direction of what would become one of his main activities: printmaking.

Soupault, who had put together a book on Guillaume Apollinaire, asked Alexeieff to illustrate it with a woodcut, to which he, a complete novice at xylography, agreed on the spot. With neither manuals nor masters available to him, and with only a few days to produce the image, Alexeieff invented the technique for himself, and on 10 December 1926 had in his hands the first of a long series of books enriched with his visual fantasies: *Guillaume Apollinaire*, published by Les Cahiers du Sud, Marseilles.

But it wasn't until a year and a half later, in June 1927, that the printmaking specialists would deal with the stylistic and technical expertise of an artist who at age twenty-six could already be considered a master. Nikolai Gogol's *Diary of a Madman*, published by Les Éditions de la Pléiade, included twenty-one illustrations in aquatint, a type of etching that makes it possible to get all the shades of grey between absolute black and white. This technique was well suited to Alexeieff's way of thinking, as opposed to the declamatory, exhibitionist, and frequently superficial attitude of the contemporary poets, painters, and musicians who populated the avant-garde. "They play the trumpet, while I play the violin", he used to say, unassumingly but lucidly.

ILLUSTRATE OR CREATE

Among the aquatints that Alexeieff produced in his life, some were splendid, others good, none mediocre. Some of the very best were *The Fall of the House of Usher* (1929), *Colloquium of Monos and Una* (1929), *The Brothers Karamazov* (1929), *The Song of Prince Igor* (1950), *Hoffmann's Tales* (1960), and *The Works of Malraux* (1970).

Apart from a handful of commissioned etchings, he produced no "original" work, preferring to confine himself to pre-existing literary texts. In the field of *static* visual art, he was an illustrator more than a painter (to some extent, we could state that he was an illustrator even in the field of dynamic visual art, i.e., in animation; but we'll talk about films later). However, a question needs to be asked here: What is an illustrator? How does an illustrator work?

The attitudes of a man of images faced with the written word are innumerable. There are those who isolate a phrase and translate it into a drawing, those who take a suggestion and develop it according to their own inclination, those who identify with the story and those who simply rebel.

To Alexeieff, the concept of the illustration was that of free, independent reinterpretation of the literary text. To some extent, he always re-wrote in images what he was asked to illustrate, so that what the readers ended up with was, in the same book, a literary version and a visual version of the story. His masterpieces came thick and fast with the texts that he felt the strongest bonds with: Hoffmann, Poe, Dostoyevsky, and the extraordinary reinterpretation in images of Pasternak's *Doctor Zhivago* (1959), which enthralled even the novelist, who was able to see it shortly before dying.

In his work as an illustrator, he used those inspirational criteria that we have already mentioned: "surrealist" spontaneity, memory (Pasternak was astonished to find in these illustrations done by an immigrant who had left Russia as an adolescent everything that he'd seen as an adult during the civil war – "I can even smell the goods wagons", he declared), and another element dear to the surrealists because it was considered free of the conscious mind: dreams.

Alexeieff's illustrations are almost invariably a voyage into the unconscious, nourished by a reading of the book that he translates into images. At times, as in the case of *Hoffmann's tales*, the aquatints are rich (dense even) in symbols, analogies, and allusions that they become real visual poems to read, re-read, and mull over until they shed even their deepest meanings. This is the mental crossroad where the draughtsman fuses into an author in his own right, abandoning the secondary role of decorator of someone else's work. We shall soon see that as a cinematographic author Alexeieff was to latch onto the work of others, from Mussorgsky to Gogol, only for his independent inspiration to shine over and above theirs.

If we examine an engraving plate with a strong magnifying glass, we can easily appreciate the basic process of the creation of the image: where the plate is smooth, the ink doesn't get caught. This is why these areas stay blank during the printing phase. Where the plate is etched, it leaves a varying amount of tiny indentations, microscopic pinholes where the black ink is deposited. To the human eye, the black of the ink combines with the white of the paper, producing a grey that is lighter or darker according to the density of the holes, in other words, according to how much ink is retained. We need to remember this to understand how and why Alexeieff came to invent the pinscreen.

CHERCHEZ LA FEMME (A WORTHY WOMAN IS THE CROWN OF HER HUSBAND)

Alexandre and Alexandra's marriage wasn't happy. Born out of a shared need for company more than for love, the young Alexeieff's age and artistic ambitions were at odds with the sedentary concept of family and fatherhood.

In 1930, Claire Parker was twenty-four. Born in Boston, Massachusetts, she was rich, good-looking, and emancipated but dissatisfied, so she left for Paris to join the group of Americans (Gertrude Stein, Ernest Hemingway, F. Scott Fitzgerald, Man Ray, etc.) irritated with the provincialism of their country, and keen to experience the intellectual stimulation of the international capital of culture. One day she found herself leafing through one of the books illustrated by Alexeieff and fell in love with his powerful, original art, realising that she had found her vocation. Shortly afterward she wrote to him asking for print-making lessons.

Their first meeting was so like the slushiest of romantic novels that one blushes to describe it in detail. Suffice to say that that instant saw the birth of a human passion and an artistic collabo-ration that was to prove itself invulnerable to the severe trials that private and external events were about to subject them to – beginning with World War II.

All the following auteur films (with the curious exception of *En passant*) would be credited to both of them. However, aca-demics and critics have always referred to them as "Alexeieff's films". This attitude was partly a result of the innate sexism in our society and partly of the need to simplify matters for record keepers, who always prefer to identify one person as the object of their discourse;[1] but the decisive element for this option was a hefty dose of historical truth. For a start, Claire Parker always openly declared her role to be, artistically speaking, no more than that of catalyst – and cheerleader – to Alexandre Alexeieff's inspiration. As often happens, the gaps better prove to us what is real. Claire left us not one unpublished sketch, no technical note, and those who knew her never saw a pencil or brush in her hand or even a notebook. Her inspiration flew into his one; it added to his one; she completed him; she corrected him. Without her, he would have been a lesser filmmaker; without him, she wouldn't have been in motion pictures.

Alexandra, meanwhile, had come across a young artist of Hungarian origin, Etienne Raïk, and had made friends with him. We have no details about this relationship in its early stages, but in his old age, Alexeieff grumbled that, while he had been in a clinic getting over an intoxication caused by the acids used in his printmaking work, his wife devoted more time to Raïk than to him. Whatever the case, the two couples, now *crossed*, had a rela-tionship of considerable harmony for many years, living opposite each other and working together on film commercials.

THE PINSCREEN (ONE)

At the age of thirty, Alexandre Alexeieff felt deeply unfulfilled. Art had been his vocation, and after several ups and downs, it had made him famous, well paid, and well integrated with the world of friends and intellectuals who shared his interests and his passions. This goal, instead of seeming to him a much-coveted achievement, gave him the feeling that he'd reached the end of the road. Every new job from an editor, which would normally have been welcome, deep down meant repeating a technique, or a style, or a creative approach that was already well trodden. Limiting himself to a formula scared him. So, he started to think about cinema.

Between the end of World War I and the early 1930s, Paris bestowed upon the new invention of the film the rank of art. It chose the first great masters: the German "expressionists", the Russian Sergei Eisenstein, and, above all, Charlie Chaplin (to whom the critic, theoretician, and filmmaker Louis Delluc in 1921 devoted his first thematic book: *Charlot*). It hosted the most original avant-garde shorts invented by the painters Fernand Léger (*Le ballet mécanique*), Marcel Duchamp (*Anémic cinéma*), Man Ray (*Le Retour à la raison*), Salvador Dalí, and Luis Buñuel (*Un Chien andalou*), not to mention Francis Picabia, René Clair, Germaine Dulac, and some others.

> Cinema – said Alexeieff in the course of a long TV interview in 1971 – was certainly considered worthy of interest by my painter and writer friends. So, I said to myself: I will make films. Alone. I don't want a large team; I'm not looking for El Dorado. Under no circumstances must my films ever be a product. They must be works of art.

One day, the fledgling filmmaker asked his wife and daughter to go and buy him 3,000 pins. This purchase naturally turned into a small comic sketch when the surprised shop assistant asked for confirmation of the number of pins ordered. Alexeieff took possession of the pins at home, and the family patiently arranged them in geometric order on a painter's canvas coated with wax. Alexeieff spread out the pins here and there until he'd formed with them the shape of Svetlana's favourite toy, a doll called Baby Nicholas, and he finally allowed himself a smile of satisfaction. The test run had been positive; the pinscreen could work.

THE PINSCREEN (TWO)

From my experience of more than thirty years of writing about Alexeieff, I can testify that the pinscreen and how it works is easy to understand when one sees it with one's own eyes, but less easy to grasp when one reads a description. I'll try to make myself clear.

The idea of the artist-inventor was to use a pinboard (though he preferred to call it a *screen*) upon which one arranges thousands of retractable pins, spread densely and set to an inclination of sixty degrees. He put a low-angle source of light at either end of the board. This way, each pin casts two shadows on the white surface, and the resulting mass of shadow makes the board completely dark. From this point on, all one has to do is to pull back certain groups of pins to reduce their shadows and make the corresponding area lighter. By pulling them out completely, any shadow vanishes, leaving just the illuminated part of the surface exposed. The artist was thus able to obtain a full range of greys in the creation of any shape. And this is where the animation comes in. Modifying the image manually and photographing it with a film camera at each new phase, the image comes to life.

It wasn't such a far-fetched idea as it might seem at first sight. Just think back to the principle of printing aquatints that we mentioned earlier on. Every small shadow cast over the surface of the boards equates with one of the tiny holes that absorb the black ink. Each white, lit up area corresponds to the bare (uninked) surface of the etched plate. In essence, Alexeieff managed to transfer the instrument that he already used for his static images into dynamic terms. He could now, definitively, make cinema out of animated prints.

THE PINSCREEN (THREE)

"This will be the film that I wanted to make but never could", Alosha (this was Alexeieff's nickname) told Claire one day. "And why not?" she asked him. "Because I haven't got enough money, and for this job, you need a lot of money". Claire's American pragmatism could not countenance an unfulfilled aspiration. "I have a letter of credit. I can finance the making of a pinscreen and the production of the film".

Together they assembled their first pinscreen and patented it (in Claire's name as the banker), thinking not just about the film that Alosha had in mind, but also letting the instrument pay for itself by selling copies of it to animators all over Europe and the rest of the world. This latter scheme, to their great surprise, never happened. That device wasn't exactly what many creators were looking for. In fact, for a long time, it was only so for Alosha and Claire. It wasn't until 1972 that the National Film Board of Canada acquired a pinscreen. For decades the French-Canadians Jacques Drouin and Michèle Lemieux were to be the only other filmmakers who would use it regularly.

UNE NUIT SUR LE MONT CHAUVE (A NIGHT ON BALD MOUNTAIN)

Russia was *far away* from Paris in 1931. In Moscow, political power was in the firm hands of Stalin, who was pitiless when it came to exiles. Many of them, gathered in various groups and ghettos (political, artistic, philosophical, religious, esoteric), spoke only Russian, excluded themselves from the France that was all around them, and chattering to each other about a return that they all knew was pure fiction. Alexandre Alexeieff frequented these groups for a while, at the start of his stay, and it was on one of those nights that he was dazzled by the piano playing of an old lady. He listened to her at first because she reminded him of his mother, also a pianist. But that evening the woman didn't play Chopin, as Maria Polidorova (Mrs. Alexeieff) used to do, but

A Night on Bald Mountain, a single-movement symphonic poem composed by Modest Mussorgsky in 1876 and arranged after his death by Nikolay Rimsky-Korsakov. The memory of that composition stuck in Alexeieff's mind, and he fantasised on it long and hard. When he decided that these gatherings of exiles were sterile and began to reconstruct his own internal Russia of the memory, choosing to live like a Frenchman among Frenchmen, *A Night on Bald Mountain* became the centrepiece around which all his nostalgia clustered.

For many days, in the darkness of his room, Alexeieff listened and listened to the recording made by the London Symphony Orchestra, conducted by Albert Coates, constantly fantasising around the piece. It was one of his ways to be a surrealist: the images surged involuntarily and dream-like from his subconscious, and he connected them later by analogy and without any rational thread to make them flow together.

He explained to Claire everything he wanted to put into the film, and she calculated the timing. It would work out as a piece of roughly forty-five minutes, which would need some trimming, as the music lasted a little over eight minutes. They set to it diligently, without any preparatory sketches that might spoil the spontaneity of the idea (the pinscreen itself, with the unpredictable but agreeably smooth touch of the steel pins, was also capable of suggesting improvisations to the artist-modeler), and at last, they were able to get down to the real work. In contrast to the tradition of animated cinema, the camera was positioned horizontally – like in shots of real images – with the pinscreen looming vertically in front of it. In a year and a half of continuous work, of reconstruction and corrections, Alexandre Alexeieff and Claire Parker made *A Night on Bald Mountain* and presented it to the public.

FEW SEE IT, MANY PEOPLE TALK ABOUT IT

The short was screened for a couple of weeks in Paris and for a week in London. Today nobody would be bothered about an event that was so palpably irrelevant. But in the 1930s there was more respect for intelligence, and *A Night on Bald Mountain* was such a novelty of a film that it caught the attention of intellectuals and journalists. To a ripe old age, Alexeieff kept a thick pile of articles and reviews published when it was first shown. In *Le Temps*, the musicologist and theoretician Emile Vuillermoz wrote:

> Among the latest offerings from the technique of cinema, we have to make a special note of this animated print essay by Alexandre Alexeieff. A masterly adaptation for the screen of Mussorgsky's *A Night on Bald Mountain*. We find in the film a series of absolutely new effects, whose importance should be stressed. (...) These animated prints reject all elements of realism. They are not photographs. Everything here is composition and transposition. But this is not even the traced drawing normally associated with animation. What we have before us is a printing technique, a dictionary of subtle nuances, of a range of greys and of blacks, whose marks of light and shade wax and wane to infinity. Instead of playing with lines and angles, the artist uses the language of surfaces, of volumes and of figures with shifting reliefs. In terms of the relationship with the music, it can be said that rarely does a conductor accept the discipline of the score with so much fidelity. Some parts demonstrate just how much can be achieved in this field when one tries to avoid the separation of two artistic disciplines born to work together. When the spectral beings arranged in a circle hold hands then raise and drop their arms, or the moment when the music surges like a rocket and then falls like rain, what is achieved is a reinforcement of musical emotion of extremely rare quality. (...) This film marks a day to remember.

Stefan Priacel wrote in *Regards*:

Two admirable artists have just put together a short film
of eight minutes' duration whose importance is such that
I consider this to be a date to write in the history of cinema. The subject of these images matters little. Let's say
that they are inspired by fantastic folklore of Ukraine,
to which Alexandre Alexeieff and Claire Parker added
their fantasies. There are hags and demons on horseback;
there are witches' sabbaths that combine musicians and
birds, horses and fireworks, landscapes that are calm one
moment and stormy the next, in one oneiric vision. But
the importance of the film lies not in the subject but in
a change in procedure whose scope is such that it could
be said to be to cinema what a beautiful painting is to a
photograph.

In Britain, in the autumn 1934 issue of *Cine Quarterly*, the great
filmmaker and producer John Grierson was beside himself with
admiration:

The film, beyond its technical interest, is a triumph of
fantasy. It's difficult to describe it, due to its startling
nature. Try to image a Walpurgis Night in which ani-
mal tracks on the ground indicate the presence of spirits,
where monsters and evil creatures appear, disappear and
tumble about by pure magic, where scarecrows dance
the fandango with their shadows on bare hillsides, where
black and white horses race across the highest heavens,
and skeletons that walk ... Every art house cinema
should show this film. It is the most astonishing, brilliant short that you will come across.

The distributors thought otherwise. They judged the film to be
very hard for the general public to cope with, and the best they
could come up with was to say that they would be willing to nego-
tiate a contract provided they had a guaranteed production of at

least six films a year, which was physically impossible. *A Night on Bald Mountain* started to make a bit of money thirty years later, when the US distributor and film specialist Cecile Starr put it on the American alternative circuit, on university campuses, and in associations passionate about art house cinema.

LIFE IN ADVERTISING

In the Europe of the 1920s and 1930s (unlike in the USA) it was quite common to show commercials at cinemas. But the European mentality of those days considered that boasting about the qualities of a product displayed slightly poor taste, so the advertisers adopted the softer approach of *making friends* with the audience. In practice, the publicity film, which could be four or five minutes long, presented itself as a show entertainment – witty, fun, original – and suggested purchasing the product only at the end, after having … forgiven the intrusion.

That meant that whoever had a creative mind could be given quite a lot of freedom so long as he was able to captivate the audience. Alexandre Alexeieff, Claire Parker, Alexandra Grinevsky, Etienne Raïk, and some other friends put their heads together and set off on this new path. Until the German invasion of France (1940) they all made a living from cinema commercials. On their return from their exile in the United States (1947), Alosha and Claire resumed that work and kept doing it for another ten years.

He didn't like advertising. It forced him to busy himself with things that had nothing to do with his inner world; it was just about selling objects. It put him in contact with clients whose myopia and arrogance he despised. For market reasons, moreover, what dominated was the use of colour, which he had always scorned, considering it a mere embellishment concerning the ideal work. And *that*, in his opinion, should be based on black and white, in other words, on the fundamental principles of yes and no, of love and hate, of good and evil, of life and death.

Despite everything, due to one of the many contradictions of the human soul, all his life he tirelessly defended the decision to devote himself to this work. He even declared that the painters of the Renaissance had no qualms about doing publicity for the Church, or court painters for their sovereigns, or the writers of *The Thousand and One Nights* for Arab merchants. Every retrospective organised in collaboration with him included his commercial films, of which he invariably showed himself proud.

These films have not aged well. They have lost any serious interest (with the partial exception of *La Belle au bois dormant*, 1935) and make patently clear the author's lack of intellectual interest. He rigorously avoids using the pinscreen, reserving it for more important occasions, and concentrates on small technical innovations to amuse himself and invent some motivation. At the risk of seeming too harsh, in my opinion Alexeieff's commercials tend towards kitsch and are best forgotten.

AMERICA AND BACK

In 1940 Hitler's troops invaded France. The day before they marched into Paris Alosha, Claire, Alexandra, and Svetlana left the country and moved to the USA, where Claire managed to get each one of them an American passport in record time. Alosha and Claire settled in the New York suburb of Mount Vernon and began a humble but happy life. Photos from those years show them smiling and head over heels in love.

Work, however, was hard to get because New York was not yet the world's capital of art and galleries, nor did it possess the cultural and worldly finesse that it would develop by the end of the century. An animator could only draw cartoons, and an artist had to paint like Grant Wood or Edward Hopper if he wanted to sell his work.

It was Norman McLaren, who had seen *A Night on Bald Mountain* in London and was then working for the National Film Board of Canada, who sought out the couple and proposed a small project to them: illustrating a Quebec folk song, *En passant*, to include it in a series that the NFBC had just got going.

For this film, two and a half minutes long, a screen with 1,125,000 pins, the largest in the whole of the career of Alosha and Claire, was specially built. *En passant* (Passing by, 1943) turned out to be a minor anomaly in the artistic production of the two filmmakers. It was the only film not to be based on a Russian story, the only one credited exclusively to Alexeieff, the only one that portrayed an external situation (like an impressionist canvas, with touches of Monet) instead of the inner movements of the mind. It has some stunning moments, like the church that suddenly becomes transparent, revealing its interior, but at the end of the day it is a lesser work; and Alexeieff himself always considered it as such.

ILLUSORY SOLIDS

The most abstract experimentation began in 1951, after their return to Paris. "Illusory" is a solid which, with long exposure time, is traced onto the cinema film by a moving source of light. The example that comes most easily to mind is the night-time photos of moving vehicles, published for many years in specialist magazines. The exposure is long, to get all the nocturnal light possible; the red tail lights and the white headlights don't register as points, rather as long luminous traces, which are "illusory" because they don't exist in reality.

Alexeieff decided to connect a tracing source (a chrome-plated metal sphere, which glowed when strongly illuminated) to a compound pendulum, whose oscillations were mathematically calculable and could, therefore, be predetermined. In this way, the different shapes that were traced in the air, one after the other, by the shining sphere could be predicted and controlled. Thus, it was possible to animate the illusory solids, those solids that were inexistent in reality. "What this is about – said the artist – is the second stage of the movement".

Though it was fascinating from a philosophical point of view, the nuts and bolts technique of illusory solids never merited more than a few seconds of film, normally used for suggestive special effects in publicity work. In 1952 *Fumées*, for the Belgian cigarette company Van Der Elst, won an award at the Venice Festival for its contribution to visual innovation.

The year 1956 was also important for our cinematic history. The prestigious Cannes Festival agreed to the request from various French filmmakers and critics, amongst them Alexeieff, Paul Grimault, and André Martin, to devote a section to animation. The *independent* (read: *non-Disney*) filmmakers had the chance to meet and find out that they had interests and goals in common. In 1960 the first festival in the world specialising in animated cinema was inaugurated in Annecy (Haute Savoy, France). Two years later saw the birth of Asifa (Association Internationale du Film d'Animation), the United Nations of the sector. Behind these initiatives invariably lay the discreet but determined will of Alexandre Alexeieff.

THE TWO GIANTS

In 1962 Orson Welles was involved with one of his many difficult projects: *The Trial*, based on the Franz Kafka novel. He realised that something was lacking, and he found it in Paris. Here is an account of the event in his own words:

(Peter Bogdanovich) – How did you manage to get the story illustrations for the prologue?

(Orson Welles) – They're images made with pins, thousands of pins. I found these two old Russian (*sic*), completely crazy, cultivated, elegant, fascinating. It was Alexandre Alexeieff and Claire Parker, husband and wife. They sat down and stuck pins in a big board. The shadow of the pins made the chiaroscuro. They were two of the kindest and happiest people in the world. In my opinion, those images are extraordinarily beautiful.

– Yes, they're really beautiful. How did you find them?

– I don't remember. I must have seen something on
television or somewhere. They were working on a film; I
think they'd been working on it for the last sixty years. I
went to see them, and I persuaded them to interrupt their
work for five months (not long, by their standards) and
stick pins for me. They did it, and they did it superbly.
– Yes. It's one of the moments of the film that I like
most.
– We should have made the whole film with pins!
With no actors. A film without actors, what you and
Alfred Hitchcock like![2]

As told by Claire Parker, the encounter had funnier touches:
After a couple of calls from the producer, Orson Welles came to
our studio. He started to look around everywhere, at all our equipment, getting more and more surprised. At first, he spoke to me
in English; then he realized that Alosha also spoke the language
well. From that moment he forgot my presence and addressed
himself solely to him. It was entertaining to see these two creative giants trying to seduce each other, to win each other over.
Eventually, they reached an agreement about how many images
were needed, how much time was needed, about how much
money was needed. Then, before leaving, Welles said to Alosha:
"Could I come here when you're working? I'll just be sitting in a
corner; I won't talk, I won't distract you. I'd like to see how you
create the prints on the pinscreen". Alosha looked at him, and
his voice became even more baritone: "One cannot refuse Orson
Welles anything – he replied as if he were pronouncing a sentence – but I know my work would suffer"! So, he parted with a
resigned smile, and we never saw him again. We found out, many
months later, that he was very pleased with the work.

Orson Welles wasn't wrong in identifying the actors as
the problem in his film. Indeed, *The Trial* has a fundamental defect: Anthony Perkins, too American, too

Hollywood, too short on nuances to cope with a role in which mystery has to turn into destiny and evil turn into life. His is a face in which one could probably read the neurosis of Freud but never, by a long way, the consummate darkness of Kafka. Many critics wrote that the prologue (based on another Kafka text, the short tale *The Judgement*) was better than the film itself. Alexeieff made it with fixed images, only slightly *enlivened*, darkened at some point in the developing process, while Welles's splendid voice narrates the story off screen.

Strange as it may seem, this one-off commissioned job turns out to us, as spectators, to be decidedly *alexeieffian*. The oneiric images of a mysterious large door, the enigmatic luck of a man trying to get through it, the atmosphere of fear that envelops the narration has much in common with *A Night on Bald Mountain*.

THE NOSE

The film which, to give credit to Orson Welles, Alosha and Claire had been shooting "for sixty years", was a short adaptation of a short novel by Nikolai Gogol. It was ready in 1963, and it was called *Le Nez* (*The Nose*).

The original story was published in 1836. The plot seems like a dream (a nightmare of castration, we students of popular Freudianism would say these days) in which a Saint Petersburg barber, one 25th of March, finds a nose in his breakfast bread. The nose starts to lead its own life, talking and socialising. The owner, his face denuded, tries to regain the protuberance he has possessed since birth, until on 7 April, when everything returns to normality.

Although it was classed within the canon of fantasy literature that had existed since the birth of humankind, *The Nose* had such a pronounced touch of surrealism that it even to some extent upset Gogol himself. Devoting the final pages to a debate on the implausibility of the affair, he did so intelligently, ironically, self-satirically, but letting slip a sneaking uncertainty, ending with these words: "However you look at things, in all this there is something truly absurd. Nevertheless, whatever you say, in this world similar events happen; seldom, but they do happen".

The setting is as always Russian culture, and this time the starting point is a piece in prose instead of a musical composition, in some sense as if Alexeieff had decided to transfer his experience as a book illustrator to the screen. (It should not be forgotten that only very recently had he produced a huge number of images for *Doctor Zhivago*, choosing to work with the pinscreen instead of etching plates.) In this film, we find all the now-familiar themes: the surreal, nostalgia, Russia, the old days of the nineteenth century, the absurdity of things, the irrational breaking into everyday life, even comedy. And it's all mixed in a wonderful black-and-white dream, using a secret process that allows the author to make the images pulse just like the light pulses in his beloved city of the White Nights and of his adolescence.

RETURN TO MUSSORGSKY

In 1972, for the first time, Alosha and Claire sent a film to compete at a festival (*The Nose* had been shown at Annecy but as a special screening). The result was bitter. The jury at the first Zagreb Festival decreed no recognition to the film by the two living legends of animation *d'auteur* and opted to award their Grand Prize to the Soviet *The Battle of Kershents*, directed nominally by the old Stalinist Iván Ivanov Vano and in practice by the unrestrained Yuri Norstein.

The work by the Parisian couple, *Tableaux d'une exposition* (*Pictures at an Exhibition*), was made up of three parts illustrating the three segments of the homonymous musical composition by Modest Mussorgsky dating from 1874.

Certainly, the jury made an error, given the film's indisputable artistic excellence. Yet in their defence it should be noted that there is no such thing as a jury that does not make mistakes.

Besides, given the extraordinary flowering of novelties coming from all the countries that attended in the early 1970s, this very personal, hermetic, black-and-white film made many, perhaps all of them, think that maybe Alexeieff was repeating himself sterilely.

As usually happens, the time has shown itself to be the best judge and the wisest critic. Removed from the emotion of its time, it reveals today all its exceptional poetic power, above all in the central piece entitled (oddly enough, in Italian) *Il vecchio castello* (*The Old Castle*). This is a masterpiece of non-narrative animation, interweaved with well-honed visual hints and with unimaginable dynamic inventions. Surprising is the play of bi-dimensionality and tri-dimensionality created by the simultaneous use of two pinscreens, one of them rotating in front of one that's static. In a letter dated 19 December 1971, announcing the completion of the film, Alexandre Alexeieff told this writer: "I think that this film is as good as *A Night on Bald Mountain*, although it's very different. You need to see it at least twenty times before you can say that you know it well. That is something that good poetry requires too".

THE MOON IS DOWN

With seventy years behind him, Alexeieff started to feel old. Claire was still smiling, displaying her natural cheerfulness and optimism, but the French Slav was showing signs of melancholy. In 1977 he mentioned that he was planning some last experiments and that he wanted to have a go at doing an animated version of *adagio* defined by the pace of its movements. He also said he was fascinated by the caressing movement of the leaves of a lime tree.

The experiments turned into the last film, *Trois thèmes* (*Three Themes*, also known as *Three Moods*), based on three other pieces from Mussorgsky's *Pictures at an Exhibition*. In the first piece, we see an ox melting away in a Russian landscape, while in the second a string of images from *Pictures at an Exhibition*. The third offers a contrast between an obtuse giant stamping out coins and a brave little flying thing (and in whom we recognise Mussorgsky) buzzing around to try to get some attention. Despite the fact that it has plenty of quality moments, this is a film made by an old man, by someone who has run out of steam. It is an attempt to summarise his artistic life and, more or less consciously, leave behind a spiritual testimonial. It is the work of a pessimist. The last *picture* in this *exhibition* shows us the heavy, rich Goldenberg producing money with his fists, while around him pants the tiny, anxious, creative Schmuyle. The former symbolises the power of the wealthy man, the latter the weakness of the artist. And the scales hang on the musical notes, ringing when the coins fall into his dish, but it changes its balance definitively when golden coins rain into the other.

"Alexeieff loved putting the moon in his films", confessed Claire Parker to the public in the soundtrack of *À coups d'épingles*[3] (*To the Sound of Pins*), a short 1959 documentary. In *Three Themes*, for the first time, we see no moon. Without giving too much importance to this element, which could have been accidental (yet, knowing Alexeieff's complex psychology, it doesn't seem likely), undoubtedly the missing moon is indicative of a farewell.

Claire Parker began to show the first symptoms of bone cancer in the spring of 1981, and after a great deal of suffering, she died in Paris on October 3 that year. Alexandre Alexeieff, beaten, survived her less than a year. He left us on the 9th of August 1982.

NOTES

1. Normally, for example, one speaks of 8½ as "a masterpiece by Fellini", overlooking the fact that for the film he was able to use uniquely talented collaborators: the scriptwriter Ennio Flaiano, the set designer Piero Gherardi, the director of photography Gianni Di Venanzo, and the musician Nino Rota.
2. Quoted from the book *This Is Orson Welles*, by Peter Bogdanovich and Orson Welles, edited by Jonathan Rosenbaum, New York: Harper Collins, 1992.
3. Play on words: *un coup d'épingle* in French is "a small provocation".

CHAPTER 7

The First Reviews of *A Night on Bald Mountain**

A NIGHT ON BALD MOUNTAIN (*Une nuit sur le Mont Chauve*) was shown in Paris in 1933, with a critical success that had few equals for a short film of just over eight minutes. It had been made in eighteen months of hard work by Alexandre Alexeieff (Kazan, 1901–Paris, 1982) and by his partner Claire Parker (Boston, 1906–Paris, 1981), photographing frame by frame the images that were created utilising a tool invented by Alexeieff himself and called écran d'épingles (pinscreen).

It was a white, square board on which 500,000 retractable black pins were fixed. They were illuminated by two light sources placed on the two upper corners. Thanks to this lighting system, every single pin cast a shadow on the surface of the board, long in proportion to its output: in this way it was possible to obtain an absolute white (completely retracted pin) or a whole range of

---

* First published in *Immagine – Note di storia del cinema*, Nuova serie, nn. 38–39, Rome, 1997.

greys up to absolute black (pin completely escaped and shadow brought up to cover the adjacent pin). The principle, identical to that of the black dots on the engraver's plate, allowed Alexeieff and Parker to get animated etchings. The artistic quality was the same as the illustrations for quality books that Alexeieff had made in the 1920s, and for which he was already famous in the restricted milieu of the sector's specialists. The construction of the pinscreen, which he had envisioned since 1929, had been made possible thanks to the funds available to Claire Parker, who entered his life in 1930. In fact, the relative patent was deposited in her name, in recognition of the importance the funding had had.

A Night on Bald Mountain was based on the homonymous symphonic poem by Modest Mussorgsky. It was one of the most fascinating and vital proposals to solve the problem of the relationship between image and sound; as such it quickly became a cult film. Often it was more quoted than seen, also because of the difficult availability of copies. Many people confused it with the episode with the same title of Walt Disney's *Fantasia*, made seven years later.

This masterpiece of the first season of animation cinema predicted with extreme significance many of those characteristics that had to mark, thirty years later, the great international wave of author animation, certainly the more important and interesting phenomenon, in terms of quality, in the world history of the sector.

Before dying, Alexeieff entrusted this writer with the collection of reviews that appeared in the press at the time of the first release of *A Night on Bald Mountain*. It was, in his words, the film's pressbook, but also the book concerning the film (the filmmaker loved to play with words, in this case on the double meaning of "book of the press" and "book for the Press"). He gave this collection a meaning of completeness as far as the critical reception of the film had been.

From it we draw here some quotations.

The musicologist and theorist Émile Vuillermoz wrote in *Le Temps* (the date is untraceable):

Among the new contributions of the film technique, an essay of "animated engraving" made by Alexandre Alexeieff, in an adaptation to the screen of the *Night on Bald Mountain* of Mousorgsky. This is a series of absolutely new effects, whose importance is worth underlining. Responding to a wish that, for my part, I have expressed very often and for a long time, the film directors periodically try to transpose a musical masterpiece onto the screen.

I will not remind my readers of the close ties that unite the grammar and syntax of sentences written for the eye with the grammar and syntax of sentences built for the ear (…) His [Alexeieff's] animated engravings reject every realistic element. Realistic. There are no photographs of reality. Everything here is composition and transposition. But it is not even of the animated drawing in the sense of drawing line that generally applies to this procedure. We are in the presence of a technique of etching, of a subtle vocabulary of nuances, of a range of grays and blacks, of a sort of chalcography or printing, whose patches of light and shadow fade and come to life to infinity. Instead of playing with lines or angles, the artist uses the language of surfaces, volumes and models with changing reliefs. (…) Very rarely I saw a director accepting the disciplines of a score so loyally. Some passages show everything that can be achieved in this field, when you don't want to separate two limbs that are made so well to get along. When the hallucinatory beings holding hands raise and lower their arms, when the music rockets and falls as rain, a musical emotion of the rarest quality is strengthened.

The technique of animated engraving is certainly of great richness and can give the spectators works of the highest interest. In the musical film it has to play a leading role. *A Night on Bald Mountain* is just a first demonstration and a first sampling of this new language. But this film marks a date that we must not forget.

The considerations of Stefan Priacel on the "Spectacles" column of *Regards* magazine (date unknown) follow:

Two admirable artisans, who are also great artists, Alexandre Alexeieff and Claire Parker, have just made a film, a small film, whose importance however is such that it seems to constitute a date in the history of cinematography. A symphonic work by the great Russian composer Mousorgsky, *A Night on Bald Mountain*, served as a theme for twelve thousand images whose projection lasts just eight minutes. The subject itself of these images does not matter. Let's just say that they are inspired by the fantastic folklore of Ukraine, to which is added the imagination of Alexeieff and Claire Parker. There are witch and demon rides, sabbaths in which dreams are mixed, musicians and birds, horses and fireworks, landscapes that alternate serene and tormented scenes. But the importance of the film is not in the subject, it is in the procedure invented by the two authors, applied here for the first time and whose scope is such that we can say that it is to the cinema what a beautiful painting is to a photograph. Alexandre Alexeieff and Claire Parker call it "animated engraving" (…) It has the extraordinary advantage of offering more than a hundred shades of gray, which is very necessary in film, given the rapidity of the projection.

This fineness of grays allows to pass from one image to another without jerks, through half-tones, giving each image a complete model. It goes without saying that the human eye is not sensitive enough to distinguish all these nuances, but thanks to this procedure it is possible to create, from one image to another, a transition identical to that of "true photography". (...) Thus it will be possible to make this art which is engraving accessible to a wide public. (...) Alexeieff, one of the most excellent contemporary engravers, is the first to realize this.

Paul Gilson also dwells on the importance of the technical procedure in an article of 18 October 1933 in *L'Intransigeant*. Gilson concludes his paper thus:

A Night on Bald Mountain is the work of two artisans who oppose the conception of work on the assembly line. This work that does not last even half an hour [half an hour, sic] represents more than a year of work. Alexandre Alexeieff and Claire Parker have sometimes lived a second of their film in one day. The witches of *A Night on Bald Mountain* can vanish with the last aquatint of the film: it remains alive as it once was the witch teacher, Itta. The Sabbath of *A Night on Bald Mountain* has the beauty of the devil.

Enthusiastic, finally, is the note that the great British filmmaker, organiser, and producer John Grierson dedicates to the film in *Cinema Quarterly* of autumn 1934:

This short film introduces a new method of animation, the particulars of which are the secret of the inventor, Alexeieff. The general effect is of animated engraving. There is a soft shadowy quality in the form, and none of the hard precision of line associated with cartoons. The forms emerge from space, they have the appearance of dissolving to other forms. Three dimensional qualities seem to be easily achieved, and models in animation can be introduced without disturbing the general style. The film, apart of its technical interest, is an imaginative performance, though difficult to describe. Imagine, however, a *Walpurgis Nacht,* in which animated footsteps indicate spirit presence, goblins and hobgoblins appear and disappear and tumble fantastically, scarecrows do a fandango with their shadows on empty hillsides, white horses and black tear across high heaven and skeletons walk. The animation is to the music of Mussorgsky. All films societies should see this film. It is as astonishing and as brilliant a short as they are likely to find.

The readers have probably observed that, while some reviewers scrupulously adhere to the dictates of the opening credits (which reads "Animated engravings of Alexeieff and Claire Parker"), others only mention the man's name. The phenomenon will be repeated in the following decades, so much so that still the name of Claire Parker is relatively little known even to specialists.

This lack has not to do with a male chauvinist bullying (Alexandre always tried to promote Claire's merits), but rather with the mentality of "Making loans only to the rich", which extended to the film the unique signature of the already accredited etcher. Luckily, this time the damage has been limited. According to Claire Parker herself and to unanimous testimony of those who knew their working method, most of the contribution, in the creative field, was due to Alexandre Alexeieff.

CHAPTER 8

Dreams of Alexeieff

IT HAS BEEN ARGUED for many decades that people dream in black and white. Today this idea is rejected, but it was common currency at the time of Alexandre Alexeieff and certainly had a basis in the consciousness of the dreaming person. The memory of nocturnal images is blurred, based more on impressions than on images, echoing badly remembered plots – then completed by conscious reinterpretation: a bit like black-and-white cinema, which has evocation characteristics much superior to realistic colour film.

It is therefore no coincidence that Alexeieff, intimately indebted to the dream and to memory for his creation, has always done – when he wanted to make art and not advertising – black-and-white films, and that he has always opposed colour in general, considering it to be ornamental and in fact irrelevant on an aesthetic level. Colour was useful only in making the works "pretty" in the eyes of culturally less well-equipped users. The opinion is personal and certainly not acceptable, but it was rooted in the artist and must be taken into account in thinking about him and his work.

A universe in black and white, then. To which the pinscreen technique attributes blurred contours, such as the images that come to us when we fall asleep; and to which we do not bring all the synaesthesia of our present body, but a sort of selected, eminently emotional and visionary participation. Alexeieff did not believe in art as a reproduction of reality, he did not believe (he often repeated that) in an orchestra's three-dimensionality. He asserted: "I play fiddle". And he built works based on free mental associations, allusions, suggestions, echoes. Like lyric poetry. Like the re-enactment of dreams. He was in good company. Although he was proudly individualistic and pursued an autonomous and unassailable inspiration, he was a frequent visitor to the surrealists, a friend for the whole life of one of them in particular and the most radical: Philippe Soupault.

The passion of the surrealists for the dream is known. When the surveillance of reason has diminished, the constraint of social issues is cancelled. In the dream activity there was no automatic writing through artifices that inhibited the conscience (alcohol, drugs, "cretinising evenings", games like exquisite corpse): the subconscious turned into surreal without translation tools.

American director Henry Hathaway directed *Peter Ibbetson* in 1935. It is the story of a man (Gary Cooper) unjustly condemned to life imprisonment, but who every night, in the misery of his prison, can free himself from the current situation and reunite with the woman he loves (Ann Harding), who dreams the same dream of him. Leaving aside the assessments on quality (not negligible), the film is remembered because the surrealists saw there one of their theoretical cornerstones. (Actually the original text was a novel by George Du Maurier.) For Alexeieff, *Peter Ibbetson* was this and something more. That bond that was retied every night also represented the mirror of an indelible devotion: his for the native Russia he had abandoned, that he could not forget – but it is more accurate to say that he refused to – and that still lived in him at times when vigilance was relaxed.

Sigmund Freud argued that all dreams are the hallucinatory realisation of a desire (Gesammelte Schriften, II, pp. 126–136). If it is allowed to force the reasoning a bit, we could say that the entire artistic/dreaming activity of Alexandre Alexeieff is the hallucinatory realisation of a return to maternal Russia. First in the form of a nightmare with *A Night on Bald Mountain*; the artist himself claimed to have understood, only after many years, that he had described the tragedy of the death of his own father in the fall of the white horse, and the consequent clouding over of his mother in the struggle between the witches. The same approach fits to the fantastic reworking of *The Nose* (from Gogol, 1963). Eventually, we see it as a sentimental and cultural evocation with *Pictures at an Exhibition* (1972) and *Three Moods* (1980).

It would be an error of perspective to consider Alexeieff as the last of the romantics, and to read his work, both cinematographic and illustrational, as a collection of sighs dedicated to the things, to the people and to the places he desired. Other components were also very incisive in him, from the experimental to the humorous to the exotic. Even the perpetual resumption of the thread of the discourse on Russia was much more reasoned and articulated than a simple devotion to the birthplace: he had a very high literary admiration towards *Doctor Zhivago*, of which he left us a splendid illustrated edition. The admiration for Solgenitsin's prose was also very high; his mindset and personal history as a political opponent (in which he could have found a reflection of himself) did not touch him on the contrary for nothing.

One could essentially say that in this author (so different yet always so identical, so elusive yet so powerful) the memory is an ethical choice, therefore pre-aesthetic and of connotative consequence of the whole work. "I am a conservative", he observed in a letter addressed to this writer, "but not in the political sense: rather in the sense that I would never want the things that really have value lost".

The selection of things that really had value (even pictorial, even cinematographic) was by Alexeieff made a priori with respect to the material creation of images; and from this mental warehouse the scene to be reproduced was then extracted from time to time.

In *Pictures from an Exhibition* and in *Three Moods* we see land-scapes from childhood, corners of the maternal house, domestic furniture, toys, and the comrades of the Petersburg cadet school in which he himself studied.

In his life Alexeieff only once made a copy from life: when he asked his wife, Claire Parker, to pose for the etchings dedicated to the *Man's Fate* of Malraux. It was for the portrait of a dead woman and he always said, laughing and almost apologetically, that he needed his most lively affection to be able to trace the mourning with a sure hand.

CHAPTER 9

Bruno Bozzetto*

His Early Years

B RUNO BOZZETTO BEGAN HIS artistic career in 1958 with *Tapum! The History of Weapons*. He was only twenty years old, and for four years he had been making narrow gauge films, learning and experimenting with animation techniques on his own. The film is admired everywhere, receives awards (in Mulhouse and Rapallo), and is favourably reviewed. In the traditionally poor panorama of Italian animated films, the name of the young Milanese became an obligatory point of reference from the first moment.

The second part of the 1950s is perhaps the most tumultuous period of Italian animation. Once the stammering of the pioneering generation had ended, and the attempts at full-length films had failed (*La rosa di Bagdad* by Domeneghini and *The Dynamite Brothers* by Pagot, both from 1949), the activity turned to theatrical advertising. The area was not vast, but the chance of survival was assured.

---

* Originally published as a booklet with the title *Animazione primo amore* (*My First Love, Animation*, Milan: ISCA, 1972). Updated and revised version.

The novelty year was 1957 when the state broadcaster RAI opened its one television channel to advertising. The prime-time program was called *Carosello*, and it was a series of installments, each one combining an entertainment "body" and a "pigtail" dedicated to praising the product. The small screen suddenly expanded the market, while the nascent economic boom sky-rocketed the demand for audiovisual advertising. Many small producers found new sap, others were born and entered the lists; the ongoing activity refined the technique of the animators, and the best ones abandoned the companies in which they had carried out their apprenticeship to set up on their own.

Bruno Bozzetto made his encounter with advertising in 1960, after another two years as an amateur. In the process of selling equipment and dedicating himself to university exams, he came across an old friend one day. He sees his work and gives him an order for the company of which he is an emissary. It is the birth of the first, very short advertising series: five episodes, based on the character of Kuko.

From this moment the activity of the "Bruno Bozzetto Film" would be split into two channels of advertising and entertainment films, in a kind of mutualistic symbiosis whereby the former finances the latter and the latter acts as promotion for the former.

It was indispensable, to keep faith with these intentions, to create an agile structure. Bozzetto needed a team: his goals were too industrial for him to work alone and too creative for an impersonal organisation like that of the American and Japanese studios of the time to be tolerated.

He manages to bring together a good number of intelligent, young and enthusiastic collaborators; with them he decides to attempt the feat that for sixteen years has disturbed the sleep of Italian animators, captivating them and rejecting them: the feature film.

In 1965 *West and Soda* premiered at the "Arlecchino" cinema in Milan. The public flows in large numbers, even if an

unpredictable fact dampens the interest: during the slow process-
ing of the animated film, Sergio Leone has made *Per un pugno di
dollari* (*A Fistful of Dollars*) and uncorked the phenomenon of
the Spaghetti western, obviously in competition with Bozzetto's
film. However, the result is positive. The team proves to be valid.
Ermanno Comuzio extends a nice compliment to the twenty-
seven-year-old author writing:

> Bozzetto seems to be the one who sums up all the Italian
> animation filmmakers, fusing in his company – more
> workshop in the Renaissance sense than industrial stu-
> dio – art and technique, that is the taste and the ability to
> create, to experiment, to propose a style, with the indis-
> pensable instrumental needs of an efficient organism.[1]

West and Soda taught an inattentive and unaware audience that
animators existed and operated in Italy, capable of producing a
film on the level of Hollywood productions. The next *VIP, My
Brother Superman* had the favour of the public as well, but in the
meantime, through the breach opened by Bozzetto, more people
had passed to feature film (the Gavioli brothers, Zac, the Cenci
brothers).

Some commentators claim that these are the least beautiful
works coming from the Via Melchiorre Gioia atelier in Milan.
Maybe. The same could be valid for TV opening titles, like the
fortunate "Donna Rosa" of the *Settevoci* show, to which another
considerable part of the notoriety of the studio is linked. However,
these were the only means of engaging the public in animation. A
difficult courtship, which pushes the author of animated films to
make concessions to the current taste to the detriment of the gen-
uineness of his own inspiration and the linguistic characteristics
of the medium (the concise character of the animated expression
is not suitable for the length of the feature film).

After *VIP* Bozzetto experienced a period of crisis, which lasts
two years and during which he makes only two short films (but

Ego belongs more to the background designer Mulazzani than to him). He comes out of the black-dog period abandoning the unloved advertising activity and devoting himself instead of making his "personal" films.

Bozzetto gives a precise indication in the humanistic direction, openly pronouncing himself for the artistic characteristics of animation as a craft. "If I have to go to the assembly line and sell a product, then I'd rather produce something else. Shoes, for example, why not".[2]

MR. ROSSI

Before 1960, the year of *An Oscar for Mr. Rossi*, Bozzetto had populated his films with bizarre figurines for the sole purpose of enriching the plot, which was the real reason of interest. Mr. Rossi, on the other hand, sacrifices the narrative structure of the film. Bozzetto's love for his creature will remain alive for decades, demonstrating how a figure born almost by chance was able to objectify the author's world well.

Mr. Rossi is enough a character as to primarily attract the interest of the viewer and make the plot pass in the second line. However, his personality, once delineated, never deepens, remains in a state of hint. Many might prefer the contemptuous diction of "caricature" and decide that a character without psychology is a failure without remedy.

This writer thinks that Mr. Rossi is a close relative of the Chaplinian tramp, of the Buster Keatonian great stone face, of the young-man-with-horn-rimmed-glasses of Harold Lloyd. In the great and fruitful tradition of the American vaudeville of 1910–1920, the animated short film by Terry and Fleischer and Disney finds its roots; from these, in turn, the Italian-drawn comedian is born, although contaminated with the great lesson of the United Productions of America (UPA) and above all of Bobe Cannon (see the stylistic analogies with *Gerald McBoing Boing*, 1951).

Bozzetto's comedy is rooted in the principles and recipes of the Californian one reel, although filtered through a European vision (with the eye more to the intellect than to the instinct, and therefore blander in the rhythms of the action), and although restrained in the graphic sign (the "I style" of the UPA against the round opulence of the "O style" of Disney): the chase (*Mr. Rossi Buys a Car*), the gag (classically formed by premise, expectation, surprise; see the episode of the bather in *Mr. Rossi to the Beach*), the absurd (the examples are multiple; think to the seller of *An Oscar for Mr. Rossi* whose face turns into a record player while he repeats his rigmarole always the same). The French scholar Jean-Pierre Coursodon, in synthesising the definition of a vaudevillian hero, provides a portrait that fits perfectly with our Rossi: "A handicapped man, who is saved from annihilation only thanks incessant stratagems typical of the oppressed, and thanks to a paradoxically enormous luck".[3]

After what has been said, it is clear why the character should not be investigated with psychological tools, which do not belong to him. Hero of vaudeville, it fulfils the task of all vaudeville heroes: it acts.

Lloyd's horn-rimmed-glasses man had rudimentary features, which indicated him as the dreamer but full of energy and practical optimism. Chaplin was the eternal dispossessed, Langdon the teenager, Keaton was so many things, perhaps all coming from the moon.

These summary and – above all – generic characteristics constituted the viaticum for which the viewer who considered himself an adolescent, or disinherited, or petty bourgeois, could identify himself in the hero and laugh with gusto at the comic aspects of his daily life; at the variations on the theme that happened to his avatar on the screen.

The secret, for the actor, was then to identify the "type" for which he felt he was cut, and then identify the actions, the facts, the experiences that were to the "type", as well as congenial and habitual. Afterward, it was only a question of turning them to ridicule. The merits of the American comedy arise from these foundations of structure; and they are the inexhaustible fantasy, the inventive genius, the acumen of observation, the mastery in orchestrating the effects. The satire of custom is lacking, and those who seek it at all costs (there have been, and there are) are guilty of cultural provincialism.

Bozzetto's man in the street is the portrait of a hot-tempered petty bourgeois, ugly and uptight because he is unable to excel in anything. A victim, almost always, of events that are everyday stuff but which turn out to be bigger than him (and, it seems appropriate to say, only him, which frustrates him even more), but he is always ready to try again. He is eternally in the quest of an ideal: that may be a hit (*Rossi Oscar*), tranquillity (*Rossi Beach, Rossi Campsite*), leisure (*Rossi Skiing, Rossi Safari*), or the desire to keep up with the times (*Rossi Car*).

The classic structure of his adventures sees a beginning, in which Rossi forms this ideal (or by dreaming, or by casually encountering it); a development, which summarises the troubles on which he bangs his head; and an ending, mostly bitter, that records his failure.

In Rossi, the viewer can identify himself, laugh at his own tics, at his own faults. There is always a certain underlying flattery alive (also ancient as the school of comedy in entertainment).

In other words, the character is too wretched to allow complete identification by the viewer. As far as satire is concerned, this is the limit of Bruno Bozzetto's satire. The type of people whom he sees in real life – and then puts on the screen – can laugh at things that no one refuses to laugh at. He will not be shamed for what he should not want to discuss publicly or for what "is no joke".

These considerations do not entail a value judgement. Every author has his own poetic world and his own ideology, and no one will want to expect from Bozzetto what Bozzetto was not born to give. We have clarified the features of his satire precisely to avoid the risk of elevating to an aesthetic criterion that it is the ferocity or yielding of the invective.

THE FEATURE FILM

For the general public, "film" is synonymous with "feature film". The approach with such a general public then passes through the Caudine Forks of the hour and a half of projection; then if we talk about animation, here is another drain: "animation" means "Disney", and "animated film" means "cinematic fable for children". (It follows that if a work is for children, it is not suitable for refined adults; consequently, it is not appropriate to disturb the aesthetics.)

Here's the crossroads: Compete with Disney by putting yourself on the same level, giving the public what they already want, or compete with Disney by denying it and trying to attract the public with a novelty? The first way leads to financial and artistic failure, the second is no less risky, but at least it allows the author to keep faith with his/her inspiration.

West and Soda and *VIP, My Brother Superman* are expressions of the second way of trying luck. Both imperfect for some commercial compromises, especially the second; but recognisably signed Bozzetto in every sequence. Both possess intelligence, vivacity, and sarcasm, in a dose that perhaps frightens some parents in search of harmless fables, but definitely have qualities for those who approach show business-land with a receptive mind.

We are facing two parodies: the parody of the western in *West and Soda*, complete with a neurotic gunslinger, a girl called Clementine (think of the namesake song), a very bad boss, redskins, and bluejackets; and a parody of the adventure comic books in *VIP*. It is a way always known to comedy if it is true that Aristophanes parodied Euripides; and that fits well with the spirit of our filmmaker, made of acute observation and propensity to demystifying laughter.

Tradition serves as a connective; using it as a support, Bozzetto can work at ease, not constrained by narrative or explanation commitments. Proceeding with another directive, we arrive at the same result. The paramount recipe of the vaudeville farce consists of choosing a physical environment as a theme, from which to draw all the possible inventions (those who know, for instance, Stan Laurel, know what incredible variations on the theme he can draw from a door that does not close). A step further, and we are at the choice of a tradition, well known to the public as a physical environment and to the exploitation of all the opportunities it offers. The parody, therefore, serves to sketch the circle.

The feature film implies narrativity, thinking in prose. The greats of the golden age of comedy had to radically transform their works when they passed from the two reels to the hour and a half of projection. In the beginning, an idea was enough, a skeleton whose pulp would have been the gags; then it was necessary to create psychologies, plots, secondary actions. In short, to embark into screwball comedy.

This way of entertaining audiences is difficult to reach, with a medium like the animated cartoon. This does not allow psychological investigations and mimic games; its linguistic features are conciseness and non-narrativity. The point is, therefore, to dilute as long as it is possible the characteristics of the short film and arrive at last at the fateful running time. Dress a large body in a tight dress, make the circle square.

Bozzetto manages quite well in the intent, in the one case as in the other. *West and Soda* is not boring; it does not suffer from showy slowdowns; it is rich in brilliant gags and acute details. At least two sequences are textbook: the aggression of the ants to Johnny, and the final duel between the hero and Despicable. The best of the film, however, lies in even more minute touches. Here are some: a completely original absurdity (the cows that open up like refrigerators, the horse equipped with a speedometer, the devil who emerges from the ground to take Despicable); and some minor characters (Socrates the drunkard dog, the two gravediggers, the moose head in the house of Despicable). On the other hand, three aggressions and violence at Clementine's house are frankly too many; the elements of gold and land tenure end up overlapping and performing the same function of pushing Despicable against the two positive heroes.

Nor Clementine herself, Ursus, Slim, or Esmeralda are satisfactorily fully expressed. Dominant is Despicable, half Shylock and half Al Capone, and also the figure of Johnny, the gunslinger in a crisis of conscience and with the Stetson eternally lowered on the face (he takes it off only once, on the diligence, and for a few tenths of a second; this writer has seen the film in slow motion and can testify that he has brown hair and a parting).

VIP, My Brother Superman had an arduous production. At first, it had to parody the adventures of The Phantom; the little Vip had to be the hero's caricature (the elements of the aquiline nose and the red costume remained); Happy Betty had to be Neapolitan and even have a boyfriend. American capital intervened, so there was a reorganisation from which the handsome SuperVip was born, then Nervustrella, Lisa, and the little songs to fill downtime. American capital volatilised.

Despite these accidents, the filigree of the film remains good, and the praises made about the previous one could be repeated. The differentiating element consists of greater thematic maturity and a broader intellectual commitment, where the former was above all characterised by imagination and youthful enthusiasm (even the dominant colours are warm in one and cold in the other).

Particularly interesting is the insert on advertising and mass communication. An insert that is perhaps disharmonious and too long, but very much in line with the underlying spirit.

The two VIPs represent the champions of human nature against massification, and massification is not the usual future danger that in dystopic narratives is vanquished in the name of the "good" present. It is precisely our present, which the island of Happy Betty portrays in perfect miniature. The scientist who carries out the demonstration would not dream of being confident on the condition of the human brain of today: his problem is to use the brain missile for good rather than for evil. To let the mind reboot itself is just not an option.

The visit that Happy Betty makes her shareholders perform through the factory gives the dismay. Midgets all the same work under a heavy yoke, and for their "holidays" they are canned in long afferent tubes (our highways?) and conveyed to places of leisure no less false and neurotic than the world they have left. Only the voice-over comment, of light humour, mitigates the impression that leaves this concentration camp world. Hope, the author seems to tell us, lies in the simple man, in the concrete conscience of each of us. The one who removes chestnuts from the fire is not the invincible giant, but the small Vip, the one who is kicked and punched, is short-sighted, and flutters for a few metres panting for fatigue. Bozzetto's humanistic spirit manifests itself in full: when the measure of man is lost, it is up to him to regain it, without hoping for anything from superheroes or semi-magical equivalents.

SHORT FILMS

Alpha Omega dates back to 1961. A schematic character, in a static shot, lives his parable from birth to death, from alpha to omega. The various enticements and the various opportunities of existence are presented to him, in the form of brief appearances: education, love, goodness, marriage, work, health. When he is close to dying, he calls the poor to whom he had not given a coin, frees the bird he had caged. The film has a slow, moving trend, in which even the smiling notes give more tenderness than joy.

The theme of man's destiny returns, much more mature and motivated, in *A Life in a Box*, which is from 1967. Here the contrast between the world of fantasy and beauty is symbolised by the vision of a very colourful nature and by a piece of music that evokes joy, and the dehumanising contemporary world. The beginning is a subtly allegoric trompe l'oeil (what appears to be a rising sun is the belly of a pregnant woman dressed in red).

Nothing in this film could be added or removed; as a whole, it is a small jewel of cinematographic poetry. The timing, the graphic and sound solutions, everything is fitting and well resolved.

In the same year, 1967, Bozzetto made the third of what we could call lyric films.

"The man and his world" was the theme that the Montreal Expo had proposed to animators around the world, to be held within the fixed duration of one minute. Bozzetto won a silver medal telling of a politician (whose face changes very quickly: Truman, Stalin, Khrushchev, Nasser, and so on) who, while speaking in public, tries to chase away a butterfly that disturbs him. At this point, an increasingly dizzying zooming backwards begins, from the speaker to the earth, to the stars, to the galaxies, until we discover that the galaxies are only a part of the body of another butterfly, similar to the first, which twirls twice and then disappears from the field. The relativity of what surrounds us, the sweetness of nature, the fallibility of man, are underlined by an excellent soundtrack.

Bozzetto's lyrical style is somewhat reminiscent of Guido Gozzano, also due to the image of the butterfly (the Turin writer died before concluding an entomological poem). In both, there is a mixture of emotion and irony, of guarded tenderness, of feeling tempered by scepticism. We should not push the parallel beyond the indication of an analogy, but it testifies how we can compare certain cinema to poetry, without blushing. *I due castelli* (*The Two Castles*, 1963) records the actions of one of two castellans who tries to storm the manor facing it. The tidy drawing and the originality of the gags (some of which will be reproduced in *West and Soda*) constitute the titles of merit of this work.

I due castelli is bare and linear; *Ego* (1969) instead is leafy and colourful. The structure of the dream, that is two thirds of the film, is based on an evocative technique that is often too subtle to be communicative. Although it shines in many points of intelligence, the film seems to be among the least personal (after all, the hand of the scenographer Giovanni Mulazzani is present perhaps more than that of Bozzetto himself), and the presence of horror elements, like the long lines of hanged people, seems to confirm it.

Sottaceti (*Pickles*, 1971) is a series of film-pill each of which portrays a concept: war, hunger, religion, et cetera. The taste of the brief apologue, of the pregnant gimmick, has always been alive in this author who claims his highest admiration for the Japanese Yoji Kuri and his short and cruel animated flashes. In *Pickles*, the expressive maturity is achieved, as well as the disappearance of the juvenile residues, at both thematic and expressive levels.

The *Conquests* sequence shows the mountain so painfully climbed collapse on the two climbers. The composition of the titles of each chapter is rhythmic and spectacular (sometimes the letters make the whims), and if the drawing is less polished than usual (Bozzetto has drawn and coloured by himself here), it is more expressive.

BEFORE THE BEGINNING

The first animation work of the man who would have been nicknamed "The Italian Disney" has to do with Disney: it's a Donald Duck cartoon. Shot in black and white, 8 mm, the film dates back to 1953 and is no more than a technical experiment. A roughly drawn Donald Duck walks (on a background that wobbles, because it was redesigned every time; no cels then) until he comes across a newspaper in the ground whose title reads: "The Martians are coming". Donald catches a sign with the sentence "Then we flee" and vanishes. This first approach would just be a curiosity if there was not a notable element: that zoom towards the newspaper headline that could not be done "in the camera" and that therefore had to be drawn every time by hand. A precise stylistic choice, already tenaciously pursued (to save the effort it would have been enough to proceed by straight cut), demonstrating the good stuff of the fifteen-year-old author.

Indian Fantasy (8 mm black and white, 1954) shows that the first lesson was useful. The rhythm is well directed by the filmmaker; the first gags make their appearance; we note the use of some cels.

In 1955 Bozzetto tried to animate puppets. It had to be a science fiction movie, with small robots and shining spaceships. It was not completed, and only a few outtakes remain. At the same time, Bozzetto tried his hand at live action. Of 1954 is *I ladri che mascalzoni* (*Thieves, What Rogues!*), based on a chase (the fugitive is a thief specialised in disguises) and made sapid by some film tricks. *Il cerchio si stringe* (*The Circle Tightens*) of the same year seems the continuation of the previous one (characterized by pursuits and camouflages that follow one another on the roofs of Milan).

These amateur films, such as the following and unfinished *Due ragni nel piatto* (*Two Spiders on the Plate*, 1958), are the anticipation of the lifelong taste for the slapstick film with actors, with camouflages and sneers of the comedian who hunt him down.

Equally significant are the documentaries on nature (*Piccolo mondo amico* [*Little World Friend*], 1955; *I gatti che furbacchioni* [*The Smartass Cats*], 1956; *Sul filo dell'erba* [*On a Thread of Grass*], 1957; *Il solito documentario* [*The Usual Documentary*], 1959).

They testify to Bruno Bozzetto's love of nature, a love that we find in the entire subsequent work, and which is also expressed in the recurring interest for insects (see the humorous book *Thousand Little Cretins*). Secondly, they prove how rooted was the graphic choice of the "very small", which we will find throughout his career (think of how many ants, or people in long shot, he has staged). Finally, the documentaries represent a further tutorial on Disney, this time the one of the series *The True-Life Adventures*. In this case, Bozzetto accepts the Disney principle of the documentary show, that is of his non-scientific nature. However, he deliberately chooses not to go into the "beautiful image", in the formal game, and to keep his style sober and close to the subject.

Last I left *Tico-Tico* and *Partita a dama* (*Game of Checkers*; both dated 1959–1960). They are already mature, as evidenced by the production date itself, following that of the often -mentioned *Tapum!*

On the rhythm of the famous Brazilian samba, *Tico-Tico* unfolds a series of semi-abstract metamorphoses, engraved on black film in the manner of Norman McLaren. At that time Bozzetto had for the first time seen the Scot/Canadian animator's films and had then had the opportunity to meet him. If it is true that *Tico-Tico* resembles *Blinkity-Blank*, it is equally true that no careful eye would miss the distance between one and the other. Nor is it only a question of technical mastery: the film of the Montreal genius is all about abstract rhythms, a challenge to human intellect, research, and evocation; while that of the young Milanese is joyful and sparkling and is anchored to the immediate intelligibility of what takes place on the screen. Equally McLaren-inspired is *Game of Checkers*, which makes use of the *Rythmetic* lesson. The pawns play the game by themselves, and during the performance they have a chance to quarrel among themselves, to show shyness or stubbornness. The theme will be resumed, albeit from a different angle, in one of *Pickles*'s fragments.

McLaren's influence will always remain latent and never manifest. It could be said that McLaren was a master of synthesis, of self-control, of dry expression; that is, that he was a much more fruitful and useful teacher than is usually the case for the stylistic and thematic models that young people choose.

THE MOUSE, THE DUCK, AND THE STRIP

Outside the borders of Italy, Mickey and Donald & Co. comic strips or books have been received very mildly, and the names of Floyd Gottfredson (Mickey) and Carl Barks (Donald) are far from being a legend. In Italy, they reigned for almost seventy years, and they also provided suggestions for Bruno Bozzetto's first films. Here are some examples. Mr. Rossi, standing on the ski lift, freezes into an ice cube (*Rossi sci*); the same, after having shattered and recomposed the camera several times, repairs it "definitively", and doesn't care of surplus pieces (*Rossi Oscar*); the scientist is segregated, and fed with bones, by the powerful who wants him at his/her services (*VIP*). In other words, the Milanese author was able to learn and reuse material from his predecessors, despite having much to create.

According to the ancient recipe, a gag consists of a dynamic structure, in which a certain fact produces a development that appears consistent and reasonable; then a twist, a "surprise" follows this development. The latter interrupts the logical trend, lets the irrational flow suddenly, and thereby generates laughter.

To us, it seems interesting that the gag mixes with emotion, the one to which Bozzetto above all points ("For me, the gag is: a surprise plus a concept").

The emotional gag is not new (Chaplin used it, and Keaton used it); but Bozzetto was able to command it with full mastery (think, for example, of that collection of gags that is *Pickles*). Some attention should instead be given to the "sound" element. The spoken word has little space. With the exception of narrative feature films, Bozzetto utilises allusive sound, vocal distortions, and synthetic effects. A cinema that makes its flag of synthesis and significance cannot be linked to the logical threads of prose.

These "special" sounds integrate the image; they are its continuation in another language. The same cannot always be said about music, even if it structurally carries out the same function as the sound effects. The music of *A Life in a Box* is skilfully appropriate, while that of *Mr. Rossi at the Sea* just doesn't work.

It is no discovery that verbal humour is very different from the visual one. One can exist when the other is absent: and so, *VIP*'s long excursus on the evils of mass communication is verbal humour, grafted onto visual support that is almost documentary.

CULTURED, NOT NEEDING BOOKS

Mr. Rossi's cinematic adventure dealing with the Oscar is a well-thought-out entertainment film: and it is also an acute satire of certain festivals and fashions. For the author, the latent danger is the uncontrolled joke: in two words, moral indifference. Only a solid culture can constitute a bulwark: meaning a sure taste, a solid ideology, a constant breadth of views. Bozzetto's constant control over his creative material is obvious. Everything in him seems spontaneous, his good taste seems innate, not a shade of a built, bookish culture. Despite the very long cinematographic militia, his works preserve that enthusiasm and the naïveté typical of the neophyte. It seems to me beautiful – because incisive – the definition that his colleague Max Massimino-Garniér once gave of him: "A cultured man without books".

The vision of the world, and the tools to interpret and recreate it, come to him from the experience of every day and from his personal history, rather than from erudition. An only child (therefore often alone) of wealthy parents, he shows in his work some classical constants of the bourgeois artist: interest in the problems of the individual (rather than of society), anxiety about the destiny of man on earth, the longing for a more natural state than the one in which he lives. The years of childhood passed not far from the ski fields and the summer hills have induced in the artist's spirit an incurable antithesis between the world he has known and loved, and the acrid world in which he operates today. The "social" part of Bozzetto's irony is exhausted in this. He scratches on the surface, mocks the symptoms instead of the disease; its controversy does not reach the root of the phenomenon and the identification of a buggy society, but it stops at the condemnation of the facts. Some may grieve and blame him. But such an attitude would mean not understanding the characteristics of our director, who presents himself as a sensitive witness of the tensions present in his time and of those that are arriving. The non-triviality, the non-contingency of Bozzetto's art are witnessed by the fact that the older works are still thematically vibrant. But that he is neither a sociologist nor a political scientist nor even a philosopher, is witnessed by the same caution of his polemic, which avoids proposing an alternative to the evils he deciphers. The alternative will have to come from the awakening of the viewer's conscience; and with this Bozzetto will have exhausted his task, as it was for – say – the South African William Kentridge (who had to do with apartheid).

Since his early years, Bozzetto seems to have a precise awareness of his function as an artist, his ideas and lucidity would become even stronger than at the beginning. In 1976, he will sign his long-length masterpiece: *Allegro Non Troppo*.

NOTES

1. Ermanno Comuzio, "Piccola storia del disegno animato italiano", in *Cineforum* 53, March 1966, p. 235, Bergamo.
2. Personal communication with Giannalberto Bendazzi, 1970.
3. Jean-Pierre Coursodon, *Keaton & Cie – Les burlesques américains du «muet»*, Paris: Seghers, 1964, p. 53.

CHAPTER 10

Address

Rossi, Mitteleuropa

I REMEMBER A LESSON I was given when I was a young critic on my debut. I was attending the preview of Franco Giraldi's film *Solitary Hearts*, starring Ugo Tognazzi and Senta Berger. At the end of the screening, I commented that Berger's performance seemed particularly good to me, especially considering that she, an Austrian with a Hollywood past, had impersonated a woman of the Lombard bourgeoisie, therefore a figure far removed from her direct experiences. Giraldi replied to me, a little paternal and somewhat ironic: "Look, it was an easy figure. It is the bourgeoisie of Mitteleuropa. In Vienna, she grew up among women of that type". Giraldi was from Trieste, Mitteleuropean par excellence.

It is my thesis that there is a bourgeois population of central Europe and that Italian animation is not wrong to believe that its Mr. Rossi is understandable and captivating even beyond Brenner to the north and beyond Opicina to the east.

This moustachioed, short-haired, red-dressed character, always a victim of frustration and small mishaps, was the pro- tagonist of several short films, comics on TV, comic books, and some television series in the 1960s and 1970s. He was born in

1960, when a short of the twenty-two-year-old Bruno Bozzetto was rejected from the festival of his family's city, Bergamo. As a "poet's revenge", Bozzetto designed the caricature of the director of that event, and around the cartoon he built the sarcastic story of an amateur filmmaker who is first despised and then accidentally honoured (*An Oscar for Mr. Rossi*).

The saga of Rossi can be read in various ways, but the first that comes to mind is that of a drawn version of the successful "Comedy the Italian way". Like Sordi, Manfredi, Tognazzi, and Villaggio, the grotesque protagonists, our hero is also a middleman; to the point that his name itself is the most widespread in the country. He is a cheap, mediocre, frustrated loser who either endures failures or consoles himself with imagination.

It is certainly not a new figure: its origins date back to the theatre piece Monssù Travet (1863), born from playwright Vittorio Bersezio's pen. But it has a specific culture behind it. Heir of the free enterprise and capitalism that has flourished in the Po Valley for a thousand years, Rossi is far from self-pity, from fatalism, from the narcissistic self-injury of Roman films. To adversity he reacts trying to assert his reasons; he perseveres and tries again instead of "getting by"; he rejects compromises. It is not surprising that Hungarian animation gave birth to his artistic brother, Gusztav. Today I know that for two centuries the political and social consonances between Northern Italy and Hungary have been innumerable, so much so that even among the Garibaldi's Thousand there were three Magyars.

Rossi has changed over time as times have changed. At first, he was a trifling thing struggling with the dreams of the 1960s: making the "little film", going to the mountains and the sea, buying a car. Later, he travelled to Venice and Africa. In the 1970s we see him engaged in affairs as an opulent businessman, with a house outside the city and a doghouse-keeper.

Then came the 1980s, 1990s, and 2000s. Probably the anti-heroic hero had its day in the advanced society of the whole world.

Animation no longer has Mickey Mouse, Bugs Bunny, Daffy Duck, and Tom and Jerry, that a few decades ago gave birth to a small but vibrant epic of the everyday life reinterpreted through zoomorphic figures.

In the 2000s and 2010s, the film characters have been of pure fantasy; reality has no grip on the public. The average citizen goes instead to the supermarket of culture, as it goes to that of food, vacation, or information. Buy and consume.

Pessimist? Not at all. Mr. Rossi and his colleagues from trans-alpine and Danuban adventures are even more important than yesterday. They are a historical document, the digital imprint of what we will call the Cold War Society. A season which is the mother of that of the new century, and still must be analysed; and that in addition to economic and political teachings, also has many ethical teachings to deliver to us. It may not have been better than the one that lived in the first half of the twentieth century and that faced dictatorships, invasions, and military conflicts. But it knew how to evolve, also and perhaps precisely because he knew how to look at itself; not infrequently with the right irony.

CHAPTER 11

The Egg of Cohl

FANTASMAGORIE, CONCEIVED, DESIGNED, AND directed by Parisian Émile Cohl in 1908, is considered by many to be the first animated film in history, and by all still a classic. For the duration of two and a half minutes, Cohl puts on characters quickly sketched, intent on being metamorphosed and playing tricks.

The non-plot plot seems to be kneaded by a surrealist in the mood for automatic writing, but in fact it is rather the umpteenth appearance of that karst river which is the art of the absurd, and which is as old as the human intellect. We see a hand drawing a small character, white on a black background. They disappear behind a man who falls from above and then sits in a movie theatre. Disturbed by the big lady's hat that occupies the seat in front of him, he tears off the feathers of the hat one by one.

From the lady's lorgnette glasses reappears the first character, who absorbs the man, then interacts with a soldier, a bottle, an elephant, a house; climbs to the first floor and from there falls materially losing its head in the impact with the pavement. The hand returns to the scene and recomposes the body, which swells like a balloon, mounts on a horse, and finally gallops away on the latter.

Fantasmagorie is one of the most viewed films in the world, first in festivals, retrospectives, and special evenings, and now on YouTube. In 2017, in the imminence of the nineteenth convention of the Society for Animation Studies (Padova, 3–7 July), I was lazily watching it on my PC.

I realised that I was seeing something new.

In the scene set in the movie theatre we were faced with a film in the film; to a *mise en abîme*, to put it in critical jargon. While the character performs the main action by removing the feathers from the lady's hat, a movie starring drawn characters passes on the screen (the screen of the room in which the action takes place). The curtain falls and rises again on abstract animated drawings.

The message is important. In this way Cohl claimed an industrial future for the medium he was creating, and foresaw the birth and success of abstract animation.

Keep in mind that in 1908 abstract animation did not exist yet, and that abstract painting itself would become fashionable only a couple of years later, with Vasily Kandinsky. It seemed to me unlikely that I would be the first, after a century or so of projections, to notice this elementary sleight of hand (focus attention on one main action and send the message through the secondary action). I sifted through the books and accessible articles on Émile Cohl. Donald Crafton[1] was the only one to describe the scene, but he didn't dwell on the meaning.

I made public this discovery with a communication at the conference in Padua, sitting at the table of speakers together with Donald Crafton. He supplemented the information, adding that the copies visible today are drawn by a single English copy found decades ago. It was probably of a larger size, so the sides had been cut in the 35 mm transfer. Here is the possible reason of the incomplete visibility of the drawn screen, otherwise unexplainable.

It is said (notice: it is pure historical invention) that Christopher Columbus would one day talk with some dignitaries of the court of Spain, and that these would diminish his enterprise by claiming that, by all accounts, anyone would have been able to do it. In response, he challenged them in another endeavour: to keep a hard-boiled egg standing on the table. Each made numerous attempts, but none succeeded. They asked Columbus to demonstrate how to solve the case. He made a slight dent at the end of the egg, tapping it lightly against the table. The egg remained straight. When the onlookers protested saying that they could do the same, Columbus replied: "The solution was before your eyes, but you didn't see it".

Our mind constantly tends to give a meaning to reality, selecting among all the stimuli those that are composed in a coherent presupposed image. This tendency entails a consequence: the particular image that the eye and the mind select ends up excluding all other possible images. If this is true, our eyes and our minds have seen the main action for 109 years, excluding the secondary one.

Consequently, I propose to name this case of hidden message in plain sight as "the egg of Cohl".

NOTE

1. Donald Crafton, *Emile Cohl, Caricature and Film*, Princeton, NJ: Princeton University Press, 1990.

Index

Note: Page numbers followed by "n" refer to notes.

Index ■ 125

Creating Modern Athens
A Capital Between East and West

Denis Roubien

Routledge
Taylor & Francis Group

LONDON AND NEW YORK

First published 2017
by Routledge
2 Park Square, Milton Park, Abingdon, Oxon OX14 4RN

and by Routledge
52 Vanderbilt Avenue, New York, NY 10017

First issued in paperback 2020

Routledge is an imprint of the Taylor & Francis Group, an informa business

British Library Cataloguing-in-Publication Data
A catalogue record for this book is available from the British Library

Library of Congress Cataloging-in-Publication Data
A catalog record for this book has been requested

ISBN 13: 978-0-367-67050-4 (pbk)
ISBN 13: 978-1-138-29166-9 (hbk)

Typeset in Times New Roman
by Apex CoVantage, LLC

This book is dedicated to those whose continuous support throughout my life made me able to write it today.

Contents

Figures

Introduction

Athens is a well-known destination for those interested in discovering the birthplace of Western civilization. Its ancient monuments have been the model for innumerable buildings and works of art all over the Western World. Therefore, visitors come prepared to find the roots of the Western world. However, what they face is something much more complicated: the ancient monuments are dispersed in a European capital with avenues bordered by neo-classical buildings, but interlaced with a traditional settlement with winding streets, Byzantine churches, mosques, and an oriental bazaar, all these inextricably tied with each other.

This book explains this image Athens offers to the contemporary visitor. It presents the process of creation of a neo-classical capital after the Greek Independence, in the place of a pre-existing multi-layered town, comprising the remains of a long history, going much beyond ancient times. It presents the treatment of the pre-revolutionary town after the Greek Independence, the connection of it with the new neo-classical city, the position of Byzantine and post-Byzantine churches in this antiquity-centred new city. It also presents the factors that influenced the implementation of the projects for the new capital: land availability, functional requirements, and the results of all of these factors in the city's evolution. Thus, it presents the passage from the grandiose plans of a European metropolis to a much more modest peripheral capital, presenting a dual character of a pre-modern Eastern town and a modern Western capital.

The originality of this book lies in its relying on unpublished archival sources which throw new light on the subject and present unknown sides of the recent history of Athens. In this way, it explains the present image of Athens and offers to modern visitors a complete knowledge of the city's evolution, which will help them understand a city which is much more complicated than a mere assemblage of archaeological sites, but also much more interesting, since it combines the testimonies of a very long history.

Part I

Ideology

The revival of ancient glory

1 The ideological background of the creation of neo-classical Athens

The different priorities between idealism and rationalism in establishing a European capital, and the importance of cultural institutions

The ideological position of Athens: the importance of public architecture

The monumental projects made for the new capital of Greece after independence (1830) are explained by the position of nineteenth-century Athens in the Hellenic world and in Europe. From the ideological viewpoint, that position is absolutely prominent among all Greek cities. Athens has a particularity that differentiates considerably the context of its evolution from all other European capitals, with the exception of Rome. This particularity is the existence of its world-famous classical antiquities. Until the mid-eighteenth century, when all the routes of the Europeans' grand tour were leading their footsteps to Rome, their acquaintance with antiquity was taking place through the Roman 'filter'. However, after the publication of *The Antiquities of Athens* by James Stuart and Nicholas Revett in 1762, the first to have systematically studied them, the Greek antiquities became widely known and attracted the interest of European antiquity lovers, representing for them the embodiment of the classical world. That coincided with the publishing in 1764 of the German art historian's Johann J. Winckelmann major work, *Geschichte der Kunst des Alterthums* ('History of Ancient Art'), which played a decisive role in their progressive reevaluation and in the reconsideration of their position vis-à-vis Rome, regarded until then as the summit of ancient culture. For European art lovers, the reasons for the existence of Athens were the natural presence of ancient ruins, the ancient names, and the memories evoked by them (Klenze, 1838, pp. 20, 420; Maurer, 1943–1947, pp. 119–127; Hederer, 1976, p. 199).[1] Naturally, the way in which Western Europeans saw Athens was one of the main reasons it was chosen as the capital of the new Greek state (Klenze, 1838, p. 397; Papageorgiou-Venetas, 1994; Bastea, 2000, pp. 6–11; Fatsea, 2000).

Furthermore, the newly appointed King of Greece was Otto (1833–1862), the underage[2] son of King Ludwig I of Bavaria. Ludwig was perhaps the greatest antiquity lover among all European monarchs, as his building programme in Munich and his collections of art suggest. The choice of Otto for the Greek throne by the Great Powers thus led to the particularly intense influence of German classicism in Greece. That reinforced the ideological context of the new capital's inception.

The transfer of the capital from Nafplion to Athens was largely due to the desire of the authorities to offer the new kingdom an ideological unity, which was lacking after so many centuries in the multinational Ottoman Empire. The sought-after ideological unity would satisfy the two main axes set at the state's inception: its reconnection with its ancient past and its entry in the family of the civilised nations of Western Europe. That unity would differentiate Greece from the East and approach her to Europe. Therefore, Greece had to erase every trace of her Eastern character and retransform on the basis of her ancient heritage. The most appropriate town for the fulfilment of that purpose was Athens, where the ancient past was present more than anywhere else. Thus, Athens was preferred to other more suitable alternatives, although it had the least geographical and financial qualifications to assume that role. Moreover, among several alternative solutions about the exact siting of the new city, the final choice was exactly the one connecting it in space most firmly with its ancient predecessor, against all practical considerations.

The new capital had to replace every Eastern characteristic with the 'Occidental' image that would express the authority of its European monarch and would incarnate the name of 'Athens', as the Western European antiquity lovers understood it. The plan of the new city would be a modern 'answer' to the medieval urban fabric, which was the outcome of a free, 'organic' development.

Especially under King Otto, the superficial Europeanization (through architecture, clothing, spectacles, etc.) preceded by a long way the respective adjustment of socio-economic structures, which, of course, needed much more time. The task of filling that gap won't be fulfilled before the end of the century, in the last years of King George I's reign (1863–1913; son of King Christian IX of Denmark). It must be underlined that all projects serving that purpose were prepared or inspired by Western Europeans or by Greeks who had spent a great part of their lives in Western Europe and were fervent supporters of that view.

Public architecture would be essential to the fulfilment of that purpose. Since the newly founded Greek state hadn't the necessary conditions of a financial development, it would have to acquire its sought-after European character through its institutions. Those were based on the institutions of the European countries that constituted the models for nineteenth-century Greece, and the most suitable representatives of those European institutions would be the buildings that would house them. This accounts for the particular importance of public architecture in Athens.

However, contrary to other European capitals, in Athens the interest centred not on administrative edifices, but on buildings housing cultural institutions, especially educational. Greece lacked appropriate buildings to house the new institutions, as well as educated people who would build those buildings and staff those institutions. The revolution had caused the destruction of the new kingdom's towns and villages. Thus, schools, university, schools of engineering, and architecture were urgently needed, just as hospitals and so forth. The new authorities had to find premises, mostly existing buildings that were rapidly restored, but more importantly, they had to seek or train literate people to get the economy and the society to move on. But, in addition to that, reborn Greece was supposed to undertake the cultural renaissance of her whole historic area – mostly included in the Ottoman Empire – and the revival of her ancient glory in the cultural domain. That was very eloquently expressed by Lysandros Kaftantzoglou, the most famous Greek architect of the nineteenth century, in his speech on the occasion of the Polytechnic's anniversary, and again much later by Dimitrios Bikelas, future first president of the International Olympic Committee, on the occasion of the fiftieth anniversary of the University of Athens (the occasions are particularly significant; Kaftantzoglou, 1847, p. 9; *Πανδώρα*, 1855, p. 555; Bikelas, 1888, p. 78; *Ιστορία του Ελληνικού Έθνους*, 1970–1978, vol. 13, p. 64). Therefore, educational buildings were given more attention than administrative constructions. Moreover, they should be as monumental as possible, in order to better express that desire and underline their symbolism.

However, others – especially the press – thought that Greece should avoid spending money on the construction of unnecessarily monumental buildings of symbolical value and focus on covering urgent practical needs, which were innumerable. From that point on, the ideological way of seeing Athens would be in a perpetual antagonism with its practical needs.

The first intention to satisfy the needs of the future new European state was expressed by the Demogerontia[3] of Athens in 1822, when the city was temporarily liberated (Kabouroglous, 1922, pp. 401–402), but the effort was interrupted by its recapture in 1827. Thus, the application of those projects began under Ioannis Capodistria, first governor of liberated Greece, before the arrival of King Otto. That time's choices demonstrate Capodistria's practical spirit, an outcome of his experience as Minister of Foreign Affairs of the Russian Empire in 1815–1821. The governor believed that the urgent needs were the construction of hospitals and the education of the major victims of the War of Independence (namely, children and especially orphans); the protection of the major asset of the Greek nation, the antiquities, which played a decisive role in the appearance of the philhellenic movement and therefore in the liberation of Greece; and finally the state's organisation. Thus, the first public edifice constructed in Aegina, first capital of Greece, in 1828, was the Orphanage (Ross, 1863, p. 26). Although simple, it was then characterised as a 'splendid structure' and housed also the Central School, the Museum, the Library, and the Printing House. In those first years of independence, priority is given to schools, while some administrative buildings were also erected in other cities.

Nevertheless, Capodistria's views were very far from the ideology not only of the Bavarian dynasty that succeeded him, but also of the scholars and benefactors, whose role in the new state was decisive. That was firstly demonstrated by the capital's master plans.

The first master plans: intentions and final development

The special position of Athens in the Hellenic world accounts for the intense idealism characterising every project during the first decades after independence. That idealism ignored the material realities of the country, for it counted on a very imminent expansion toward all territories inhabited by Greeks and a consequent spectacular change of circumstances. Thus, the same idealism is reflected in the first propositions made for the new capital's city plan. Only after the events related to the Crimean War, in 1854, the Greeks, disillusioned in regard to the role of the Western European powers, started accepting that the expansion of the Greek state and the creation of a big country wasn't for the immediate future. That had at least one positive outcome: the Greek authorities concentrated their efforts not in obtaining more resources for Greece by expansion, but in enhancing whatever resources Greece already had. That resulted in some serious efforts to create infrastructures.

The first official plan made in 1833 (Figure 1.1) was commissioned by the Greek government from the Greek architect Stamatios Kleanthes and his German colleague Eduard Schaubert, pupils of Carl Friedrich von Schinkel. In this plan, the Royal Palace is situated at the top of a triangle, like the Palace of Versailles. From the palace's square three streets depart radially: Piraeus, Athena, and Stadium. Stadium Street, the triangle's right side, connects the palace to the ancient stadium, while Piraeus Street, the left side, ensures the connection with Athens's homonymous ancient port.

Athena Street is the triangle's bisector. It links visually the Royal Palace to the Acropolis, with the interference of the market, which, as its position and size suggest, was destined to become the modern city's centre. At the same time, it is the new city's main street. Along with two narrower parallel

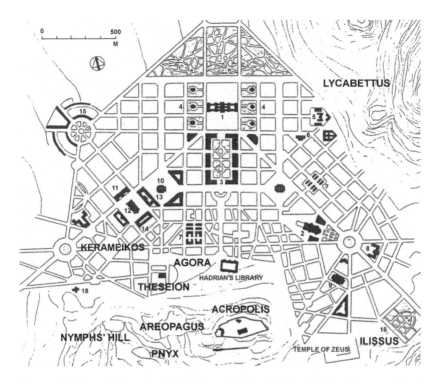

Figure 1.1 Plan of Stamatios Kleanthes and Eduard Schaubert for the new city of Athens

Re-drawn by the author, using several versions of the plan, with the addition of location names: 1. Royal Palace; 2. Cathedral; 3. Central Market; 4. Ministries; 5. Garrison; 6. Mint; 7. Market; 8. Academy; 9. Library; 10. Stock Exchange; 11. Parliament; 12. Church; 13. Post Office; 14. Headquarters; 15. Oil Press; 16. Botanical Garden; 17. Exhibition Hall; 18. Observatory.

streets, Aeolus and Areopagus, it would link it to the old one, through its penetration into the latter. Also Hermes Street, the triangle's base, would penetrate the old urban fabric.

However, the realisation of the Kleanthes and Schaubert project would be too costly, because of the expropriations it would entail for the creation of wide avenues and extended gardens and squares on private land. Consequently, in 1834 the Bavarian architect Leo von Klenze, official architect to King Ludwig I of Bavaria, undertook to adapt it to Greek realities (Figure 1.2). Von Klenze maintained the urban triangle. The role of Athena Street as the main link between the new European capital and the old Ottoman

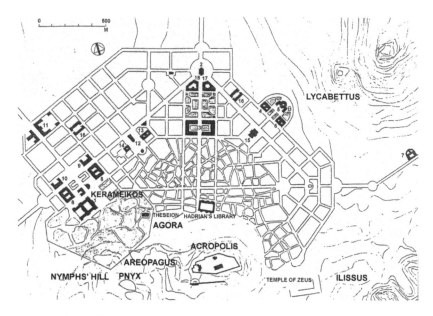

Figure 1.2 Modification of Kleanthes and Schaubert plan by Leo von Klenze

Re-drawn by the author, using several versions of the plan, with the addition of location names: 1. Royal Palace; 2. Cathedral; 3. Central Market; 4. Academy; 5. Library; 6. University; 7. Exhibition Hall; 8. Ministries; 9. Senate; 10. Parliament; 11. Camp; 12. Church; 13. Post Office; 14. Prison and Police; 15. Theatre; 16. Markets; 17. Bishop's Palace; 18. Schools.

town remained untouched and was even accentuated, since only one of the two other streets penetrating into the old urban fabric – Aeolus Street – was maintained, considerably diminished in width.

The financial condition of the Greek state: the economic position of Greece in the Hellenic world

If the ideological context accounts for the first master plans of Athens, the financial realities of the new state explain under which circumstances the capital was created. The Greek kingdom included the poorest provinces of Hellenism. The great financial centres of Hellenism in the first half of the nineteenth century, such as Constantinople, Smyrna, and Salonica, had remained out of the kingdom. The prominent position of Hellenism in the economic life of the Balkans and the Near East was due to the Greeks of the Ottoman Empire, the Ionian Islands,[4] and European cities. That fact is corroborated by numbers: the inhabitants of Greece constituted no more than one quarter of the Greek nation. That demonstrates the restricted importance of the Greek economy within the whole Hellenic world under King Otto. Furthermore, the Greeks of the diaspora were also considerably wealthier than those of the Greek state (*Ιστορία του Ελληνικού Έθνους*, vol. 13, p. 18; Svoronos, 1976, p. 91).

However, the Greek state had undertaken tasks surpassing its capacities. The reasons were its inversely proportional ideological position in the Hellenic world – since it included Athens – and the heavy heritage of which it was expected to prove worthy. The even partial realisation of those tasks became possible mainly through the donations of wealthy citizens. Those came almost entirely from the Greeks of the diaspora, who desired to offer a part of their fortunes for the glory of their country and, why not, their own as well. Donations were, therefore, important in the choice of the public buildings to construct and defined their form and construction quality, according to the benefactors' preferences. Naturally, those preferences leaned toward the buildings constituting the symbols of the power and wealth of the bourgeoisie of big European cities, which the Greek upper class (where the benefactors belonged) wanted to imitate. Some of the most characteristic of those buildings were theatres, town halls, and parliaments, symbolising the bourgeoisie's cultural interests and increasing civic rights.

The lack of money for the necessary expropriations didn't permit the application of a general city plan. That led to the gradual elaboration of several partial ones, with the intention to proceed step by step, according to each time's possibilities (Letter by Gregorios Petimezas, G.S.A., 26 August 1848; Bastea, 2000, pp. 84–85, 105, 126–127; Fatsea, 2000, pp. 271–272).[5] But even those projects had to be simplified or even abandoned. Therefore, perhaps the greatest difference between the initial plans and the finally realised ones is the difference of their public spaces and of the latter's architectural surroundings.

Practical intentions expressed by the Bavarian dynasty

The absence of civic buildings of 'European standards' in Athens at the arrival of King Otto made it necessary to put some priorities, since it was impossible to cover all needs immediately. The official documents and city plans indicate that, at first, the Bavarian dynasty wanted to follow Capodistria's steps in the reconstruction of Greece (Government Gazette, December 1833, 3 March 1834, 17 August 1834, 19 May 1835, 25 January 1836, 30 March 1841, 18 June 1836, 31 December 1836, 9 November 1843, 16 March 1838, 22 September 1843; G.S.A., 21 September 1834). They all reveal the intention to construct buildings satisfying the state's urgent practical needs. The Minister of the Interior, immediately after the government's arrival in the new capital, ordered the establishment of a temporary Civil Hospital (G.S.A., 21 February 1835). King Otto, in a decree of his, stipulates as priorities the edification of barracks and a Mint (G.S.A., 22 October 1833). He also observes to von Klenze that in his city plan there is no provision for a Military or a Civil Hospital (G.S.A., 22 October 1834). The Military Hospital is the first monumental public building constructed in Athens, before the Royal Palace's construction even began.

Although Ministries are essential for a capital city, and they appear on both master plans and their construction was repeatedly proposed, not a single Ministry was built in Athens until the end of the twentieth century. In 1844 a group of architects proposed the plot opposite the northern side of the Royal Palace for the Ministries and the Courts of Justice (Figure 1.3). They mention that each minister had of old given the necessary information about each building's plans (G.S.A., 30 June 1844). Moreover, the Minister of the Interior mentions in 1851 a project, according to which he proposed the construction of two buildings, one for the Ministries of the Interior, the Marine, and Justice, and another for the Ministries of War, of Foreign Affairs, and Public Education. The buildings were to be 'spacious,

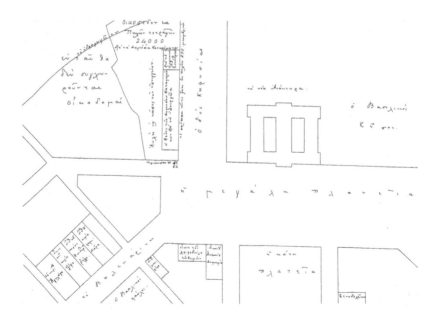

Figure 1.3 The plot opposite the northern side of the Royal Palace, at the plan's left. The plan accompanies the document of 30 June 1844

General State Archives, City Plan, file 1; re-drawn by the author

grandiose, safe, appropriately divided and will decorate the capital and especially its more splendid part' (G.S.A., 23 September 1851).

However, in at least one case, the Ministry itself considers unnecessary the edification of a building that would house it. A document of the Ministry of Finance to the Ministry of the Interior is eloquent:

> Since the offices of the Ministry of Finance and the Treasury occupy already the upper floor of the Establishment of the Mint, which is unnecessary to the Mint, and in which there is all the necessary spaciousness, we consider completely unnecessary to erect an establishment for the office of the Ministry of Finance.
>
> (G.S.A., 27 September 1844)

That rather short-eyed view is in complete contrast with the previous one, according to which the Ministries are expected to 'decorate' the capital.

Similar was the fate of the Courts of Justice. Their edification had repeatedly been announced, while in 1858 it was decided to erect them on the southern side of the Market (Government Gazette, 30 October 1858), next to the south-eastern part of the Varvakeion Lyceum.[6] However, those too, like the Ministries, would have to wait a century and a half.

The practical spirit undermined by idealism

Despite the theoretical demonstrations of a practical spirit, the antagonism between priorities emerges already in the Mint's case, one of the first public constructions of Athens. The decision for its edification wasn't so simple, according to the Danish painter Martinus Rorbye, who writes in 1836:

> Everybody claims it, for it is the only decent building the Government disposes of. One day it is said that it will function as a mint, the next day that it will become an oil press, the other one that it will be the Regent[7] Armansperg's house etc.
>
> (Haugsted, 1985)

That confusion doesn't mean that the authorities didn't really prefer to give priority to the buildings of greatest symbolical value. Such a spirit is revealed by a decree of 1834 (Government Gazette, 16 June 1834), defining the public institutions that will be founded 'in Athens, the seat of the government, of the academy of sciences, of that of fine arts and of the pandidakterion'.[8] The list contains the following: (1) Central Public Library, (2) Central Public Museum for the Antiquities, (3) Coin Cabinet, (4) Cabinet of Natural History, (5) Cabinet of Instruments of Physics and Mathematics,

(6) Chemical Laboratory, (7) Anatomy Theatre, (8) Chirurgic Cabinet, (9) Model Collection, (10) Painting Collection, (11) Copper Engraving Collection, (12) Observatory, (13) Polytechnic Collection. The priorities are evident. The Academy (here there is additionally a distinction between an academy of sciences and one of fine arts) and the 'pandidakterion' are a given, while next to them are also placed the Library and the Museum, establishments necessary to a country of such cultural ambitions. Those are followed by everything necessary to the function of the major institutions of higher education, although one could argue that in a state with non-existent technology, it would be difficult to profit from any scientific discovery made by the Observatory. Even Kaftantzoglou, who wrote much on the creation of the new city of Athens (Kaftantzoglou, G.S.A., file 214; Kaftantzoglou, 1839; 1858), proposed the hill of Lycabettus[9] for the installation of the Observatory, whereas he omitted many other important buildings.

The summit, however, is the Academy, perhaps the first public institution it was decided to found in Greece. In 1825 some distinguished citizens from the Ionian Islands sent a letter supporting the idea (Biris, 1966–1967, p. 151). Before the Revolution was finished, twenty-one scholars and fighters signed the 'Project of an Academic Establishment', submitted to the Greek administration.

The way the Greek scholars imagined the Academy is revealed in a document of the Minister of Education addressed to King Otto. It concerns the petition of the Court's doctor, Dr Röser, for its foundation: 'All educated men of Greece were always wishing that the day would come when an academy would be founded on the ruins of Plato's academy, in order to concentrate as in one home the scientific elements dispersed in Greece, which would flow from it on the country' (G.S.A., 20 May 1833). It is evident that their conception of the Academy is based more on a verbal association with the ancient 'Akademeia' than on the homonymous institutions of modern Europe, with a vague idea that it would be a cultural institution of a very high level. Also, its mention of an 'Academy of Fine Arts' in a document of the Court of Appeal is a further indication of the confusion about that institution (G.S.A., 11 February 1850).

It is characteristic that the siting and the choice of the plot, issues so complicated and time-consuming in the case of most public buildings, don't seem to have been the object of many discussions in the Academy's case. On the contrary, even before the donator's[10] appearance, the location and the plot had already been chosen, as is mentioned by the previously listed document of the Court of Appeal. Moreover, a part of the land where the Academy was built was offered by the Municipality of Athens, after a donation of another part by the Petraki Monastery (Laios, 1972, p. 182).[11] It is noteworthy that the Municipality of Athens desperately needed land and buildings for functions far more urgent than the Academy. A decree stipulated the obligation of the municipality to indemnify the private plots that have been or will be expropriated for a municipal use (G.S.A., 24 November 1836). Also, in 1843, the Ministry of the Interior asked from King Otto to approve the extension of the city plan to the north-east of the Royal Palace. In the opposite case, it couldn't be permitted to the owners to build there, and the municipality would have to spend considerable sums of money to indemnify them (G.S.A., 12 June 1843).

The other great cultural institution of Athens, whose foundation was decided early, is the University. Its building was constructed – not at all by coincidence – in a previously decided architectural complex with the Academy, called Athenian Trilogy, the complex of three cultural buildings predicted in both master plans (Figure 1.1, nos. 2, 8, 9, and Figure 1.2, nos. 4, 5, 6). It was inaugurated in 1837 in its temporary premises, the house of Kleanthes, at the foot of the Acropolis (Figure 1.4). Its foundation was announced in 1836 as 'Otto's University' (Government Gazette, 31 December 1836). It is noteworthy that no other institution bore the King's name.

Figure 1.4 The house of Stamatios Kleanthes
Photograph by the author

It is impressive that none of the numerous modifications proposed for the city plan of von Klenze touched the Athenian Trilogy. It was even attempted to build the fourth of those buildings, the Theatre, exactly where this was predicted by that project, on the plot where the Mint was finally constructed (today demolished; Haugsted, 1985, p. 76).

Another institution that was judged important was a school of architecture, which as the Minister of Education writes in 1835 (G.S.A., 31 December 1835),[12] was necessary in Greece more than anywhere else: first, he says, there was a great lack of houses due to the destructions caused by the Revolution; second, those who would undertake the task of reconstruction should receive an education worthy of the ancient heritage, represented by the city's antiquities. Those needs started being satisfied soon by the engineers of the Military School and the craftsmen of the School of Arts, the future Polytechnic (today's National Technical University).

However, while a university and an academy were being founded, destined moreover to be housed in the monumental buildings of the Danish architects Christian and Theophil Hansen respectively, there was only one high school. That is very indicative of the haste to acquire higher cultural institutions without taking into consideration the country's real needs. Nevertheless, in 1836 the German architect Ludwig Lange designed a high school (G.S.A., 25 April 1836); however, it was never built. As for the school buildings in general, the First Primary School for Boys of King Otto's reign and the Second Primary School for Boys of King George I's reign were the only buildings constructed specifically for public schools of elementary education in the Greek capital throughout the nineteenth century. Furthermore, it is surprising that, despite the great importance attributed from the beginning to libraries, within the intense interest in education, the edification of a monumental permanent building to house the National Library delayed considerably.[13] Nevertheless, already in 1835 a decree was published 'about the constitution of a public library in every public school of the State' (Government Gazette, 18 September 1835).

Another building whose edification delayed surprisingly was the Archaeological Museum, although in King Otto's time the interest in the antiquities is clearly more intense than under Capodistria (Government Gazette, 28 June 1834). Three plans by Schaubert are conserved, dating from 1834. They represent propositions for guard rooms in the archaeological sites, including special rooms for travellers and the temporary keeping of antiquities (G.S.A., Ottonian Record, Ministry of Education, L, file 44). Also von Klenze had designed, according to King Otto's wish, a 'National Glyptothek' at the south-eastern end of the Acropolis, where the Acropolis Museum was later constructed (Klenze, 1838, p. 471). Nevertheless, the projects remained theoretical, and in 1853 the Minister of Education writes to King

Otto that 'even the visitors, observing the need for a building concentrating in one the remains of fine arts, and in order that the latter should be easily understandable to those visiting them, criticise the delay of such a necessary building' (G.S.A., 7 April 1853). However, from the following year (1854) the government started inscribing in the state's budget 10,000 drachmas annually for that purpose (Government Gazette, 26 October 1853). On the same issue, the newspaper 'Ελπίς' writes in 1861:

> We don't need any new antiquities, Sirs, but to guard and arrange the existing ones, which are dispersed in all the angles of the city and in derelict churches, in uncovered vaults, in humid basements and completely in the open air under the influence of the atmosphere and at the disposition of anyone they are damaged, destroyed, stolen.
>
> (*Ελπίς*, 12 December 1861)

At the end of the Bavarian dynasty, the most important material possessions of Greece were still homeless.

The influence of the Athenian upper class

At the same time, priority is often given to buildings that weren't of urgent need, but constituted the symbols of the bourgeoisie of big European cities. Their edification was expected to give Athens a more European aspect, erasing its Ottoman past. The most characteristic of those buildings are the theatres. In the country where theatre was born, the interest in it was particularly intense in the decades preceding the revolution. Theatre was considered by the scholars as the best school for the people, as it was in ancient times. That resulted in many efforts to revive that ancient tradition, especially in the great centres of Hellenism. After independence, the Athenian upper class regarded the theatres as symbols of their 'Europeanization'. Of course, they were forgetting that the European capitals they wanted to imitate acquired their grandiose theatres after other more urgent buildings of public use. In Athens, the theatre almost preceded even a public construction of fundamental importance for the very existence of a state: the Mint, which, as mentioned previously, was built on the foundations of a building initially destined to be a theatre. Christian Hansen writes in 1835, almost a year before the aforementioned information by Rorbye:

> The theatre I started over here for the Government is so advanced, that the foundations have reached the ground's surface. But the local newspapers criticise intensely the Government for building a theatre

in Athens, while there are neither schools nor other necessary buildings. It was thus decided not to go further with the theatre for the
time being.

(Haugsted, 1985, p. 76)

In many cases the press has been the voice of reason, while it is noteworthy
that the schools are placed in the first rank of necessary buildings.

Nevertheless, from that same year started the function of short-lived
improvised theatres. Furthermore, despite the previous reactions, a decree
of 1838 (Government Gazette, 22 August 1843) ceded to Iosif Kamilieri
gratis a plot, where he was obliged to erect at his own expenses within six
months a stone theatre according to the plan that would be given to him
by the government. Thus, the government ceded a plot to a citizen for the
construction of a theatre, while there was such a shortage of public land.
Moreover, the government would interfere in the theatre's plans.

A decree of 1839 transferred all the previous concessions to Vasilios
Sansoni,[14] an Italian, who in the same year received a subvention from the
municipality and from the Royal Palace Treasury (Karykopoulos, 1971,
p. 75; Kairofylas, 1978, p. 32). That provoked a storm of protests in the
press, who spoke of a purposeless waste of public money at the moment
Greece was tending a 'hand of beggary' to Europe (Kairofylas, 1978).
In 1844 that theatre was bought for 23,000 drachmas (Kairofylas, 1978,
p. 33) and became known as 'Boukoura theatre', from the name of its new
owner. It was the only stone theatre of King Otto's reign. Soon, however,
it didn't satisfy the Athenian society. The Mayor Georgios Skoufos considered it shameful that Athens didn't have a decent theatre, whereas Her-
moupolis had the 'Apollo' and Corfu had the 'San Giacomo' (Kydoniatis,
1985, p. 18). In 1856 it was thus decided by law to build a new theatre
in the middle of the never realised People's Garden of the general city
plan. The building, designed by the French architect François Florimont
Boulanger, was founded in 1858 as a National Theatre, and was expected
to cost 400,000 drachmas. Finally, the Municipal Theatre was built at the
same place a little later.

Another demonstration of the Athenians' effort to rival the European
metropolises, disregarding their city's urgent needs, is the haste to orga-
nise expositions, symbols of progress for that time's society. In 1860 was
thus erected a wooden building for industrial and agricultural expositions
(Vrettos-Papadopoulos, 1860, p. 84) in the area of Zappeion, the future
permanent exhibition hall. The universal expositions intensely interested
the Athenian public, and the newspapers 'Αιών' and 'Αθηνά', already from
1851, had given in sequels the events of the Great Exhibition of London of
that year.

The neglect of the buildings of welfare

Yet the most impressive is perhaps the little importance attributed to the buildings of welfare. With the exception of the Military and the Civil Hospital, built from the first years of King Otto's reign and which were far from covering the capital's needs, all the other institutions of welfare were not housed before the reign of King George I or later. A newspaper writes in 1835 that 'the Athenians look after balls, as the fashion goes today; but they didn't care to found a hospital, and the poor patients suffer and die in the streets' (Biris, 1966–1967, p. 74). The appeal of the doctor Mayor Anarghyros Petrakis in 1836 for the financial contribution of the citizens to the edification of the Civil Hospital took place only after the gastro-choleric epidemic of 1835, which rendered the needs more urgent (Kydoniatis, 1985, p. 160).

Things weren't better for other institutions of welfare. While hunger and analphabetism encouraged the abandoning and killing of babies, the municipality waited until 1848 to found an orphanage for abandoned babies (Biris, 1966–1967, p. 205). The self-owned building of the Municipal Foundling Hospital took a long time more (1872–1875), while orphanages for older children were built towards the end of King Otto's reign: the Queen Amalia Orphanage in 1855–1857 (Government Gazette, 25 June 1855) and the Hatzikonsta Orphanage in 1856. Even those, however, were built because of the abrupt increase of orphans after the terrible cholera epidemic that attacked the Greek capital, like the whole Europe, in 1854. The letter of Maria Ypsilanti and Zoe Soutsou to Queen Amalia mentions the cholera and exposes their plan to found a girls' orphanage (G.S.A., 17 January 1855). Furthermore, the Hatzikonsta Orphanage was created by a private donation (of the homonymous couple and K. Vranis). There was no support from the state, as is indicated by a petition of the institution's administration to the Ministry of the Interior (G.S.A., 9 September 1862). In it, the institution asks, again, to be exempted from the debt for the construction of pavements, and mentions that this would be the first financial benefaction offered from the government to the Orphanage. Finally, we have the edification of the Eye Hospital in 1847–1854, imposed by the increased frequency of eye diseases, due to the city's insufficient cleanliness. A little before its expulsion, the Bavarian dynasty made its last spasmodic moves to found institutions of welfare, finally realised under its successors (Government Gazette, 30 September 1861; 19 May 1862).

The Bavarian dynasty's heritage

The best testimony of the Bavarian dynasty's heritage in the capital's functional organisation is a list submitted in 1859 by the Minister of the Interior to King Otto, enumerating the plots needed for public buildings (G.S.A., 30

July 1859) and including the following: (1) Ministry of the Interior; (2) Prefecture; (3) Direction of the Administrative Police; (4) Post Office; (5) Five Buildings of the Police Sub-division; (6) Seven Police Stations; (7) Establishment for the Imprisonment of the Personally Detained; (8) Establishment for the Imprisonment of Those Convicted for Minor Penalties; (9) Prison for Women; (10) Barracks of the Gendarmerie; (11) Ministry of Finance; (12) Customs; (13) Mint; (14) Revenue Office; (15) Establishment for the Concentration of All Judicial Authorities; (16) Ministry of the Marine; (17) Establishment for the Bishop and the Synod Building; (18) High School and Hellenikon School; (19) Zosimaion High School;[15] (20) Archaeological Museum; (21) School of Teaching; (22) Public Library; (23) Ministry of War; (24) Barracks of the Infantry; (25) Barracks of the Artillery; (26) Barracks of the Cavalry; (27) Four Primary Schools for Boys; (28) Four Primary Schools for Girls; (29) Four Local Markets; (30) One Central Market. Twenty-five years after the installation of King Otto, the most necessary buildings were all missing. On the other hand, in the same year the foundations of the Academy began to be dug.

The contradiction between the priorities and the capacities and needs of Greece appeared when it was endeavoured to put the completed buildings in function. It was then realised that their operation was far more difficult than their edification. That became more evident under King George I, when many of the buildings programmed by the previous dynasty were completed and the problem of their function was put forward. Nevertheless, already in King Otto's time there is one characteristic example. In 1858, the Minister of Education reports to King Otto that 'our Observatory, which since a long time had ceased to work, and the worst, almost fell apart, for firstly it lacked instruments completely and secondly the existing ones were partly damaged, has resumed its function since last year'. And he continues saying that 'apart from the meteorological observations, for which the Observatory's service can suffice, it cannot undertake any greater task, demanded by science, due to the lack of sufficient personnel' (G.S.A., 15 May 1858).

Finally, we should point out not only the complete lack of a service network in Ottonian Athens, namely of streets, illumination, telecommunications, transports, but also the absence of serious efforts to cover those needs, which in other European capitals were considered to be perhaps more important than the needs in public buildings, at least in the central streets and squares, where those buildings stood. In Athens, public buildings preceded the urban network. That was criticised by the press, with the observation that 'we wear gloves with dirty shirts' (M., 1858). It is impressive that until 1858, parallel to Stadium Street, in the area that concentrated several important public buildings, there was an uncovered stream. The Greek capital was thus tormented by dust in summer and mud and stagnating water in winter (*Αθηνά*, 17 November 1852). Garbage was usual in the streets of Athens of that time, which suffered from water shortage. The absence of organised slaughterhouses, of a cleaning service and the existence of farms in the direct neighbourhood of the city, underlined the contrast with the monumental buildings. That demonstrates the specificities of the evolution of Athens and the difference of the Greek upper class from the European bourgeoisie they imitated. That evolution couldn't follow the rhythms of Western European cities, which were the Greek capital's models. That gap will start being bridged many years after King George I's accession to the throne.

The situation under King George I

In the late nineteenth century, that time's more rational spirit led to the gradual abandon of idealistic projects and the domination of more practical ones. That spirit was due both to the new dynasty's different antecedents and the generally more practical views prevailing then, as a result of the progress of science and technology. But it was also due to the realisation that Greece wouldn't become the big country they imagined at the time of independence.

The faster approach of the Greek upper class to the European bourgeoisie under King George I had a direct impact on the priorities concerning public architecture. That upper class was dominated by a spirit of progress. Moreover, after King Otto's fall in 1862, the decline of construction activity of the immediately previous period – due to the political instability – turned into a complete inactivity, which accumulated imperative construction needs (Russack, 1942, p. 127). The new dynasty thus found many unfinished buildings, with the political instability and the lack of funds leading to real abandon. A characteristic instance is the University: although almost completed at King Otto's fall, in 1863 it is reported to be in a poor condition, partly because of the temporary functions it was housing (Frearitis, 1889, p. 12). A similar image of abandon was given by already finished buildings, and led to a financial decadence by the turbulent times. Thus, in 1869 the Queen Amalia Orphanage is called a 'ruin' (Burnouf, 1869, p. 465).

Additionally, the new dynasty inherited urgent needs for buildings whose construction hadn't even started yet. The continuous efforts of the previous reign to construct the necessary administrative buildings carried on thus undiminished. In 1865 a decree approved the edification of a public establishment for the office of the General Post, the Telegraph, and the Prefecture (Government Gazette, 27 January 1865). A subsequent decree (Government Gazette, 7 April 1866), referring to the previous one, approved the necessary changes and additions to the establishment that would be edified, so that it would become useful for the offices of the Ministry of the Interior and the General Direction of the Post.

As for the Courts of Justice, for many years several decrees announced their edification. That, however, wasn't realised before the late twentieth century, whereas in most European capitals the Courts are among the most monumental civic buildings. The first related decree of King George I's reign dates from 1875 (Government Gazette, 3 March 1875) and declares 'the building of the courts in the capital of the State' a 'task of public need', designating the plot next to the Arsakeion School for Girls.[16] Another decree followed in 1876 (Government Gazette, 24 June 1876) and the edification started in 1877, but was interrupted by the reactions of the Arsakeion's direction (Galatis, 1957, vol. 2, chapter 1, pp. 18a–19). In 1889 the Prime Minister Charilaos Trikoupis attempted to transform the Municipal Hospital into a Palace of Justice, and the German architect Ernst Ziller prepared the respective plans (*Ακρόπολις*, 22 March 1889). That project wasn't realised either, yet the efforts continued. In 1901, the Law 'About the edification of judicial establishments' was published (Government Gazette, 15 February 1901), destined to execute the 1898 testament of the benefactor Andreas Syggros about the edification of Courts of Justice, followed by the related decree (Government Gazette, 13 March 1901). The same year we are informed that the barracks of the artillery, lying in Kifisias Avenue (today's Queen Sophia Avenue), is going to be transferred, and the 'palace of Justice' would take its place (*Ελλάς*, 1901, p. 66). Finally, 'Result of the launched international competition for the preparation of a project for a Palace of Justice that will be erected in Athens' was published in 1912 (Government Gazette, 6 March 1912). However, for the same reasons, the projects were never realised.

Another imperative need was that of a Museum. Immediately after the new king's arrival, the Statute 'About the edification of the Museum' was published in the Government Gazette, the Statute 'About the edification of the Museum',[17] according to the plans of Panagiotis Kalkos (Government Gazette, 11 October 1863), which was finally built on the Acropolis in 1874. However, the lack of library buildings will persist, and the National Library won't be finished before 1902, while the edification of the Parliament's Library wasn't decided prior to 1911 (Government Gazette, 25 May 1911).

Nevertheless, the most urgent need concerned the hospitals and became acuter with the increase of the capital's population. Due to the spirit of progress dominating the upper class all over Europe, benefaction was no longer expressed by the edification of monumental public buildings, but manifested a preference for institutions of welfare, not so much grandiose and luxurious, as functional. Many foundation decrees demonstrate that tendency (Government Gazette, 15 November 1863; 20 March 1869; 16 November 1878; 4 May 1881; 3 December 1899), sealed by the edification of a hospital. It is the new Municipal Hospital (1904–1909), which was allegedly the most perfect in the East (East meaning the Balkans and Asia Minor) and on a par with the newest hospitals of Europe, fulfilling all contemporary demands of hospital architecture. Its construction budget amounted to 3,797,400 drachmas (Paraskevopoulos, 1907, pp. 521–523), making it the first public building that cost more than the most emblematic construction of neo-classical Athens, the Academy, which had cost 3,360,000 drachmas (Biris, 1966–1967, p. 154).

The Athenian upper class under King George I

The advanced development of the Athenian upper class rendered necessary the construction of buildings constituting from then on symbols of the power and wealth of that class all over Europe. Such buildings were the town halls and the markets. The City Hall of Athens had no permanent premises throughout King Otto's reign. Under King George I, however, the moment came for it to acquire its own building. As for the market, 1879 saw the start of the gradual edification of the new Municipal Market, in Athena Street, in the direction of the city's expansion to the North. That market, half-finished still, started functioning far earlier than expected. The night of the 8th to the 9th of August 1884, a fire, the cause of which was never clarified, completely destroyed the oriental-style old market, and with it, a characteristic part of Ottonian Athens, replaced by a building expressing the spirit of its time.

Nevertheless, despite the more practical spirit dominating in the time of King George I, the phenomena of imitation and consequently of bad evaluation of the capital's needs didn't disappear. Thus, in the turn of the century Athens disposed of a number of theatres excessively disproportionate to its population, in comparison with those of the European metropolises. Moreover, the Municipal Theatre (1873–1888) was erected at a time of prosperity of the opera, like the great European opera houses.

Finally, the Athenian upper class saluted with enthusiasm the inauguration of the grandiose Zappeion Exhibition Hall in 1888. The excessive haste to edify a building of expositions, while there were other urgent needs, is criticised by Kaftantzoglou:

> In our country [. . .], where agriculture, industry and all the other arts are in swaddling clothes, and there is no study or care to reinforce them, it is decided boisterously and hastily to found a permanent palace for the Olympics[18] in order to expose the Greek products, because of the unfortunately dominating in our country undiscerning imitation of everything foreign.
>
> (Kaftantzoglou, 1880, p. 6)

The Zappeion, however, clearly satisfied the desires and ambitions of the Athenians, whose interest in universal expositions had been demonstrated since their beginning.

End of a reign and of an era

The most certain indication that the choices made on the subject of the Athenian public buildings, especially under King Otto, weren't so realistic, is offered by the dysfunction or even uselessness and partial or total abandon of some buildings, after their completion. Since most of them were choices of the Bavarian dynasty completed under King George I, those problems appeared only then. Some others, however, constituted choices of his time, fulfilling older desires.

The most characteristic example is the Academy, the most monumental and most onerous of all. In 1885 Iphigenia Sina, the widow of Simon Sinas,[19] offered through Ziller, who supervised the construction, the building's keys to the Prime Minister Theodoros Diligiannis, along with an endowment of 800,000 drachmas. However, the latter avoided accepting the offer, judging that, after the exhaustion of that sum, the cost of the institution's function would be unbearable for the state's finances (Biris, 1966–1967, p. 154). Considering that the Academy first functioned only in 1926, it seems that the huge donation of the Sinas couple, which could have been employed for the satisfaction of numerous urgent needs of Athens, was consumed for a building of no practical use. For decades the Academy's only merit was being a masterpiece of classicism and probably the most important architectural jewel of modern Athens. According to Émile-Louis Burnouf, principal of the French School of Athens, many Athenians regarded the Academy as a demonstration of wealth and a monument of vanity, in a country without roads (Burnouf, 1887, p. 554). On the other hand, several people regarded the empty masterpiece as a glorious proof of the position of culture in the young and replete with hopes state and a precursor of the cultural renaissance of the East, which Greece was undertaking. From that viewpoint, that building fulfilled its purpose more than adequately.

Another characteristic example is the Zappeion Exhibition Hall. The Universal Exposition of 1903, just 15 years after the building's inauguration, even though the best organised, was also its last great activity. In the following years it rarely fulfilled its purpose. Closed for years, it became a ruin, housing functions irrelevant to its destination, like barracks, a warehouse of provisions, a hospital, laboratories, public offices, a refugees' shelter, a school, and finally an asylum (Kydoniatis, 1985, p. 145; *Ζάππειο, 1888–1988*, 1988, p. 30).

The ideological frame defining the Greek state's priorities disappeared definitely only in 1922, when the whole ideological network that nourished the Hellenism of modern times collapsed, with the destruction of the Greek communities of Asia Minor and the end of every aspiration to a great Greek state spreading across all territories of the historic presence of the Greek nation. Only the abrupt landing in that cruel reality proved capable of turning the Greek state's and people's desires and efforts to more realistic goals. Therefore, that date corresponds roughly to the end of classicism as a style and as an ideology in Greece.

Notes

1 Leo von Klenze mentions a message of the Minister of Foreign Affairs I. Rizos to him, referring to the glory associated with future citizens linking his name to the inception of the new plan of Athens.
2 Since Otto was a minor when he became King of Greece, a three-member Regency Council was installed until 1835, when he came of age. That council was composed of Bavarian court officials.
3 An administrative body during Ottoman domination in Greece.
4 Under British control from 1814 to 1864.
5 In 1843 the newly appointed architect of the capital, Gregorios Petimezas, was assigned the design of a general plan of Athens, putting together the various partial plans. He was assisted by the surveyor J. Beck.
6 A public school for boys founded with a donation of Ioannis Varvakis, a wealthy Greek of Russia.
7 See note 2.
8 The name indicates that it would be an education institution of different levels, without more specific information.
9 The highest hill of Athens.
10 Simon Sinas, a wealthy Greek of Vienna.
11 The Petraki monastery lies on the southern slope of the hill of Lycabettus.
12 Also more documents of a similar content in the same file.
13 It was built in 1885–1902.
14 The first name is Hellenized.
15 It would be financed by the Zosimas brothers.
16 Founded thanks to the donation of Apostolos Arsakis, a wealthy Greek of Romania.
17 It means the Acropolis Museum.
18 That was the name of the expositions.
19 See note 10.

Bibliography

Bastea, E. (2000). *The Creation of Modern Athens: Planning the Myth*. Cambridge: Cambridge University Press.
Bikelas, D. (1888). Le cinquantenaire de l'Université. *Revue des Etudes grecques*, 1(1), pp. 78–85.

26   *Ideology*

Biris, K. (1966–1967). *Αι Αθήναι*. Athens. Book published by the author.
Burnouf, E.-L. (1869). La Grèce en 1869. *Revue des deux mondes*, 81, pp. 458–482.
Burnouf, E.-L. (1887). La Grèce en 1886 – I. Son état matériel. *Revue des deux mondes*, 79, pp. 547–572.
Fatsea, I. (2000). *Monumentality and its shadows: A quest for modern Greek architectural discourse in nineteenth-century Athens (1834–1862)*. PhD. MIT.
Frearitis, K. (1889). Τα κατά την αποπεράτωσιν και ανακαίνισιν του Εθνικού Πανεπιστημίου. In: I. Pantazidis, ed., *Χρονικόν της πρώτης πεντηκονταετίας του Ελληνικού Πανεπιστημίου*. Athens, p. 12. Book published by the author.
Galatis, S. (1957). *Ιστορία της εν Αθήναις Φιλεκπαιδευτικής Εταιρίας*. Athens. Book published by the author.
General State Archives (G.S.A.), City Plan, file 1, 24 November 1836, 30 June 1844, 27 September 1844, 26 August 1848; file 7, 11 February 1850; file 13, 9 September 1862.
G.S.A., Ottonian Record, Ministry of Education, L, file 34, 20 May 1833; file 35, 15 May 1858; file 43, 17 January 1855; file 44; file 45, 7 April 1853; file 57, 25 April 1836.
G.S.A., Ottonian Record, Ministry of the Interior, file 188, 21 February 1835; file 208, 23 September 1851; file 211, 31 December 1835; file 212, 21 September 1834; file 214, 12 June 1843, 30 July 1859; file 221, 22 October 1833, 22 October 1834.
Government Gazette 41, December 1833; 11, 3 March 1834; 22, 16 June 1834; 22, 28 June 1834; 29, 17 August 1834; 23, 19 May 1835; 20, 18 September 1835; 2, 25 January 1836; 86, 31 December 1836; 6, 30 March 1841; 27, 18 June 1836; 81, 31 December 1836; 82, 31 December 1836; 38, 9 November 1843; 9, 16 March 1838; 30, 22 August 1843; 34, 22 September 1843; 36, 26 October 1853; 26, 25 June 1855; 51, 30 October 1858; 59, 30 September 1861; 28, 19 May 1862; 36, 11 October 1863; 40, 15 November 1863; 8, 27 January 1865; 27, 7 April 1866; 15, 20 March 1869; 13, 3 March 1875; 28, 24 June 1876; 64, 16 November 1878; 39, 4 May 1881; 266, A, 3 December 1899; 31, A, 15 February 1901; 60, 13 March 1901; 121, A, 25 May 1911; 82, 6 March 1912.
Haugsted, I. (1985). Η αρχιτεκτονική σχολή της Κοπεγχάγης. In: Y. Tsiomis, ed., *Αθήνα πρωτεύουσα πόλη*. Athens: Ministry of Culture, pp. 74–81.
Hederer, O. (1976). *Friedrich von Gärtner, 1792–1847*. München: Prestel.
Kabouroglous, D. (1922). *Αι παλαιαί Αθήναι*. Athens. Book published by the author.
Kaftantzoglou, L. *Esquisse d'un plan pour la ville d'Athènes propre à remplacer le projet en exécution si mal conçu et impossible à recevoir jamais sa totale organisation*. G.S.A., Ottonian Record, Ministry of the Interior, file 214.
Kaftantzoglou, L. (8 March 1839). *Σχεδιογραφία Αθηνών*. Αιών.
Kaftantzoglou, L. (1847). *Λόγος εκφωνηθείς κατά την επέτειον τελετήν του Βασιλικού Πολυτεχνείου, επί της κατά το τρίτον καλλιτεχνικόν έτος εκθέσεως των διαγωνισμών*. Athens. Book published by the author.
Kaftantzoglou, L. (1858). *Περί μεταρρυθμίσεως της πόλεως Αθηνών γνώμαι*. Athens: S. Pavlidis and Z. Gryparis.
Kaftantzoglou, L. (1880). *Τα Ολύμπια εν Φαλήρω και το νυν μεταρρυθμιζόμενον Ζάππειον*. Athens. Book published by the author.

Kairofylas, G. (1978). *Η Αθήνα και οι Αθηναίοι (1834–1934)*. Athens: Φιλιππότης.

Karykopoulos, P. (1971). *Αθήνα, Το χωριό που έγινε πρωτεύουσα*. Athens. Book published by the author.

Klenze, L. von (1838). *Aphoristische Bemerkungen gesammelt auf seiner Reise nach Griechenland*. Berlin: G. Reimer.

Kydoniatis, S. (1985). *Αθήναι, παρελθόν και μέλλον*. Athens: Πνευματικό Κέντρο Δήμου Αθηναίων.

Laios, G. (1972). *Σίμων Σίνας*. Athens: Γραφείον Δημοσιευμάτων της Ακαδημίας Αθηνών.

M. (3 August 1858). *Μακάριοι οι λέγοντες εις ώτα ακουόντων*. Αθηνά.

Maurer, G. L. von (1943–1947). *Ο ελληνικός λαός, εις τας σχέσεις του δημοσίου, εκκλησιαστικού και ιδιωτικού δικαίου, προ του Απελευθερωτικού αγώνος και μετ'αυτόν μέχρι της 31ης Ιουλίου 1834*. Athens.

Papageorgiou-Venetas, A. (1994). *Hauptstadt – Athen: ein Stadtgedanke des Klassizismus*. München: Deutscher Kunstverlag.

Paraskevopoulos, G. P. (1907). *Οι Δήμαρχοι των Αθηνών (1835–1907)*. Athens. Published by the author.

Ross, L. (1863). *Errinerungen und Mitteilungen aus Griechenland*. Berlin: R. Gärtner.

Russack, H. H. (1942). *Deutsche Bauen in Athen*. Berlin: Wilhelm Limpert Verlag.

Stuart, J., Revett, N. (1762). *The Antiquities of Athens and Other Monuments of Greece*. London: Henry G. Bohn.

Svoronos, N. (1976). *Επισκόπηση της νεοελληνικής ιστορίας*. Athens: Θεμέλιο.

Vrettos-Papadopoulos, M. (1860). *Αι νέαι Αθήναι – Athènes moderns*. Athens: P. A. Sakellarios.

Αθηνά (17 November 1852).

Ακρόπολις (22 March 1889).

Ελλάς (1901). Leipzig: K. Baedeker.

Ελπίς (12 December 1861).

Ζάππειο 1888–1988 (1988). Athens: Ministry of Finance, Committee of Olympics and Legacies.

Ιστορία του Ελληνικού Έθνους (1970–1978). Athens: Εκδοτική Αθηνών.

Πανδώρα (1 March 1855).

2 The relationship of the neo-classical city with the antiquities

The idealistic era of King Otto

While the initial plans of Athens – including the significantly less famous plan of Kaftantzoglou (Kaftantzoglou, 1839) – predicted a balanced distribution of monumental buildings within the urban fabric, according to all rational principles of their time, today's situation shows a very clear displacement of those buildings along an axis formed from the North to the South by the avenues Patision, University (Panepistimiou), and Amalias, including most monumental buildings: the Archaeological Museum, the Polytechnic, the Council of State (former Arsakeion), the National Library, the University, the Academy of Athens, the Catholic Cathedral, the Numismatic Museum (former mansion of the archaeologist Heinrich Schliemann), the Bank of Greece, the Parliament (former Royal Palace) with the National Garden, and the Zappeion Exhibition Hall. That change from a triangular to a linear layout resulted from the desire to reconnect with the ancient past. According to that concept, every important building in Athens had to be worthy of the ancient ruins. Namely, it should be positioned according to their location and have the best view towards them, even more so since the ancient monuments were the stylistic prototypes of the modern ones.

General projects

In the Kleanthes and Schaubert project, the new city is planned with a complete respect of antiquities. The architects propose the demolition of an important part of the Ottoman city. That would permit the excavations for the discovery of the ancient town, as they mention in their memorandum. They say, 'the transfer of the new city onto the plateau to the North has the advantage of letting free to future excavations the ground of the ancient city of Theseus and Hadrian' (Russack, 1942, p. 189). In their plan, the densely built area between the Acropolis and Hadrian's library (Karydis, 1981) appears unbuilt, and the street network depends on the ancient sites. Therefore, as mentioned previously, Athena Street connects the Royal Palace to the Acropolis and the ancient Agora. Stadium Street connects the palace to the ancient stadium, while Piraeus Street ensures the connection with Athens' homonymous ancient port. Apart from the Royal Palace, no other public building lies on the plan's visual axes. Here the antiquities become 'points of view', playing the role held in other capitals by public buildings. The latter, although substantially bigger than ancient monuments, keep a clear distance from them. Moreover, there are no new monumental constructions like triumphal arcs and so forth, which confirms the respect of antiquities. Nevertheless, the plan's intense symmetry reveals that the architects ignored the ground's inclination towards the south-west and the concentration of most historic sites in the same direction vis-à-vis the city's historical core.

The German architect Alexander Ferdinand von Quast made observations on the Kleanthes and Schaubert project and offered another proposal (Quast, 1834, pp. 32, 34), perhaps the most idealistic among all. Although he never saw the Greek capital, he took, like many of his countrymen, a vivid interest in what was to him the revival of the most glorious city of all time. Naturally, he had no idea of the state in which the object of his admiration was in his time, like many visionaries who occupied themselves with the creation of modern Athens.

Von Quast believed that the modern city should expand at some distance from the ancient one, along the axis connecting the latter with the port of Piraeus to the south-west of the Acropolis (an opinion that was also shared by Anastasios Goudas, who published a manual about the medical chorography and the climate of Athens; Goudas, 1858, pp. 8, 11–12; see Fatsea, 2000, p. 81). He sustains that the new capital's civic buildings must be concentrated in the same place in order to create an important impression. Therefore, he imagined them at the foot of the Acropolis. He suggested a viaduct linking the Cathedral on the ancient court of the Areopagus to the Acropolis' Propylaea, namely religious to political power, since the Royal Palace was to be built on the Acropolis, according to the project of Carl Friedrich von Schinkel. Von Quast positioned the Cathedral on the Areopagus, where Saint Paul had preached. Like others, he was imagining the cultural institutions on the shore of Ilissus (Plato, Phaedrus),[1] mentioning also the spring Kallirroe. Naturally, he ignored the lamentable state of the river and the spring in his time.

When von Klenze undertook to modify the Kleanthes and Schaubert project, apart from changing the scale of streets, gardens, and squares to minimise the expropriation cost, he proposed a town of a size permitting the antiquities to prevail. He connected the Royal Palace directly to them, positioning it in Kerameikos, one of the most sacred archaeological sites of Greece. The royal residence would have a direct visual relationship with the Acropolis, the ancient parliament of the Pnyx, the Areopagus, and the Royal Garden, including the Theseion (temple of Hephaestus, Figure 2.1). He relocated the cathedral and introduced the cultural buildings to their actual location. He was also the first to insert into the plan the Boulevard, the city's largest and most official avenue, today's University Street.

Von Klenze seems to take more into account the particularities of the Athenian landscape, since the plan's symmetry is now adapted to them. On the other hand, unlike his predecessors, he seems to have overlooked the location's functionality. He took an interest only in the positioning of the Royal Palace, and sited other official functions just to fill the plan, since he writes that it would be easy to place the missing buildings in such an extended area (Klenze, 1838, p. 444). Unfortunately, in that he was very much mistaken, as will be explicated later.

Figure 2.1 The temple of Hephaestus

Photograph by the author

Partial projects

Contrary to the existence of practical principles in the Kleanthes and Schaubert project, the following partial projects for separate parts of the capital demonstrate an effort to site important public constructions on locations of great archaeological and historical value, without an equal interest in functionality. This is clear in von Klenze's project for the Pantechneion (Museum), which he placed in 1835 at the same place he had previously proposed for the Royal Palace, in Kerameikos (Hederer, 1976, p. 144).[2] It is noteworthy that he chose the same location for a totally different building from the one he himself had previously proposed.

Much later, in 1857, the zone of Kerameikos was indicated by the government for the edification of the Academy. The choice was accompanied by enthusiastic comments on the location's qualities, ignoring, however, any practical aspect. It was sustained that the site was 'prominent' and 'extremely safe' (*Ήλιος*, 2 February 1857). Others, however, considered as a big sin the creation of modern Athens on the ruins of the ancient one. Moreover, the vicinity of the classical monuments would reduce the building's architectural value (*Φιλόπατρις*, 12 January 1857). Nonetheless, in 1865 it was proposed to erect the Archaeological Museum at the same place. Additionally, Queen Amalia wanted to incorporate the temple of Hephaestus, lying in the same area, into the Royal Garden, but abandoned the idea after the reactions generated by the threat to the antiquities.

Similar issues emerged with the Observatory, built on the Nymphs' Hill, notwithstanding the vivid objections of the Academy of Munich (Biris, 1966–1967, p. 131). According to the professor of Athens' University Georgios Vouris, speaking at the Observatory's foundation ceremony, the edifice would be close to the Pnyx, where the ancient astronomer Meton had his 'heliotropium' (Laios, 1972, p. 108). This gives an idea of the emotion caused by such comparisons and, especially, by the pride that no other city could boast of such a privilege.

Apparently, only ideology could overcome the obstacles in the positioning of public functions, at least those associated with famous ancient buildings. The Athenian Trilogy (Figure 2.2, nos. 8, 18, 31, Figures 2.3–2.5) constitutes the most debated case, since it would include the major cultural foundations, which would be associated with their ancient predecessors.[3] The Trilogy's components were the only public buildings constructed at the site predicted by all the city plans, although not in the initial combination. The selected location was – as they thought at that time – next to the ancient Lyceum,[4] close to the Stadium and Ilissus, a direct reference to the historical continuity between ancient and modern Greece. Only for them

32   *Ideology*

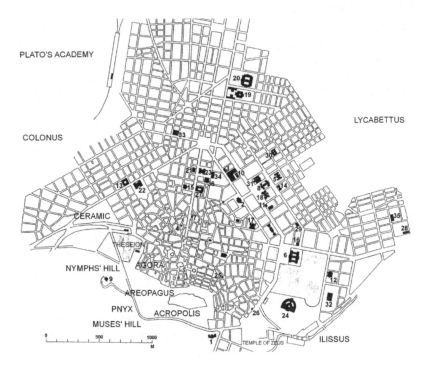

Figure 2.2 Athens towards the end of the nineteenth century. The public buildings are numbered in chronological order.

Drawn by the author: 1. Military Hospital; 2. Mint; 3. Royal Printing House; 4. Criminal Court; 5. Civil Hospital; 6. Royal Palace; 7. First Primary School for Boys; 8. University; 9. Observatory; 10. Arsakeion School for Girls; 11. Eye Hospital; 12. Queen Amalia Orphanage; 13. Hatzikonsta Orphanage; 14. Papadopoulos Lyceum; 15. Varvakeion Lyceum; 16. Military Pharmacy; 17. Parliament; 18. Academy; 19. Polytechnic; 20. Archaeological Museum; 21. City Hall; 22. Municipal Foundling Hospital; 23. Municipal Theatre; 24. Zappeion Exhibition Hall; 25. Second Primary School for Boys; 26. Schools of the 'Ladies' Club for Women's Education'; 27. Municipal Market; 28. Annunciation Hospital; 29. Court-Martial; 30.Chemical Laboratory; 31.National Library; 32.Crown Prince Palace; 33. Royal Theatre; 34. National Bank; 35. Marasleion School; 36. Central Post Office

did von Klenze put limits to possible changes of his plans, discouraging the transfer of cultural institutions from there (Papageorgiou-Venetas, 1994, p. 148). Therefore, they were the only buildings to resist to the innumerable displacements of public functions, remaining at the supposed location of one of the most illustrious institutions of antiquity.

However, more practical minds were against siting public functions close to the antiquities. The Minister of Justice mentions in 1834 three buildings

Figure 2.3 The University of Athens
Photograph by the author

Figure 2.4 The Academy of Athens
Photograph by the author

Figure 2.5 The National Library
Photograph by the author

belonging to the government, suitable to house the Courts of Justice. But they were in the excavation zone, where even repairs were forbidden. The question was whether to repair those buildings, when that wasn't allowed to the citizens (G.S.A., 1 July 1834). The following year the Minister of Justice writes that the church of Saint Mary of Kandilis, which would be repaired and house the Supreme Court, wasn't suitable, for it was close to the monument of Lysicrates (Figure 2.6), where it was expected to find antiquities (G.S.A., 14 April 1835).

Despite these justified objections, some projects proposed the construction of public buildings not just close to the antiquities, but even above them. The first and best known is von Schinkel's aforesaid project. Despite his great knowledge and estimation for classical antiquity, his enormous palace would destroy ancient monuments. Moreover, the Military Hospital was supposed to have been built above the Odeon of Pericles and the existence of a mosaic in its basements is reported (Vrettos-Papadopoulos, 1860, pp. 68–70).[5]

Figure 2.6 The monument of Lysicrates
Photograph by the author

The view towards the antiquities

However, after it was accepted that locating official functions in archaeological sites presented practical obstacles, efforts tended towards ensuring them the best view to those sites. In perhaps no other city in the world was the issue of view and orientation of major architectural monuments put as seriously as in Athens. For nineteenth-century classicists, Greeks and foreigners, Athens was the most privileged city from that viewpoint, having a natural environment of rare beauty and charged with historical and mythological memories unique in the world (Klenze, 1838, pp. 388–389; Maurer, 1943–1947, p. 99; K., 1853; Ross, 1863, p. 244; Hessel, 1874, p. 23; see also Fatsea, 2000, which argues about K. being Koumanoudis). The great diversity of the Athenian landscape, dotted with hills, rendered it extremely sensitive in human interventions. It was said about the hills that they played the role of pediments or frames for the monuments. If the latter were too small, they would disappear, while if they were too big, they would overwhelm the landscape's elements (Villard, 1875, pp. 13–14).

Once the uniqueness of the Athenian landscape was realised, the creators of the new capital wanted to enhance it and relate monumental buildings to it. Already King Otto, in his speech of 23 May 1833, when he placed the foundation stone of his palace, mentions the view to monuments (Σωτήρ, 18 March 1834). Also Kaftantzoglou refers constantly to the advantages of the Athenian landscape. As he sustains, his propositions for the new city aim to ensure a better view (Kaftantzoglou, 1839). He believes that the new capital should be built west of the Pnyx, in order to have the optimum visual relationship with the antiquities and the historic sites (Kaftantzoglou, 1858, p. 11).

The desire to relate the monumental architecture of Athens to its historic landscape was more intense in the case of the Royal Palace, because of its great symbolic value in a regime of absolute monarchy. The view through the columns of the Parthenon was one of the reasons why von Quast approved of von Schinkel's bold project (Quast, 1834, p. 32).

The German architect Friedrich Stauffert (Stauffert, 1844) and the German archaeologist Ludwig Ross (Ross, 1863, p. 159) made similar remarks about the view from the royal residence of the Kleanthes and Schaubert project. Their palace would have a view to the Acropolis, the Areopagus, the Nymphs' Hill, the Pnyx, the modern city, Piraeus, the islands of Aegina and Salamis, the Olive Forest where Plato's Academy had been, and the mountains of Parnes, Lycabettus, and Hymettus.

Similarly, von Klenze writes about the area proposed by him that no other European capital presented such advantages for siting a royal residence, giving a full description of all interesting views (Klenze, 1838, pp. 442–443, 481). On the contrary, about the location proposed by Kleanthes and Schaubert, he thinks that the view is very disadvantageous (Klenze, 1838, pp. 436–438). Moreover, the view was decisive in the selection of the Royal Palace's final site (Αθηνά, 12 February 1836, 7 March, 1836; Stauffert, April 1844). Finally, the location Lange had proposed for the royal residence isn't known exactly, but the plans indicate that he imagined it at the foot of Lycabettus (Kokkou, 1983, p. 136). Thus it would have had approximately the same view as the realised building (Klenze, 1838, pp. 447–448).

The royal couple took care to ensure that advantageous view, which no other monarch in the world had the privilege of contemplating. According to a document addressed to the Queen,

the height of the ministerial building above the ground on which it will be constructed is 18 metres 40/100. The height of the And.Koromilas house above the same ground is 17 metres 50/100. The height of the Anarghyros house above the same ground is 18 metres 70/100. The height of the floor of the big balcony of the Royal Palace above the same ground is 23 metres 90/100, so that the floor of the aforementioned balcony will be 5 metres 50/100 above the roof of the ministerial building. (G.S.A., Ottonian Record, Ministry of the Interior, file 215)

Also the University is clearly oriented to the Acropolis, as Stauffert observes (Stauffert, 1844). According to the text accompanying the publication of its plans in 1851, 'the happiest among us are the students of Athens', because of the historic sites they contemplate from the University's Propylaea (Vakas, 1925, p. 27; see also Villard, 1875, p. 14). Also, the lithography of the Eye Hospital by Christian Hansen reveals the same interest in the building's relationship with the landscape of Attica. The same goes for the perspective view of the Observatory by his brother, Theophil.

The south-western orientation offered the richest view to the Attica basin and to the Saronic gulf. That was intensified by the ground's inclination towards the bed of Cephisus, the main river of the Attica basin. The final siting of official edifices demonstrates that that view was aimed at in most cases, contrary to the initial project's homogeneity. That goes also for unrealised projects, like that of Kleanthes for the Arsakeion. Contrary to Kaftantzoglou's realised project (Figure 2.7), Kleanthes put the main façade to

Figure 2.7 The Arsakeion School for Girls
Photograph by the author

the south-west, although the opposite one, which became the main façade, was on the Boulevard (Galatis, 1957, vol. 1, chapter 7, p. 4, which includes a plan of Kleanthes' project). Finally, for the Eye Hospital, the south-western orientation was preferred to the north-western initially proposed, as the aforementioned drawing by Christian Hansen reveals.

The shortage in public land overturned most efforts based on specific principles. However, the buildings housing cultural functions overcame that problem and were built where intended, not by the initial plans, but by the following projects, forming the aforementioned axis. To them is added the Royal Palace, which housed the power from which all the other functions were supposed to emanate: the power of the enlightened king, protector of the arts and science, as he is depicted in the centre of the whole composition – the frieze of the University.

The situation under King George I: the gradual fading of idealism

At the time of George I's reign, the sources indicate that idealistic principles trying to associate monumental buildings with antiquities recede. This accords with the realistic spirit characterising that reign.

An exception to that is the Archaeological Museum. As already mentioned, thirty years after von Klenze's projects first for the Royal Palace and then for the Pantechneion, it was again proposed to position the building most closely related to the ancient monuments in Kerameikos, for which Lange made a project. Even a decree was published in 1865 (Government Gazette, 8 March 1865).

But the idea was abandoned because of the objections, especially about the location. Kaftantzoglou, who was a member of the related committee, writes that when that site was proposed in 1857 for the construction of the Academy, the Paris Institute sustained that 'the spots and sites around the Acropolis should stay untouched and sacred'. Therefore, 'when it was a question of choosing the location of any public building in Athens, the prevailing idea should be the initial one, for which Athens was assigned as capital of Greece; namely, because of its ancient monuments' (*Ελπίς*, 25 March 1865). It is noteworthy how that text interprets the idea of the choice of Athens 'because of its ancient monuments': in order to protect them and not connect them to modern buildings in a harmful way, which is a very different approach from that of the 1830s.

Much later, in 1888, when the final building at Patision Street was almost finished (Figure 2.8), Theophil Hansen presented a grandiose project for a Museum on the southern slope of the Acropolis. That project was equally

Figure 2.8 The National Archaeological Museum
Photograph by the author

rejected, because of its overwhelming budget, but also because it was too late to change the location. Other propositions predicted the transformation of Hadrian's Library into a museum or the construction of a new building on the hill of Ardettus, above the ancient Stadium.

Nevertheless, also under George I there is a case of a public building built on ancient ruins, as happened with the Military Hospital during Otto's reign. That was the Zappeion Exhibition Hall, which occupied the supposed place of Hippia's Baths, in spite of the Archaeological Society's protests (Kaftantzoglou, 1880, p. 8; Vernardakis, 1902, pp. 38–39). The reactions of architects and archaeologists demonstrate, though, that monuments are now treated in a more 'scientific' way than during Otto's reign. Now it isn't only their value which is recognised, but also the dangers they encounter as a result of their inclusion in the modern city.

There is no written evidence of an interest to orient official buildings towards the archaeological and historic sites. However, one can observe the orientation of the three more monumental edifices of that time, the

Polytechnic (Figure 2.9), the Archaeological Museum, and the Zappeion Exhibition Hall (Figure 2.10). Apart from those, though, the interest seems to focus now rather on the landscape's natural beauty. Now, even simple citizens express an opinion about it, in accordance with the middle class's

Figure 2.9 The Polytechnic (National Technical University)

Photograph by the author

Figure 2.10 The Zappeion Exhibition Hall
Photograph by the author

demand for better living conditions. Thus some citizens ask for the cancellation of the construction of a cavalry barracks in Ares square, observing:

> Not only do we neglect, but we even destroy whatever we have without expense, while the civilised nations of Europe pay great expenses to replace by art whatever nature has deprived them of, in favour of the really human life they lead.
>
> (G.S.A., 10 December 1869)

An official document concerning the view from the Royal Palace indicates a similar change in the authorities' priorities. The document addressed by the Ministry of Education to the Ministry of the Interior about yet another proposal for the siting of the Archaeological Museum is illuminating:

> We wish to have exact information about the public sites extending below the Royal Palace towards the sanctuary of the Olympian Zeus, and a plan of them also featuring their surface. As these sites seem

suitable for the construction of the National Museum, it is necessary to level them vis-à-vis the Royal Palace, in order to make clear which height can be achieved by a building erected there without it impending the view of the sea from the upper uncovered portico of the Royal Palace.

(G.S.A., 2 October 1864)

Although practical principles appear in buildings, not housing cultural functions, and thus less connected to ancient prototypes, the interest in the antiquities seems now more scientific and less idealistic, and the antiquities are no longer just a romantic decorative frame for the modern city.

Notes

1 One of the three rivers going through the Attica basin (the others being Cephisus and Eridanus), a favourite promenade of the ancient Athenians, due to its beautiful nature and numerous sanctuaries.
2 He writes that the northern slope of the Acropolis was determined as the location of the Pantechneion.
3 The equivalence was, of course, imaginary, since for instance the Academy had very little to do with the homonymous ancient institution of Plato.
4 The ancient Lyceum, Aristotle's school, was discovered in 1997, more in the South than it was thought until then.
5 However, the recent excavations for the construction of the new Acropolis Museum proved that what they believed to be the ruins of Pericles' Odeon belonged in fact to dwellings of early Christian times. The Odeon was discovered earlier more to the north.

Bibliography

Biris, K. (1966–1967). *Αι Αθήναι*. Athens. Book published by the author.
Fatsea, I. (2000). *Monumentality and its shadows: A quest for modern Greek architectural discourse in nineteenth-century Athens (1834–1862)*. PhD. MIT.
Galatis, S. (1957). *Ιστορία της εν Αθήναις Φιλεκπαιδευτικής Εταιρίας*. Athens.
General State Archives (G.S.A.), City Plan, file 14, 2 October 1864; file 15, 10 December 1869. Book published by the author.
G.S.A., Ottonian Record, Ministry of the Interior, file 215.
G.S.A., Ottonian Record, Ministry of Justice, K, file 29, 1 July 1834, 14 April 1835.
Goudas, A. (1858). *Έρευναι περί Ιατρικής Χωρογραφίας και Κλίματος Αθηνών*. Athens. Book published by the author.
Government Gazette 17, 8 March 1865.
Hederer, O. (1976). *Friedrich von Gärtner, 1792–1847*. München: Prestel.
Hessel, C. (1874). Reiseskizzen aus Griechenland. In: *Program des königlichen Gymnasiums zu Wetzlar*. Wetzlar: Ferd. Schnitzler, pp. 1–26.
K. (1853). Καθολικόν Πανόραμα των Αθηνών. *Νέα Πανδώρα*, 67(3), pp. 440–445.

Kaftantzoglou, L. (8 March 1839). *Σχεδιογραφία Αθηνών*. Αιών.

Kaftantzoglou, L. (1858). *Περί μεταρρυθμίσεως της πόλεως Αθηνών γνώμαι*. Athens: S. Pavlidis and Z. Gryparis.

Kaftantzoglou, L. (1880). *Τα Ολύμπια εν Φαλήρω και το νυν μεταρρυθμιζόμενον Ζάππειον*. Athens. Book published by the author.

Karydis, D. (1981). *Πολεοδομικά των Αθηνών της Τουρκοκρατίας*. PhD. National Technical University of Athens.

Klenze, L. von (1838). *Aphoristische Bemerkungen gesammelt auf seiner Reise nach Griechenland*. Berlin: G. Reimer.

Kokkou, A. (1983). *Σχέδια αθηναϊκών κτιρίων. Προτάσεις που δεν εφαρμόστηκαν.* In: *Νεοκλασική πόλη και αρχιτεκτονική*. Thessaloniki, Greece: Aristotle University of Thessaloniki, pp. 135–144.

Laios, G. (1972). *Σίμων Σίνας*. Athens: Γραφείον Δημοσιευμάτων της Ακαδημίας Αθηνών.

Maurer, G. L. von (1943–1947). *Ο ελληνικός λαός, εις τας σχέσεις του δημοσίου, εκκλησιαστικού και ιδιωτικού δικαίου, προ του Απελευθερωτικού αγώνος και μετ΄αυτόν μέχρι της 31ης Ιουλίου 1834*. Athens.

Papageorgiou-Venetas, A. (1994). *Hauptstadt – Athen: ein Stadtgedanke des Klassizismus*. München: Deutscher Kunstverlag.

Quast, A. F. von (1834). *Mittheilungen über Alt und Neu Athen*. Berlin: George Gropius.

Ross, L. (1863). *Errinerungen und Mitteilungen aus Griechenland*. Berlin: R. Gärtner.

Russack, H. H. (1942). *Deutsche Bauen in Athen*. Berlin: Wilhelm Limpert Verlag.

Stauffert, F. (1844). Die Anlage von Athen und der jetzige Zustand der Baukunst in Griechenland. *Allgemeine Bauzeitung, Ephemeriden*, 1, pp. 2–8, 2, pp. 17–25.

Vakas, P. (1925). *Ι.Παρατηρήσεις επί του νέου σχεδίου της πόλεως Αθηνών του εκπονηθέντος παρά της επιτροπής υπό τον κ.Π. Καλλιγά ΙΙ.Μελέτη επί της αρχιτεκτονικής του κτιρίου του Πανεπιστημίου*. Athens. Book published by the author.

Vernardakis, A. (1902). *Το μέλλον των Αθηνών*. Athens. Book published by the author.

Villard, F. (1875). *Impressions de voyage. Lettres sur l'Attique*. Guéret: Dugenest.

Vrettos-Papadopoulos, M. (1860). *Αι νέαι Αθήναι – Athènes moderns*. Athens: P. A. Sakellarios.

Αθηνά (12 February 1836, 7 March, 1836).

Ελπίς (25 March 1865).

Ήλιος (2 February 1857).

Σωτήρ (18 March 1834).

Φιλόπατρις (12 January 1857).

Part II

The treatment of the pre-revolutionary town

3 The connection of the new neo-classical city with the old one

The treatment of Byzantine and post-Byzantine churches and pre-revolutionary houses

The connection of the new neo-classical city with the old one

The plan of Athens is formed by two different patterns set next to one another: an irregular one, made of narrow winding streets, which surrounds the Acropolis and corresponds to the city's age-long part; and a regular one, made of three combined orthogonal grids, which surrounds the former and corresponds to the new city designed in the nineteenth century. The heart of the contemporary city's commercial and social life lies within the older irregular urban fabric, despite the presence of the capital's more official buildings in the modern city. However, that was hardly the purpose of those who undertook the creation of the modern capital in the nineteenth century.

The importance attributed to the new public buildings imposed their emancipation from the old city, where the small and irregular plots and the narrow and winding streets were totally unsuitable for the construction of the edifices that should reflect the new capital's symbolic role. On the contrary, the new city would have large and regular plots, inserted in an urban fabric whose form would permit the official buildings to function better. The latter would be thus able to fulfil their destination in 'consecrating' the new, modern, and European city as opposed to the old pre-modern one. Applying these principles, the new city's creators tried to replace the existing 'organic' pattern with their rational orthogonal plan. However, the comparison of their plans with the finally realised one demonstrates that these intentions weren't realised.

The existing urban fabric had to be preserved and taken into account, due to the state's incapacity to pay for the expropriations necessary to its total extinction. That resulted in the need to connect the two parts. That was done mainly through the aforementioned penetration of three of the streets of the new city into the old one. Hermes, Athena, and Aeolus Streets would be modern streets, which would stand out through their straight tracing and their width, as well as through their architecture. According to a decree of 1836 (Government Gazette, 15 May 1836), along these three main axes of the old town, but also along Stadium Street and Piraeus Street of the new city, as well as around the main squares (namely, Otto Square, today's Concord Square; and Ludwig Square, today's City Hall Square), it was compulsory to construct two-storey buildings, at a time when one-storey houses were numerous. Those buildings had to be in an uninterrupted row, while their plans had to be submitted to the city's surveyor engineer. Moreover, the three new streets of the old city were the only ones where it was compulsory to modify the limits between the plots, in case that was necessary for the creation of orthogonal buildings, while the same disposition was valid in all the streets of the new city. Precisely in the same streets (the three of the old town and all those of the new city), a plot had to have a surface of at least two hundred square piques,[1] in order to be constructible. Hermes, Athena, and Aeolus Streets were destined since the beginning to be the central commercial arteries. Their crossing constituted the heart of Athens throughout the whole reign of King Otto (G.S.A., 22 February 1838, 25 February 1840; K., 1853, 442b).

The question arising is why the new city wasn't created on the parts of the Attica basin where monastic land, which had become public after the abolition of a large number of monasteries (an unpublished decree of 25 September 1833), could offer the necessary plots. One answer could be the psychological factor. The plans of Athens attempted, for the first time in the city's history, to displace its gravity point from its eternal cradle, in the shadow of the Acropolis, towards the north. From the ancient agora to the Ottoman bazaar, the city's heart was indissolubly tied to the area at the sacred rock's foot. To focus on the immediate past, the market of Ottoman Athens included not only the commercial, but also the administrative centre of the city. Its surface covered the area from Andronicus Kyrristus Clock[2] and the Madrasa[3] up to the western wall of Hadrian's Library. It was there that lay the places of worship (churches and mosques), the administrative buildings (Voivodate and Demogerontia), the Customs, the Court of Law, and also the coffee-houses, the baths (fundamental places of social contact during the Ottoman domination),[4] the hostels, as well as the dwellings of the upper class. In a city which memories of millenaries wanted limited around the Acropolis, it was very difficult to accept that the new realities and the new role reserved to Athens imposed its emancipation from its ancient narrow limits. It is illuminating to consider the question posed by several eminent personalities: would a city not built in the shadow of the Acropolis have the right to bear the name of Athens?

However, apart from the ideological side, there was a general distrust in the city's prospects. Most personalities didn't believe that Athens would ever achieve the size predicted by the Kleanthes and Schaubert project (Kaftantzoglou, 1842; Kaftantzoglou, 1858, p. 13). However, that size, in terms of population, was already overcome before the end of King Otto's reign. As for the surface of the approved plan, the predicted size was overcome before the end of the century, while in the case of the built area, it was overcome much earlier. However, innumerable examples prove the Athenians' disbelief. In 1834–1835 the plots of Stadium Street were being sold at 1–2 drachmas per square pique, and those of Hadrian Street (Adrianou, the old city's main street) at 10 drachmas per square pique (Stasinopoulos, 1973, p. 367). In 1839, the year the University's construction began, the price of the plots in the Boulevard was of 40 cents per square pique (Karykopoulos, 1971, p. 86). Several years later, the Catholic vicar of Athens reacted vividly against the choice of the location for the future Catholic cathedral of Saint Dennis in the Boulevard (next to number 11 of the plan in Fig. 2.2), calling the site 'savage'. Another example is the report of the Minister of the Interior about the violation of the prohibition to construct in the plots around the Royal Palace. According to this, that site lies 'in the environs of Athens' (G.S.A., 15 January 1851).

As a result of the previously listed items, not only were temporary public functions being established in the old urban fabric – which was natural, since at the government's arrival, there were no buildings in the new city – but there were also attempts to construct new public buildings in the old city's heart, as is witnessed by a report of the State Secretariat for the Interior to King Otto (G.S.A., 22 February 1838). According to that, the Ministry of War had proposed to that of the interior to provide it with a convenient location, with the purpose of constructing there a building capable of containing the Place Commandment, the Gendarmerie, the Governor's office, and that of the municipality. Therefore, it defined a location situated in the intersection of Hermes and Aeolus Streets. Another report of the Ministry of the Interior to King Otto on the same subject (G.S.A., 25 February 1840) proposes the 'plots of Kaisariani workshops[5] situated in Athena and Hermes Streets' for the construction of the same building, calling, moreover, the place 'central', which it is, even today. It is the same logic found in the report of the Minister of Education to King Otto on the subject of the location of the Varvakeion Lyceum (Fig. 2.2, no. 15; G.S.A., 29 May 1856).[6] According to that, the proposed site (which was finally selected) 'compared to the majority of the city quarters seems to be more central than that determined next to the University'. Likewise, in a report to King Otto about renting a building for the Public Library, the Minister of Education rejects the building housing Zentner's technical school on Pireaus Street,[7] judging it not central enough (G.S.A., 6 April 1839). An exception to all that disbelief is the case of the wealthy Greek businessmen living abroad. Those, coming to settle in Athens after Independence, preferred to keep with their new houses an ostentatious distance from the existing city, in which it was very difficult to acquire large plots, because of the urban fabric's density.

Under King George I, the Greek capital's particularities compared with the rest of Europe are less obvious. At his arrival, and even more during his long reign, Athens isn't any more the small dismantled town of 10,000 people found by the Bavarian dynasty. It has more than 50,000 inhabitants at the beginning and more than 150,000 at the end of the reign. Now we can speak for the first time of the plan's 'emancipation' from the old urban fabric. The urban fabric expands rapidly, followed by a visible tendency of the public functions' network to expand as well.

The growth of Athens resulted in the need of bigger buildings and therefore of bigger plots. But the splitting up of the urban fabric in small blocks from the beginning made it impossible to construct those buildings in the city centre. Moreover, those small blocks had been occupied at that time almost entirely by private properties, since the state hadn't succeeded in acquiring the plots predicted for public buildings.

Nevertheless, conservatism didn't lack at that time either. When the definite location of the Archaeological Museum was chosen in 1866, many members of the responsible commission thought it wasn't central enough and consequently unsuitable for the museum (Ragavis, 1894–1930, p. 158). However, even before the plot's offer by Helen Tositsa, a newspaper (*Ελπίς*, 30 March 1865) had proposed the same location, predicting that 'later [. . .] it will become central, because the city has started spreading towards the well aerated plain under Lycabettus hill'.

Unfortunately, the lack of funds, along with the disbelief in the city's future, didn't permit the realisation of most of those projects. Public functions were disengaged too late from the old urban fabric to positively influence the modern city's development, which happened in a random way, and according to the possibilities of the moment, without any central planning.

The position of Byzantine and post-Byzantine churches in the new city of Athens

The intense idealism characterising the new Greek state after independence focused on classical antiquity and put the medieval past in a controversial position. On the one hand, Byzantine and post-Byzantine churches housed the actual religion of the Greeks, who had long ago abandoned the religion of their ancestors. On the other hand, these churches represented an architecture that wasn't appreciated by classicists, having nothing to do with the proportions, symmetry, and perfectly elaborated surfaces of the monuments of classical antiquity. Thus, many of them were demolished, in order to permit the creation of the modern regular urban fabric. On the other hand, those that remained had to be adapted to the new dominant aesthetic ideas. Therefore, many of them were enlarged and neo-classical details were added, in order to adapt them to the new demands. In several cases, the urban fabric was modified, in order to permit their insertion in the modern city. That was necessary, because of the position churches had in the urban fabric during Ottoman domination, when their presence had to be discreet, and thus they were hidden in the interior of blocks. In one case, the changes were so extensive that the building became totally unrecognizable: it is Saint Eleousa (Virgin Mary of Mercy), a church of the sixteenth to seventeenth century, which was transformed into the Assizes in 1837 by Christian Hansen (Figure 3.1). And yet, though a modest building, its entrance is an exact copy of the entrance of the Erechtheion. On the other hand, after entering the building, one is faced with the three niches of the sanctuary, again functioning as a church, after the return of the building to the Church and its conversion into the Archdiocese's Library. The building's relationship with the neighbouring Athena Street and the old urban fabric is an excellent instance of the position of churches built under Ottoman domination in the city of Athens. A similar instance as for its position in the

Figure 3.1 The former Assizes in Saint Eleousa Street in Psyrri, which resulted from a transformation of Saint Eleousa church

Photograph by the author

urban fabric is the seventeenth-century church of the Prophet Elisha, built as the private church of the Logothetis-Chomatianos mansion. The urban fabric surrounding it is perhaps the best preserved from Ottoman times, very instructive about the organisation of Ottoman Athens in little clusters of buildings around churches. At the moment, the buildings forming this block are being transformed into a Museum of Greek Folk Art.

The most characteristic instance of insertion in the modern urban fabric is the church of Kapnikarea, dedicated to the Virgin Mary (Figure 3.2). The eleventh-century Byzantine church was destined to be demolished for the opening of Hermes Street. But King Ludwig interceded for its preservation and the street was modified, forming a little square surrounding the building. An additional problem was the fact that Byzantine buildings are on a level substantially lower than the modern city's. Therefore, the square is organised in two levels, one at the church's level and the other making the transition to the modern city. The same organisation is to be found around the churches of Saint Theodors (eleventh century), Saint Asomatoi (archangels, eleventh or twelfth century), and Saint Catherine (eleventh century; Figure 3.3). The latter's square presents the additional interest of including ancient ruins, on an even lower level. That leads to the square's organisation in multiple layers, in order to include three different levels of the city's history.

Figure 3.2 The church of Kapnikarea

Photograph by the author

Figure 3.3 The church of Saint Catherine
Photograph by the author

The relationship of all these churches and even more the relationship of other less significant ones with the urban fabric makes it clear that the first plans didn't intend to give them a prominent position in the modern city. In the Kleanthes and Schaubert plan, the blocks surrounding each old church leave a space of a regular geometrical shape, which, moreover, is different from one church to another, revealing a very conscious care of arranging that space. However, that space is impressively small compared with the vast squares predicted for the insertion of new official buildings, including the new churches (probably neo-classical). That indicates an intention of putting the old (non-neo-classical) churches in a clearly subordinate position vis-à-vis the modern city. One could argue that these churches were a source of embarrassment to the plan's creators, who had to combine the respect to the official religion with the desired promotion of classicism and the disappearance of buildings not fulfilling its aesthetic requirements.

Unfortunately, numerous churches in a bad condition or hindering too much on the application of the new plan or the revelation of ancient ruins (like the twelfth-century church of the Prophet Elias) fell victim to the still inexistent appreciation of medieval art. Naturally, that was even more so with Turkish buildings, which disappeared in their majority, apart from those who could find a satisfactory new use.

Finally, another unfortunate occurrence was the treatment of surviving churches which were found to be too small to serve the needs of an increasing population. Those were enlarged with neo-classical extensions, completely disfiguring them. In most cases these additions have been removed (like in the church of Saint Asomatoi, the eleventh-century church of Saint Apostles in the Agora, and the twelfth-century church of the Gorgoepikoos; Figure 3.4). In some cases a neo-classical bell tower is preserved, like that of the post-Byzantine church of Pantanassa, in the middle of Monastiraki Square, added as late as 1911, marking the delay in the appreciation of medieval architecture (Figure 3.5). In other cases, the neo-classical extension was preserved, like in the church of Saint Catherine and the eleventh-century church of Saint Nicholas Ragava (Figure 3.6). Many other minor Byzantine and post-Byzantine churches, totally obscure in the modern city, demonstrate the way their architecture was seen in the time of the creation of modern Athens.

Figure 3.4 The church of Gorgoepikoos

Photograph by the author

Figure 3.5 The church of Pantanassa
Photograph by the author

Figure 3.6 The church of Saint Nicholas Ragava
Photograph by the author

The treatment of pre-revolutionary houses

The pre-revolutionary houses of Athens were typical specimens of the traditional architecture of the Ottoman times, with very old roots, going back to the Byzantine times and even further back. The basic characteristic of all of them was their introvert character, adapted to the social conditions of their time, which imposed an increased need for privacy. On the contrary, neo-classical houses had a public 'zone', comprising mainly the living room and opened to the exterior through the characteristic balcony. Therefore, the pre-revolutionary houses that had survived the destruction had to undergo important modifications in order to be adapted to the new era. Very few of them managed to preserve their original form; others sadly disappeared, yielding to the wish to supplant the pre-modern town by the modern one. The most sumptuous among the latter was the Mertrud mansion, which disappeared to permit the opening of Athena Street (see below).

The dwellings of the middle and lower classes preserved up to a certain degree the traditional typology and morphology, particularly in their parts that had no contact with the street. That happened because their inhabitants remained attached to the architectural tradition, creating only neo-classical façades, with the purpose to demonstrate their 'Europeanization'. That, of course, was facilitated by the fact that those houses were often half-destroyed pre-revolutionary structures, which were just repaired after Independence. They changed considerably only as far as the façade was concerned, where the degree of Europeanization and acceptance of modern ideas by their inhabitants was 'judged', and therefore also their approximation to the upper class. The latter's representatives adopted neo-classicism with enthusiasm and unconditionally in their mansions, which were built according to the plans of famous neo-classicist architects with 'European' education, thus constituting the models for the houses of the other inhabitants of the capital.

In case a new street penetrated the old urban fabric or an old street was enlarged, the new façade or even a totally new building was inevitable. Therefore, the buildings of Hermes, Athena, and Aeolus Streets, for instance, had fronts that resulted from the streets' tracing. Consequently, the buildings constructed in them were mostly new, with an entirely neo-classical typology and morphology. However, the possibility has to be taken into account that the new tracing left perchance a part of the old building untouched, due to the position it found itself in relation to the new street's front. The archival sources reveal that in several cases, during the opening of Hermes, Athena, and Aeolus Streets in 1834, wherever it wasn't necessary to demolish the whole pre-existing building, only a part of it was expropriated and demolished, in order to pay just for that part and thus limit the expropriation cost. That is revealed by the documents fixing each owner's compensation (G.S.A., City Plan, file 1, October 1834; comprehensive list of the owners of the properties expropriated for the opening of Athena and Hermes Streets). The same happened in the 1860s, during the widening of Hermes Street, as the archival sources again reveal (G.S.A., City Plan, file 11).

In such cases, it would be justified to assume that a new façade was constructed, on the new construction line, while behind it the previous structure was preserved as much as possible. Additionally, it is even more possible that older structures survived in the rear part of the plots that resulted from the opening of the new streets, in case the new block included a sufficient part of the pre-revolutionary one. Surveys and comparison of plans strongly support this supposition.

One of the very few houses having preserved its pre-revolutionary form is the Benizelos mansion, in Hadrian Street. It is the oldest house of Athens, dwelling of one of the city's most prominent families. It dates from the fifteenth to sixteenth century, with seventeenth-century additions, thus constituting the best example of the transition from Byzantine to post-Byzantine architecture (Figure 3.7). The court from which the communication of the ground floor rooms is ensured and the open corridor of the first floor, ensuring the communication between the rooms of that level, are considered as direct survivals of the typology of the ancient Greek house. This building

Figure 3.7 The Benizelos mansion
Photograph by the author

features the great difference between the architectural tradition and the classicism that dethroned it.

Another pre-revolutionary house having preserved its original form is the dwelling of the English general Sir Richard Church, leader of the Greek forces in the revolution (Figure 3.8). It was the property of the English

Figure 3.8 The house of Sir Richard Church

Photograph by the author

Figure 3.9 Pre-revolutionary house, view from Tripodon Street
Photograph by the author

historian George Finlay and constitutes a unique preserved specimen of a pre-revolutionary tower in Athens. The sources[8] testify the existence of several such buildings in Ottoman Athens, from which only this one is preserved.

Another instance is a house whose back side, with the court, is visible from Tripodon Street (Figure 3.9). The first floor corridor is closed with glass, a common practise after independence. On the same street (no. 28) is the building housing the Elliniki Etairia (Society for the Environment and Cultural Heritage). The restoration campaign revealed that behind the purely neo-classical façade, there were several pre-revolutionary phases, and the house was built on ancient foundations, today accessible to visitors (Kizis, 2004, pp. 188–205).

Notes

1 Unit of measurement, equal to 64 cm, common in nineteenth-century Greece.
2 Roman hydraulic clock.
3 Muslim religious school functioning during the Ottoman domination.

60	*The treatment of the pre-revolutionary town*

4	At the end of Ottoman times at least five baths were functioning in Athens: those of Rodakio, of the Wheat Market, of Kyrristou Street, one at the location where the Voivodate was built later, and one on the Acropolis.
5	It is meant that they belong to the monastery of Kaisariani, situated in the outskirts of Athens.
6	It contains an extract of the report made by the commission assigned the construction of the school and submitted to the Ministry 31 March 1851.
7	Apparently the School of Arts, namely Vlachoutsis house, in Piraeus Street. It was founded by the Bavarian Lieutenant Engineer Friedrich Zentner.
8	See Chapter 5.

Bibliography

General State Archives (G.S.A.), City Plan, file 1, October 1834, 8 May 1836; file 5, 15 January 1851; file 11.

G.S.A., Ottonian Record, Ministry of Education, L, file 48, 6 April 1839; file 57, 29 May 1856.

G.S.A., Ottonian Record, Ministry of the Interior, file 208, 22 February 1838, 25 February 1840.

K. (1853). Καθολικόν Πανόραμα των Αθηνών. *Νέα Πανδώρα*, 67(3), pp. 440–445.

Kaftantzoglou, L. *Esquisse d'un plan pour la ville d'Athènes propre à remplacer le projet en exécution si mal conçu et impossible à recevoir jamais sa totale organisation.* G.S.A., Ottonian Record, Ministry of the Interior, file 214.

Kaftantzoglou, L. (9 August 1842). Esquisse d'un plan pour la ville d'Athènes (Letter, Constantinople, 5 August 1842). *Αιών*.

Kaftantzoglou, L. (1858). *Περί μεταρρυθμίσεως της πόλεως Αθηνών γνώμαι.* Athens: S. Pavlidis and Z. Gryparis.

Karykopoulos, P. (1971). *Αθήνα, Το χωριό που έγινε πρωτεύουσα.* Athens. Book published by the author.

Kizis, I., ed. (2004). *Αποκατάσταση μνημείων. Αναβίωση ιστορικών κτιρίων στην Αττική.* Athens: Έργον IV.

Ragavis, A. (1894–1930). *Απομνημονεύματα.* Athens. Book published by the author.

Royal Decree of the 9th April 1836, Government Gazette 20, 15 May 1836.

Royal Decree (unpublished) of the 25th September 1833.

Stasinopoulos, E. (1973). *Ιστορία των Αθηνών.* Athens. Book published by the author.

Ελπίς (30 March 1865).

4 Housing a European capital in a small Ottoman town

The use of the pre-revolutionary buildings of Athens for housing the official functions of the new capital

The housing of public functions in Athens under King Otto

When the capital was transferred to Athens, 13 December 1834, there were no buildings appropriate to house the state's services. Therefore, those functions had to be satisfied by churches, mosques, ancient monuments, and requisitioned houses. Since the destruction of Athens during the revolution was due to the Turks, but also because the Turks, as dominants, had the largest and most solid buildings, most of the rare constructions that had been preserved were Turkish: the Madrasa, immediately to the east of Hadrian's library and the Roman Forum; the Kati's[1] seat, next to the Library's north-eastern corner; the mosque of the Wheat Market (Fetihie), in the precinct of the Agora (Figure 4.1); the Voivoda's[2] seat, next to the Library's gate; the Tzistarakis mosque, at its north-western corner (Figure 4.2); and finally, the baths: that of the Wheat Market, next to the homonymous mosque; that of Rodakio, at the place of today's Archdiocese; and that lying until today in Kyrristou Street. Those buildings satisfied the extremely urgent needs of the newly founded capital for the additional reason that after the Turks' departure, they had become useless.

The government arrived in the middle of winter in a city lacking the necessary infrastructure to receive them. The urban fabric was thus hastily repaired, without the slightest programming (Kaftantzoglou, 1839), although it had been proposed to limit as much as possible during the first months the number of authorities that would be installed in Athens (G.S.A., 30 November 1834). Nevertheless, on 15 November 1834 the government asked for 280 houses for the needs of their services, which would be transferred to Athens in a few weeks, whereas the total number of houses was no more than a thousand (Miheli, 1994, p. 166).

The extremely urgent needs are clearly presented by the information that two houses[3] situated perpendicularly to Athena Street, thus cutting it in

Figure 4.1 The mosque of the Wheat Market (Fetihie)
Photograph by the author

Figure 4.2 The Library of Hadrian and the Tzistaraki mosque, today a museum
Photograph by the author

two, were bought at a high price by the government in 1834 in order to be demolished and thus permit the opening of that street. However, the lack of a military hospital made necessary the temporary cession of the previously listed houses to the Ministry of War, for the hospitalisation of the soldiers (G.S.A., 16 September 1836), thus blocking the new street. Similar problems were caused for many years later by other temporary functions. Some citizens complained about two temporary public buildings 'next to the small Catholic church' (former tekke[4]), used the first as a museum of plaster casts and the other as a military prison, or according to others, as furnaces or a bakery. They complained that those buildings were narrowing the street and causing dangers to the traffic (G.S.A., City Plan, file 11, September 1861).

Even before the capital's transfer, the Minister of Finance proposes to the Ministry of War a mosque and a Turkish school – evidently the Madrasa – which could be used as public buildings (G.S.A., Ottonian Record, Ministry of War, MB, file 331, August 1834). After the government's arrival, the exploitation of empty Turkish buildings started. The Voivoda's seat was transformed into barracks. The old Madrasa, already from the last years of the Ottoman domination, served also as a prison. More Turkish buildings of Athens were used as prisons, like the Tzistarakis mosque, which initially housed the band of Otto's guard. The Madrasa, after its partial destruction during the revolution, was rebuilt by King Otto in 1834 and used thereafter permanently as a prison (G.S.A., 30 December 1844). However, it was mainly the mosques, for the natural reason of being some of the best built and more spacious buildings of Ottoman Athens, which were among the first choices to house the new functions. Therefore, the Minister of Education asked from the Ministry of War the cession of a mosque of the market ('where the military musicians were', thus referring to the mosque of Tzistarakis). He wanted to install there the 'Public Library', which, until then, was housed in a church (G.S.A., 20 April 1837; it must be the Gorgoepikoos). The library's ephore, however, Georgios Gennadios, proposed to the Ministry of Education another mosque of the market, occupied by the pioneers (G.S.A., 13 May 1837). The Minister of the Interior also references the same mosque when he writes that the Eparch of Attica, in 1835, proposed for the temporary housing of the Civil Hospital the mosque lying next to the Wheat Market, occupied then by soldiers.

Likewise, the baths attracted also the authorities' attention. The Prefect of Attica and Beotia S. Skoufos wrote to the Ministry of the Interior that the big bath (the bath of the Wheat Market) could, due to the 'beauty of its construction', be used either to house the Supreme Court or some other Court of Justice, or the Council of State. He also thought it was 'most suitable' for the National Archives and for a Public Library (G.S.A., 22 September 1834). Subsequently, the Minister of the Interior wrote to King

Otto, adding to the previous propositions of the Prefect the idea of trans-forming the bath into barracks (G.S.A., 9 October 1834). Moreover, the Ministry of Finance mentioned in a document addressed to the king that the small bath was ceded to the Ministry of Justice in order to serve as a court of justice (G.S.A., 20 November 1834). A little later we learn that the aforementioned big bath was already full of boxes and packages of books from the royal library. Since the place was humid and unsuitable for books, permission was asked to transfer the books to the cathedral (at that time it was the Gorgoepikoos) and to another neighbouring church (G.S.A., 22 December 1834). The Cathedral was also proposed by the library's superintendent, along with another church, a dependency of the Kaisariani monastery (G.S.A., 20 November 1834). Some months later we know that the Cathedral was already being used as a library (G.S.A., 11 April 1835), while the next year the same happened with the church of the Kaisariani monastery (G.S.A., 18 September 1836). The same use was also served by the church of Saint Nicholas, which was at the location of today's Cathedral (Biris, 1966–1967, p. 214).

About the churches, one could observe that the urgent need to house the capital's official functions set aside the possible hesitations and objections to the use of sacred places for the satisfaction of totally profane needs. Therefore, the Minister of Justice wrote to the regency that his incapacity to find houses suitable to house the Courts of Justice obliged him to turn towards the old churches. He proposed to that use the churches of Saint Eleousa, Saint Athanasius, and Chrysokopidis[5] at Psyrri; that of Vlastarou[6] next to the Theseion; and that of the Saint Asomatoi next to the Bazaar Gate (ancient gate of Athena Archegetis in the Roman Forum; G.S.A., 4 January 1835). And indeed, as the Minister of Foreign Affairs wrote to King Otto, Saint Eleousa was transformed into the Assizes, the church of 'Christos Kopidis'[7] into a Court of Appeal and Saint Athanasius into a Court of First Instance (G.S.A., 4 April 1835). Ioannis Travlos (Travlos, 1960, p. 240) places the Court of First Instance in Panaghia Vlassarou, the Supreme Court in Christokopidis, and the primary school in Saint Athanasius. Moreover, he mentions that the monastery of Osia Filothei, the dependency of the mon-astery of Penteli, and Saint Spyridon became barracks, and the Sotira of Dikaios become straw storage. The document of the Ministry of Education addressed to the Ministry of War must mean the Petraki Monastery in its proposition to transform the monastery under Lycabettus into a Military Hospital (G.S.A., 22 March 1834). However, as the Minister of Education wrote, the monastery seemed to be 'among those which will be preserved' and therefore couldn't be used as a Military Hospital. Therefore, it was proposed to use the Daphni monastery,[8] a monastery which was 'stable and spacious' (G.S.A., 12 April 1834). Finally, though, the Ministry of Finance informed the Ministry of War that the Lycabettus monastery would be available (G.S.A., 10 June 1834).

Apart, however, from housing the state functions, equally imperative was the need to house the antiquities, while awaiting the construction of a museum. Already since 1830, the General Ephore of Antiquities Kyriakos Pittakis had started concentrating in the Byzantine church of the centre of the Athenian market, the so-called Megali Panaghia (Great Virgin Mary), in the middle of Hadrian's Library, the ancient remains he was finding in the area. In 1837 the space in front of Hadrian's Library was fenced and served as an open air museum, since its wall had already been liberated from most of the shops that were using it as a support. The Ministry of Education mentioned to King Otto that the church of Megali Panaghia was used as an antiquity warehouse, and that the conservator had proposed to put the antiquities in the Theseion (G.S.A., 14 November 1834). In 1853 Pittakis informed the Ministry of Education that 'the Theseion, Hadrian's portico, the Tower of Winds,[9] the Propylaea, the tank in front of the Parthenon and the Powder Magazine at the northern wall of the Acropolis and the Turkish house next to the aforementioned Powder Magazine' contained a great number of antiquities (G.S.A., 6 March 1853). The accumulation of the antiquities in the Propylaea and the Theseion is mentioned in a very disparaging way by the French traveller Edmond About, who adds that a very small mosque was used as a warehouse of the casts of the marbles stolen by Lord Elgin (About, 1854, p. 266).

The competent authorities turned even to the rare private dwellings which, with their size and construction quality, could, in a rudimentary way, house public functions. Naturally, the small number of those dwellings, along with the very acute needs, posed the problem of which services to house first in them. On the other hand, that situation engendered intense controversies between the different state services about the ownership of those buildings. Additionally, the eviction of the owners in the middle of winter, along with the evictions for the opening of streets, caused great social unrest (*Aθηνά*, 14 November 1834; *Aθηνά*, 1 December 1834). Another problem was the payment of rents, which were often very high, like that of the house of Kleanthes (G.S.A., 22 August 1835). A document mentions that it had been rented as a High School (G.S.A., 8 January 1835), while another one proposes the building's purchase, in order to use it either for the High School, or for the Seminary, or as barracks, as a hospital or for any other public need (G.S.A., 7 September 1835). The Minister of the Interior, however, claimed that the Kleanthes house couldn't serve as a Ministry because of its 'eccentric' place and its internal layout, nor as a hospital, because it was too humid (G.S.A., 5 October 1835). That house had been visited by the Minister of Justice during his research for buildings suitable to house the capital's Courts of Justice, as he writes to the regency (G.S.A., 4 January 1835, 20 January 1835). Finally, the Ministry of Education writes to King Otto that the order had been given to transfer the library to the Kleanthes house, which however was then occupied by the High School (G.S.A., 20 November 1834). In 1836 the High School was transferred from the Kleanthes house to the Botsaris (or Votzaris) house (G.S.A., 12 November 1836), which was bigger and more central (G.S.A., 11 February 1837) and was built in 1835 at the angle of the streets Kapnikareas and Ploutonos (Miliarakis, 1885, p. 26).[10] In 1837 the Kleanthes house hosts the inauguration of the University, which stayed there until 1841, when it was transferred to its final building (Ross, 1863, p. 107).

Another one of the capital's best houses was the newly built Kontostavlos mansion in Stadium Street, where the Parliament was built later. From 1834 to 1836 it served as temporary royal residence, while from 1836, when King Otto was married to Amalia, until 1842, when the construction of the final Royal Palace was completed, the royal couple lived in the Dekozis-Vouros mansion, united with the neighbouring Afthonides house, at Mint Square (today's 25th of March Square or Klafthmonos; Figure 4.3). The unification project was sent by Friedrich von Gärtner (Buchon, 1847, p. 93). Some

Figure 4.3 The Dekozis-Vouros mansion, today's Museum of the City of Athens, temporary royal residence (1836–1842), in 25th March Square

Photograph by the author

appendices were also added, like an octagonal dance hall and a kitchen. After the political change of 1843, when the king granted a constitution, the Kontostavlos mansion housed the Parliament and the Senate until 1854, when it was destroyed by fire. Two more of the best private buildings of Athens were the Vlachoutsis houses in the numbers 35 and 38–40 of Piraeus Street. When the Polytechnic was founded in 1837, it was installed in the first one, while a 1839 document mentions that the Vlachoutsis house – apparently the other one – housed the Archaeological Museum and the Museum of Natural History (G.S.A., 21 March 1839). Moreover, several other documents of the years 1836 and 1837 refer to the purchase of one of the two Vlachoutsis houses, which would serve to house the antiquities (G.S.A., Ottonian Record, Ministry of Education, file 44).

The Military School was also housed in private residences. In the period 1854–1857 it functioned in 'Ilissia', the mansion of the Duchess of Plaisance,[11] while in 1894 it was installed in the Vlachoutsis house, until its final installation in its own building at the Champ de Mars (Pedion tou Areos). Also, a part of the Public Library was initially housed in a private residence (Diaggelos house; G.S.A,. 25 October 1839, 19 April 1839, 15 December 1840), until in 1842 when King Otto approved its, again, temporary transfer to the University (G.S.A., Ottonian Record, Ministry of Education, file 48), in the upper floor of its just finished front wing (Biris, 1966–1967, p. 214). Likewise, the Arsakeion was housed in a house of Miaouli Street, close to Hermes Street (Biris, 1966–1967, p. 138; Fountoulaki, 1979, p. 113), since its foundation in 1836. Moreover, the City Hall was housed initially in the Demogerontia (Lambikis, 1938, p. 25), and afterwards in several houses in the city centre and later in a building built in the place of the demolished church of Saint Athanasius at Psyrri (Lambikis, 1938, p. 47; Biris, 1966–1967, p. 207).[12] Those transfers took place from the creation of the Municipality of Athens until 1872, when the City Hall's building was finished. As for the other municipal institutions, in 1838 the municipality founded a rudimentary orphanage, which was housed in rented private buildings (Biris, 1966–1967, p. 148). For the Municipal Foundling Hospital, founded in 1859 (Stavropoulos, 1985, p. 128), the municipality rented a private building, situated next to the Cathedral, and later another one next to the church of Saint Theodors (Biris, 1966–1967, p. 205). In addition, the Hatzikonsta Orphanage was housed for decades in the house of K. Vranis (Markezinis, 1966, vol. 2, p. 383). As for the hospitals, in the 'Panorama' of Athens, designed by Stademann (1835–1836), are marked the houses, next to one another, where the hospitals had been installed (Stavropoulos, 1985, p. 128). Even prisons were installed in the houses of Athens, according to a document of the Ministry of War to the Ministry of the Interior, where the former mentions having been informed of the latter's intention to rent private houses for that purpose (G.S.A., 29 March 1846). One of them was the Karatzas house in Sarri Street.[13] Finally, even hotels satisfied the capital's needs for public functions. The hotel 'Byron' in Aeolus Street thus housed the Observatory in the years 1839–1842 (Kydoniatis, 1985, p. 153).

However, the use of those constructions wasn't so temporary, since it was often decided to make extended repairs to them, which reveals the conscience that the permanent building would still take time. The Minister of Education mentions thus the insufficiency of the temporary High School, because the pupils had almost doubled within a year. He judges, therefore, that the creation of two more big teaching rooms is absolutely necessary (G.S.A., Ministry of Education, file 57, August 1838). A proof that the use of those buildings wasn't so temporary is given by the consecutive approvals of renewal of the renting of the Votzaris house for the High School (G.S.A., 26 October 1840, 14 July 1841, 17 June 1842, 3 July 1843). The state's incapacity to construct a new building is proved by a document of A. Botzaris[14] to the Ministry of Education about the rent arrears for his house (G.S.A., 20 February 1847). Moreover, King Otto approved the extension of the prison of Athens (Madrasa; G.S.A., 6 December 1836). That was done to the west, on the plot lying east of Aeolus Street (G.S.A., 28 February 1837).

Twenty years after the capital's transfer to Athens, the situation of the temporarily installed services wasn't much better, according to About. He writes that the ministries and the courts were installed, one above a shop, another on the first floor of a tavern, yet another in a dirty house in an infamous street (About, 1854, p. 244).

The housing of public functions in Athens under King George I

Despite the progress made under King Otto, the needs which had to be covered under King George I were still numerous and imperative. Dwellings continued to cover a large part of the needs in public buildings. The decree 'On the purchase of a house to be used by the Ministry of the Marine' (Government Gazette, 18 November 1869) allows the government to buy the house of Ioannis Skylitsis, next to the garden of the Ministry of Finance, in order to use it as a public institution. After all, even the majestic building of the National Bank is the outcome of the unification of two dwellings. Finally, a private residence temporarily served the housing needs of the kings. The Crown Prince Constantine and Princess Sophia, after their marriage, settled temporarily in the then newly built Negreponti mansion, in Constitution Square.

The Courts continued to be housed in temporary premises, churches, and houses, whose condition, moreover, wasn't good, judging by the request of the competent minister to the Direction of the Police of Athens and Piraeus to examine the condition of the Levidis house, which housed the courts (G.S.A., City Plan, file 18, February and October 1870).[15] Equally illuminating is the decree defining as meeting place of the Athens Criminal Court during the first session of that year the house of Alexandros Kontostavlos, lying in Thoukydides Street (Government Gazette, 16 March 1884).

It is characteristic, though, that especially now many needs are satisfied by public edifices built for other purposes. A good example is the University, which since 1842 (namely, long before its completion in 1864) up to 1903 hosted the National (Public) Library, and from 1854 to 1862 both chambers of Parliament, which were temporarily housed in the yet unfinished rear wing (Biris, 1966–1967, p. 149), after the fire that burned down the old Parliament. In 1858 it had to cede to the Archaeological Society the great anatomy auditorium on the ground floor for housing the library and the archaeological collection (Kokkou, 1977, p. 182). When, in 1863, the Archaeological Society had to remove the antiquities from the arcades of the University's internal courtyard, where they were until then, they placed them in the courtyard of the Academy. In 1864, however, the Senate of the University requested the society to leave the anatomy auditorium as well (Kokkou, 1977, pp. 184–185). In 1865, the society transferred all its collections to the Varvakeion (Kokkou, 1977, p. 186), but the space wasn't enough there either. Thus the society put antiquities in the Theseion, the Acropolis, near the guard room of Les Invalides, in confined archaeological sites and in the courtyard of the Archaeological Museum, which was under construction. Since 1874, they transfer antiquities to the west wing of the newly built Museum. However, at the beginning of 1875, with the increase in the number of pupils of the Varvakeion, they are forced to abandon two rooms, and in 1880 the entire building, apart from the basement. In 1881, many antiquities were transferred to the Polytechnic, where antiquities were exposed since 1877, and which increased in 1889 and 1890 (Kokkou, 1977, pp. 186–188). The Polytechnic also housed the Museum of the Historical and Ethnological Society of Greece (*Ελλάς*, 1901, p. 60; Eleftheroudakis, 1930, p. 69). The same building housed the National Gallery (Eleftheroudakis, 1930, p. 69). The Academy also housed the large coin collection of Greece (*Ελλάς*, 1901, p. 57; Eleftheroudakis, 1930, pp. 54, 69) and the Byzantine Museum (Eleftheroudakis, 1930, p. 69).

The dethronement of King Otto made available the kingdom's largest building: the Royal Palace. A proposal for its utilisation is directly linked with the destruction by fire of the Parliament. Thus, the architects Gerasimos Metaxas and Kaftantzoglou, in a report to the Ministry of the Interior, state that it was envisaged to temporarily use the first and largest ballroom of the Palace for the meetings of the National Assembly. It was found out that the room was smaller than the University's main hall, while its almost square shape wasn't suitable. Moreover, the cost of its reform would be large and would entail destroying almost entirely the expensive decoration. On the other hand, any expense made for reforming the University's hall will be useful for the future, while in the case of the Palace it would be futile, and additionally, its future restoration would be very costly. They suggest to temporarily transfer the University's classrooms to the Palace's southern underground rooms. As for the Natural History Museum, this is only temporarily in the University, while its place is in the Senate (!). If other difficulties for the University's hall arise, the best solution would be to build a shed like the one of the Olympics' Exhibition, but in a more suitable location, so that it can be used in the future for other purposes (G.S.A., 27 October 1862). The Minister of the Interior writes to the Prefect of Attica and Beotia that in the court of the Parliament, which is under construction, there is a shed, which the former government had ordered to turn into a provisional Parliament (G.S.A., City Plan, file 13, October 1862). The idea, however, to use the University for housing the provisional Parliament (as well) prevailed, since there is a 'Budget of the expenditure required' (G.S.A., City Plan, file 13, October 1862). The above shed was surviving in 1877, as Lieutenant Engineer A. Abeler writes to the Direction of Engineering of Attica, mentioning that the cover of the roof consisted of cloth (G.S.A., 17 October 1877).

Finally, also hospitals were temporarily housed in public buildings of other destination. Thus, in 1881 the west side of the Polytechnic was turned into a temporary hospital (*Αιών*, 1 April 1881), while a small part of the Aretaieion Hospital, after an elementary equipment was installed, functioned during the Greek-Turkish war of 1897 as a temporary hospital for the wounded, by the mission of the Russian Red Cross. Likewise, a temporary hospital of the Greek Red Cross had functioned in the Varvakeion (Stavropoulos, 1985, p. 131). The capital's hospital needs will begin to be met largely only from the late nineteenth and the early twentieth century, with the construction of large units in the area of Ambelokipi and around.

The temporary installation of public functions, especially in new buildings of a different destination, reveals perhaps better than anything else the contrast between ideological-symbolical background and actual needs in nineteenth-century Athens and the insistence on creating a capital expressing a non-realistic image of the centre of reborn Hellenism, rather than a modern capital satisfying practical needs.

Notes

1 Muslim judge.
2 Governor.
3 The houses of Ioannis Vlachos and Vartholomaios Mertrud.

4 Gathering place of a Sufi order.
5 Known also as Christokopidis.
6 The correct name is Vlassarou.
7 See note 5.
8 A Byzantine monastery of the eleventh century, west of Athens, World Heritage.
9 The Kyrristus Clock.
10 Botsaris had also another house in Athens, still existing at the angle of Myllerou and Kerameikou Streets in the quarter of Metaxourgeio.
11 Sophie de Marbois-Lebrun, Duchess of Plaisance (1785–1854), spent the last twenty years of her life in Athens.
12 Lambikis informs us that up to 1872 the City Hall was housed in a private dwelling at the southern corner of Kapnikarea Square.
13 Sarri, Kriezi, and Leokoriou.
14 This is the way he himself writes his name.
15 The specific courts are not clarified.

Bibliography

About, E. (1854). *La Grèce contemporaine*. Paris: Hachette.

Biris, K. (1966–1967). *Αι Αθήναι*. Athens. Book published by the author.

Buchon, J. A. (1847). *La Grèce continentale et la Morée*. Paris: Gosselin.

Eleftheroudakis (1930). *Ελλάς (Οδηγός Ταξιδιώτου)*. Athens.

Fountoulaki, O. (1979). *Stamatios Kleanthes (1802–1862)*. Karlsruhe. Book published by the author.

General State Archives (G.S.A.), City Plan, file 3, 6 December 1836, 28 February 1837, 30 December 1844; file 11, September 1861; file 13, October 1862, 27 October 1862; file 18, February and October 1870; file 20, 17 October 1877.

G.S.A., Ottonian Record, Μ-Γ, file 74, 22 March 1834, 12 April 1834, 10 June 1834.

G.S.A., Ottonian Record, Ministry of Education, file 37, 20 February 1847; file 44, 14 November 1834; file 45, 6 March 1853; file 48, 20 November 1834, 11 April 1835, 18 September 1836, 19 April 1839, 25 October 1839, 15 December 1840; file 57, 8 January 1835, 22 August 1835, 7 September 1835, 5 October 1835, 12 November 1836, 11 February 1837, August 1838, 21 March 1839, 26 October 1840, 14 July 1841, 17 June 1842, 3 July 1843.

G.S.A., Ottonian Record, Ministry of the Interior, file 205, 22 September 1834, 9 October 1834, 20 November 1834, 22 December 1834; file 213, 16 September.1836; file 216, 30 November 1834.

G.S.A., Ottonian Record, Ministry of Justice, file 29, 4 January 1835, 20 January 1835, 4 April 1835.

G.S.A., Ottonian Record, Ministry of War, MB, file 192, 29 March 1846; file 269, 20 April 1837, 13 May 1837; file 331, August 1834.

Government Gazette 46, 18 November 1869; 100, 16 March 1884.

Kaftantzoglou, L. (8 March 1839). *Σχεδιογραφία Αθηνών*. Αιών.

Kokkou, A. (1977). *Η μέριμνα για τις αρχαιότητες στην Ελλάδα και τα πρώτα μουσεία*. Athens: Ερμής.

Kydoniatis, S. (1985). *Αθήναι, παρελθόν και μέλλον*. Athens: Πνευματικό Κέντρο Δήμου Αθηναίων.

72   The treatment of the pre-revolutionary town

Lambikis, D. (1938). *Τα εκατό χρόνια του Δήμου Αθηναίων*. Athens. Published by the author.

Markezinis, S. (1966). *Πολιτική Ιστορία της Νεωτέρας Ελλάδος 1828–1964*. Athens: Πάπυρος.

Miheli, L. (1994). *Πλάκα. Ιστορική μνήμη και μυθοπλασία*. Athens: Γνώση.

Miliarakis, A. (1885). Αι προ πεντηκονταετίας μεγάλαι των Αθηνών οικίαι. *Εστία*, 19, pp. 23–27.

Ross, L. (1863). *Errinerungen und Mitteilungen aus Griechenland*. Berlin: R. Gärtner.

Stavropoulos, A. (1985). Η νοσοκομειακή και νοσηλευτική πολιτική στην Αθήνα τα πρώτα ογδόντα χρόνια της ως πρωτεύουσας. In: Y. Tsiomis, ed., *Αθήνα πρωτεύουσα πόλη*. Athens: Ministry of Culture, pp. 128–134.

Travlos, I. (1960). *Πολεοδομική εξέλιξις των Αθηνών*. Athens. Published by the author.

Αθηνά (14 November 1834).

Αθηνά (1 December 1834).

Αιών (1 April 1881).

Ελλάς (1901). Leipzig: K. Baedeker.

Part III
Creation of the new city
The actual circumstances

5 The role of land availability

The time of King Otto: the issue of national land

The financial condition of the Greek state throughout the nineteenth century accounts for the problems encountered when it was attempted to apply the approved projects for Athens. In 1835, the German[1] lieutenant Wilhelm von Weiler was given the order to draw the outlines of the public buildings' positions on the approved city plan (G.S.A., Ottonian Record, Ministry of the Interior, file 213). Very soon, though, those plans would be upset by the lack of necessary land. In the area covered by the old town of Athens and its immediate surroundings, where the new city was positioned, the greatest part of the land initially belonged to the Turks, although they were always clearly fewer than the Greeks. The nationalisation of Turkish land after independence didn't affect the Turkish properties in Athens. Therefore, when the Turks left the city, they sold their properties to those possessing the necessary capital: mainly Greeks of the diaspora and some Western Europeans. The Greek state was incapable of purchasing any of this land (Maurer, 1943–1947, pp. 119–127), hence the almost complete lack of public plots in the capital. However, in the area beyond the new city, an important part of the land belonged to the Church, especially to Petraki Monastery, which eventually donated a part of it for the construction of public buildings. That happened much later, though, when the city expanded towards this area under King George I. Under King Otto, the Greek capital was confined in an area not including these plots. The property of the Church was therefore not able to provide a solution to the problem.

Organisation problems, speculation, and arbitrary actions

Therefore, the state had to find other ways to acquire the necessary land. The government, apart from the purchase of land for the edification of public buildings, also had to pay for the expropriation of the plots necessary to the opening of the new streets. The documents concerning the opening of Hermes and Athena Streets (G.S.A., City Plan, file 1, October 1834, January 1836, 8 May 1836) mention extremely low sums. That is perhaps explained in part by the constructions' description: among sixty-nine properties, there are nine towers, twenty-one houses, thirty-one hovels, five huts, five shops, seven workshops, five barns, and an oil press.

In some cases only a part of a structure is indemnified. That suggests an effort to limit the amount to be paid, which would be certain to generate the owners' reaction. However, all the owners of the sixty-nine properties reacted likewise: they didn't agree with the sums offered to them, and moreover, their petitions demonstrate their feeling that injustice was done to them. It is understandable that the poor 'anonymous' owner of a hovel reacted to the government's intentions to destroy his humble dwelling and offer him a little sum just for a 'room' or an angle of it. However, it is more difficult to explain the exactly same reaction coming from well-known distinguished members of the pre-revolutionary Athenian upper class, whose wealth is indicated by the estimated value of their properties. This applies here especially to Ioannis Vlachos, representative of the indigenous upper class, and Vartholomaios Mertrud.[2] The latter was one of several wealthy citizens of foreign origin (in this case probably French), who had become members of the local 'aristocracy' in the last years of Ottoman domination, when several foreigners had settled in Athens. The houses of Vlachos and Mertrud, the latter one of the largest and most luxurious mansions of pre-revolutionary Athens, are expropriated for sums about forty times higher than the average sum offered to the other owners; therefore, one could wonder how much more these houses could be really worth, especially since the Mertrud mansion had been destroyed during the revolution.

The sums and the descriptions included in the aforementioned documents suggest that the indemnifications that had to be paid at the very beginning, when a great part of the buildings were just huts and hovels, the product of the precipitate reconstruction of Athens after the revolution, weren't that high, and a quick and organised effort could have rendered the procedure possible.

However, that didn't happen. The cause was the desperate dysfunction of the state machine, which, in that case, was mainly generated by the lack of an official register. That rendered equally difficult the exchange of land, which could have permitted a better positioning of public functions, without paying for the plots. The result was confusion and complications in the process of indemnification, as well as a huge encroachment on public land, which complicated things even more. In 1842 the Minister of the Interior was thus asking his ministry's services if the plot of a citizen was included in the precincts of the new Royal Palace (G.S.A., 7 December 1842). In 1847 the plot occupied by the Royal Palace's stables – along with the indemnification – was claimed by two citizens (G.S.A., City Plan, file 3, 1847). In 1852 the Court of First Instance of Athens contested the ownership of the plot containing the University's garden and asked from the owner to prove it (G.S.A., 15 November 1852).

Apart from the problems of ownership, the absence of an official register generated also doubts in relation to the boundaries of the claimed plots. According to a report addressed by the Minister of the Interior to the Ministry of Finance, there was a problem in indemnifying the owners of the plots of the Royal Palace, for the boundaries had disappeared and the state might therefore pay twice or even three times for the same plot (G.S.A., City Plan, file 7, March 1853). In the same spirit, perhaps, the Ministry of Finance pointed out to the Ministry of the Interior the necessity of preparing a perfect topographic map of the area of the Royal Palace, the Royal Garden, and their annexes, in order to facilitate any future acquisition (G.S.A., 5 July 1862).

Likewise, there was also the problem of defining the jurisdictions, and therefore the obligations to indemnify between the authorities, mainly between the government and the Municipality of Athens. According to a decree,

> the obligation to indemnify the private plots that have been or will be expropriated with the Government's approval for a municipal use, and in particular for the edification of a holy church, establishments of welfare, Schools, markets, gardens, and every other municipal establishment lies with the municipality.
>
> (G.S.A., 24 November 1836)

It seems, however, that there have been disagreements about those jurisdictions. In 1850, the Court of Appeal of Athens wrote a report on the indemnification of the owners of the plots occupied since 1838 for the edification of the University. According to that report, there was a disagreement between the University and the municipality about the indemnifications for the University's square, each one claiming it was the other's responsibility (G.S.A., 11 February 1850).

The state's dysfunction rendered it also vulnerable to speculation, a problem concerning the totality of the Athenian market (*Αθηνά*, 12 August 1839; Mendelssohn Bartholdy, 1876, vol. 2, p. 706). Particularly developed was the speculation in the land market, for after Athens became the capital, in those first years when a rapid progress was expected, there was a spectacular increase of the demand for plots, notably around the Royal Palace. That increase is mentioned by the American missionary John Henry Hill[3] in his petition to be indemnified for such a plot (G.S.A., 11 April 1837). Note that Hill was indemnified in 1845 for his plot occupied by the Royal Palace (G.S.A., 11 May 1845); in the same year, however, the indemnification of the other owners was still pending (G.S.A., City Plan, file 2). Hill had also to be indemnified for a plot of his occupied by the Royal Printing House (G.S.A., City Plan, file 1, September 1837). The price of the plots around the Royal Palace thus rose from 0.60 francs per square metre to 200 (Burnouf, 1887). There is also the information that the price of a plot in 1834 was higher, for according to the Kleanthes and Schaubert project, it would be close to the Royal Palace (G.S.A., City Plan, file 3, 1847). Additionally, there is a testimony that the compromise with the owners of the plots occupied by the Royal Palace and the Royal Garden was impossible, because of their 'avidity' (G.S.A., 16 December 1846). Certainly, no one could foresee that development, when before the capital's transfer, 126 prominent inhabitants of Athens declared in a letter addressed to the Minister of the Interior that they were ready to offer as much of their land as would be necessary for the edification of public buildings. Furthermore, they were committing themselves to contribute to their edification with all their means, relying on King Otto's justice for any indemnification that could be given to them (G.S.A., 11 March 1833).[4]

The consequence was the rapid increase of land prices in Athens at an inconceivable rhythm. Those prices differed disproportionately from one area to another, for the most important building, the Royal Palace, was finally positioned in a location that totally overturned the plan's symmetry (Kaftantzoglou, 1842; G.S.A., 28 November 1853, 10 February 1848). The purchase of plots in specific locations by the government, according to the approved city plan, thus became not just difficult, but practically impossible. As a result, the state lost every control and consequently any possibility of applying an organised city planning. The high prices of the central plots contributed to the gradual 'detachment' of public functions from the old town – contrary to the initial tendency – since the prices of land were inversely proportional to the distance from the city centre. One such instance is the Queen Amalia Orphanage, whose plot was bought with the founders' contributions in 'the surroundings of Athens'. That happened in 1855, when that location was apparently considered to be very remote. In any case, with the city's gradual expansion, the prices of plots increased little by little also in more remote areas. Such a case is the plot of the future Polytechnic. In 1837 it was bought for 65 Spanish thalers, whereas in 1843 it was on sale for 10,000 thalers (*Μεγάλη Ελληνική Εγκυκλοπαίδεια 'Πυρσός'*, 1927, p. 169). At its last sale to Helen Tositsa, in 1858, its price was 48,000 thalers (240,000 drachmas; Stasinopoulos, 1973, p. 364). Both the above instances belong to the last period, when it was gradually becoming believable that the city would soon expand towards its surroundings, which intensified the efforts to give the capital the missing infrastructure.

However, apart from the citizens' speculation, there are also some indications that even the state committed some arbitrary actions, like the Regency's decree of 11 July 1833. According to this, Athens was defined as the state's seat, and the Kleanthes and Schaubert project was approved with small modifications. That decree set the terms for the expropriations demanded by the project's implementation, including the following one: the owners of all plots necessary for the edification of public buildings would have to cede them for 20 cents per square pique, paid by the Public Treasury. According to another condition, the private plots that wouldn't be constructed within a specific deadline would become public property (G.S.A., 26 September 1833). We thus observe on the one hand the definition of an extremely low price for the indemnification of the owners – although, even in that way, the state wouldn't be able to pay the amount – and on the other hand, an attempt to acquire plots gratis, using methods that were certain to generate reactions. The same situation is revealed by the protest of the owner of a plot lying next to the prison housed in the former Madrasa, who states that the government occupied his plot in order to guard the prison (G.S.A., 21 June 1848). The Ministry of War displays a similar mentality when it proposes to the Ministry of the Interior to define the plots necessary for the edification of the barracks for the capital's garrison. According to that document, the government should 'occupy' them, in order to avoid all eventual obstacles (G.S.A., 8 February 1846).

The unsettled indemnification petitions

As a result of the state's financial incapacity and lack of organisation, numerous indemnification petitions and protests from the affected owners were pending for years (G.S.A., City Plan, files 1–20). The comparison between the date of edification of a building and the dates of the respective documents reveals impressive delays in payment, reaching even decades. Thus, there are many indemnification petitions concerning the plots occupied by the Royal Palace bearing dates up to 1845 and even one dating from 1846 (G.S.A., 17 November 1846), as well as from 1848 (G.S.A., City Plan, file 4). Furthermore, before the indemnification of the owners of the plots occupied by the Royal Palace's main edifice was settled, a similar issue arose with the Palace's gardens. The indemnification of the respective owners was pending until 1851 (G.S.A., City Plan, file 5) and 1852 (G.S.A., City Plan, file 6), and even 1860 for some cases (G.S.A., City Plan, file 10). In addition to those, there were also the plots occupied by the Royal Palace's dependencies, such as the court's 'factories',[5] east of the Royal Garden (document dating from 1851 and concerning the same unsolved issue, G.S.A., City Plan, file 6), and the court's pharmacy (G.S.A., 29 March 1852). The latest information in relation to the indemnification of the owners of the Royal Palace's land displaces the unsolved issue in 1862, the year of the Bavarian dynasty's expulsion (G.S.A., City Plan, file 12).

Despite the severe lack of money, the authorities proceeded to the occupation of more plots, in order to arrange the Royal Palace's surroundings. That resulted in many petitions for indemnification or construction permit by the owners of the neighbouring plots. Those plots, as their owners state, weren't granted a construction permit (G.S.A., City Plan, file 2 [1845–1846], file 3 [1847]). There is a report on the indemnification of the owners of the plots of the block lying opposite the Royal Palace: it explicitly states that, according to a decree of 1837, the buildings for the ministries were to be erected there (G.S.A., 22 November 1848). However, in 1843, the Ministry of the Interior asked from King Otto to approve the city plan's extension to the Royal Palace's north-east. In the opposite case, it couldn't be permitted to the owners to build there, and the municipality would have to spend considerable sums to indemnify them (G.S.A., 12 June 1843).

Additionally, the indemnification of the owners of the Military Hospital's plots was pending at least until 1844 (with many documents on the same subject, G.S.A., Ottonian Record, M-Γ', file 107; see also Stauffert, 1844). A decree of 1834 (G.S.A., 14 September 1846) concerning that building is mentioned in 1846, and the issue was still unsettled in 1852 (together with documents from 1844, 1845, and 1846 on the same subject, there is also one from 1851, G.S.A., City Plan, file 5; also a related document dating from 1852, G.S.A., City Plan, file 6). Similar petitions related to the Mint (G.S.A., City Plan, file 3448; see also Stauffert, 1844) and to the Royal Printing House were pending in 1847 (G.S.A., 30 May 1847, 22 August 1847; see also Stauffert, 1844). A similar issue concerning the University square (G.S.A., 17 July 1851) existed in 1848–1849 (related documents dating from 1848–1849, G.S.A., City Plan, file 6) and in 1851. Finally, in 1847 and 1852, there was a pending indemnification for a plot occupied when the Madrasa prison was extended (G.S.A., 8 April 1847, 3 May 1852).

However, the Royal Garden continued to expand, whereas the indemnification of the owners of the plots occupied by its first part was still unsettled. That first part started being shaped and planted in 1839 south of the Royal Palace, in an area of only 30 acres that was expropriated to that end (Biris, 1966–1967, p. 67). However, extensions of the garden are reported in 1843 and 1845 (G.S.A., 12 January 1843, 5 October 1845). The extension must have been continuing at least until 1848. That year, some minister (perhaps of the interior) asked the Royal Chamberlain's office to limit the planting of the Royal Palace's gardens (which were being extended) only to the plots

The role of land availability 81

already acquired, until they could order the members of the pertinent committee to complete their duties (G.S.A., City Plan, file 4, July 1848). There was a similar insistence on occupying plots for the edification of the Church of the Saviour (Figure 1.2, no. 2),[6] although it was obviously impossible to indemnify their owners, who protested continuously (G.S.A., 24 March 1840, 5 February 1841, 27 June 1841, 15 April 1843, 11 April 1844, 23 November 1844, 24 January 1845). The state's incapacity to impose the law, along with the exhaustion of the owners' patience, led also to arbitrary actions on their behalf, particularly construction activities without a permit (G.S.A., 15 January 1851, 23 January 1851). Naturally, the unpaid indemnifications constituted a systematic violation of private property and caused great social unrest (Finlay, 1836, pp. 94–96).[7]

Preference for public land or cheap private land

In order to avoid those complications, it was tried to employ public land as much as possible. The buildings of immediate necessity had to be realised wherever land was public or could be bought cheaply. That was formulated officially in a decree stipulating that building plots should be elected above all among the grounds belonging to the state (Government Gazette, 28 December 1836). Such plots weren't only the pre-existing ones, which in one way or another became the state's property, but also plots that were created through a change of the land's use and therefore belonged to no one. Such cases were the backfilled streams, but also the land remaining after the demolition of the so-called Haseki wall, which enclosed the pre-revolutionary town.[8] A characteristic instance is the first and absolutely urgent public building: the Mint. Since there was no money for the expropriation of the surrounding plots, it was built at the eastern edge of the future homonymous square. There, the demolition of the wall and the backfilling of the nearby stream offered some new national land (Biris, 1938–1940, p. 33). The Royal Printing House was perhaps also built on a national plot, for, in a plan of that time, the contiguous plot towards the Boulevard is characterised as a location for public buildings (Figure 5.1) (G.S.A., City Plan, file 5). The University may also be a similar case, since the foundation stone was put in 1839, in the location where the Academy was built later (Biris, 1966–1967, p. 116). It is therefore possible that some national plot existed there, explaining the insistence on that site (Archives of the Catholic Archdiocese of Athens, 458, 461).[9] Moreover, it was initially decided to erect the Eye Hospital next to the Civil Hospital (Kardamitsi-Adami, Papanikolaou-Christensen, 1993, p. 56),[10] possibly because the plot was going to be offered by the municipality (Kardamitsi-Adami, Papanikolaou-Christensen, 1993, p. 48).[11]

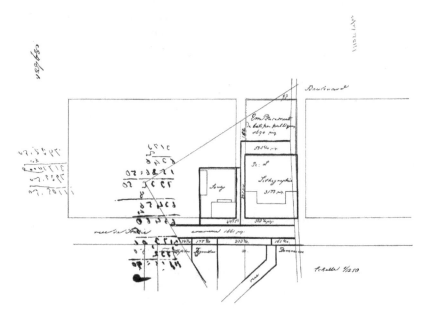

Figure 5.1 The plot towards the Boulevard is characterised as a location for public
buildings

General State Archives, City Plan, file 5; re-drawn by the author

A document by the Ministry of the Interior states that public land was
almost nonexistent within the boundaries of the new city. This information
may be an additional explanation of the initial 'confinement' of the first public functions in temporary installations within the old town's narrow limits
(G.S.A., 13 November 1835). According to the same source, the only public
land found out of the old town by the city's architect and the general curator
was in the area of the gate of Boubounistra (close to the Royal Palace's final
location). That may be a reason for the choice of the final location, since the
site is characterised as very suitable for public buildings. Certainly, the four
acres mentioned in that document were far from sufficient for the edification of the capital's largest building. Yet the existence of four acres of land
'ready' for construction could be a powerful motive. That, of course, applies
if that land was finally included in the Royal Palace's area, which isn't con-
firmed. Nevertheless, the fact that no other public edifice was erected close
to the gate of Boubounistra reinforces that assumption.

Equally important was the role of public land in siting the Varvakeion
Lyceum. The report of the Minister of Education addressed to King Otto

on the plot 'behind Philadelphia' is characteristic: 'since the greatest part of this plot belongs to the state, many thousands of drachmas will be economised in favour of the building, whereas, in a different case, they will be spent for the purchase of a private plot' (G.S.A., 29 May 1856). The report was followed by a decree. There, the scale bent towards the block lying on the southern side of the commercial market and belonging to the state in its major part. The decree according to which, the block lying east of the University Square, was defined as the location of the aforementioned building, was revoked (Government Gazette, 30 July 1856).

Finally, there was the land belonging to abolished monasteries, a relatively small part of which, as has been explained, was within the city's limits. The Ministry of Education thus proposed some of it to King Otto for the edification of the High School (G.S.A., 22 August 1835).

However, it was obvious that the scarce public land couldn't satisfy the numerous needs of a capital, where all official buildings and public spaces had to be created from zero. However, in case a private plot had to be bought, it was mainly chosen according to its price. The low price of sale, because of the owner's necessity, therefore explains the insistence on locating the Ministries on the plot lying north of the Royal Palace (G.S.A., 30 June 1844, 7 October 1844). The final abandon of every effort to position public edifices according to the initial projects was sealed by the report addressed by the 'committee for the completion of the Project of the city of Athens' to the Ministry of the Interior. According to this, the committee found it more advantageous not to define at that moment the location of public establishments as it was initially asked, but guided by the city's tendency and the service's needs, to define and purchase the necessary plots at an 'appropriate' time. The 'appropriate' time could allude to the fluctuation in the prices of materials and plots according to circumstances, as is also pointed out in the aforementioned documents.

The role of donations in the realisation of public buildings

Donations played also a role, albeit smaller, in the acquisition of public land, and consequently influenced the siting of at least some public buildings. Hence, the Civil Hospital was built on a plot donated by Domnitsa Soutsou (Miliarakis, 1885, p. 26). Furthermore, after much research for the appropriate location for the Polytechnic, the choice was finally determined by the aforementioned donation of Helen Tositsa, who purchased the necessary plot in 1858 (*Ήλιος*, 20 December 1858). On the other hand, the plot of the Arsakeion was purchased in 1839 from the monastery of Zoodochos Pighi (Source of Life) of the island of Andros (Galatis, 1957, vol. 1, chapter 7,

p. 2). Afterwards, however, the monastery offered gratis another part of the plot that had remained in its possession (Galatis, 1957, chapter 7, p. 3). Nevertheless, it must be underscored that donators offered land where they happened to have it, or they purchased it according to their own criteria, disregarding the positioning predicted by the approved city plan.

Consequences on the city plan

As a consequence, it became impossible to apply the rational town planning for the new city expressed by the various projects. The decision to build public establishments wherever plots were available, along with the always restricted financial means, had some serious implications: not only the random displacement of public buildings contrary to their initially balanced distribution in the city plan, but also the latter's 'shrinkage'. The width of streets and the surface of spaces for public use were diminished, as well as the area reserved for future archaeological excavations (Finlay, 1836, p. 67),[12] in order to restrict as much as possible the respective indemnification demands. The most famous victim of that necessity was the People's Garden, continuously diminishing by consecutive modifications of the city plan. Its disappearance was nearly completed in 1856 in favour of the Municipal Theatre: as mentioned previously, it was decided to build the latter in the remaining part of the garden between Athena Street and Apelles Street (Apellou; Figure 5.2). The main reason for the garden's gradual diminution was the effort to avoid indemnifying the owners of the necessary plots, as was explicitly stated by the Minister of the Interior to King Otto. Simultaneously, other plots had been ensured for the same purpose in more remote – and consequently cheaper – locations. Such was the area between the Royal Garden and the Temple of Zeus. Additionally, the Court Council had promised to ensure some land of a similar surface lying between Athens and the suburb of Patisia (at the north of the new city; G.S.A., 26 June 1851). It is obvious that the previous location, situated entirely out of town, couldn't offer real alternatives to the necessity of creating an urban park in the city's heart.

In the case of the Royal Palace, the state's incapacity to indemnify the owners of the neighbouring plots entirely overturned the initial planning. As mentioned previously, the latter included the concentration of administrative buildings (mainly the ministries) around the royal residence. In no case did it predict the presence of private constructions, even of the upper class, next to the Royal Palace. Von Klenze went as far as to declare clearly that the latter should be built as far as possible from private buildings (Klenze, 1838, pp. 438–439). However, that aim wasn't only forgotten in the end, as the following evolution of Constitution Square demonstrates, but even ran

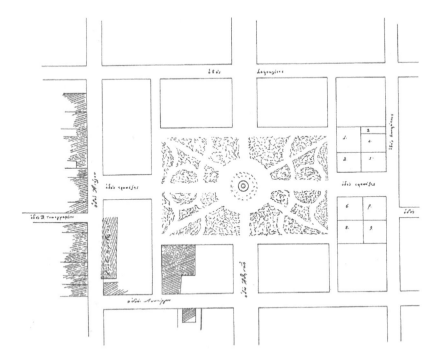

Figure 5.2 The People's Garden in a drawing dated 31 May 1857, where the numbered plots are destined for the (Municipal) Theatre

General State Archives, Ottonian Record, Ministry of the Interior, file 214; re-drawn by the author

the risk of being overturned to a significantly larger extent. This is suggested by the petition of an owner, who asked King Otto 'to be given the permission to build between the two royal palaces or to be indemnified' (G.S.A., 30 December 1838).[13] Yet the most characteristic instance is that of a plot lying in such direct contact with the Royal Palace, that a part of it had been occupied by the edifice itself. The repeated petition of the owner either to be indemnified or to be given permission to build reveals that the state's incapacity to indemnify the owners could have led to the most inconceivable compromise (G.S.A., City Plan, file 1).[14] That situation explains the surprising for European standards proximity of private mansions to the Royal Palace. That proximity was very much desired by their wealthy owners, but wasn't the intention of the authorities. The outcome was a very characteristic public space of the Greek capital, very different from the surroundings of other European royal residences.

Finally, perhaps the most extreme case where the state's financial difficulties played a decisive role in the choice of a public function's location is the Observatory. The Minister of the Interior N. G. Theocharis reported to King Otto that

> the ambassador of Austria Mr. Prokesch [. . .], if the building has to be created solely with the offer of the aforementioned Mr. Sinas, considers that it is necessary to designate the location for its edification in a different place, where it won't be necessary to make special expenses for the construction of a road and as such is considered the Nymphs' hill, next to the Areopagus.
>
> (G.S.A., 30 April 1841)

That means that the reasons for the choice of the Nymphs' hill, instead of the initially proposed Lycabettus, were perhaps less idealistic than what is believed.

The time of King George I

The issue of the plots is, perhaps, the most characteristic common point between the reigns of King Otto and King George I concerning the urban organisation of nineteenth-century Athens. The state's incapacity to expropriate private plots remains unchangeable, as in the case of the Zappeion Exhibition Hall. In 1869 a project of law was introduced in the Parliament concerning the cession of a national plot for the construction of the Zappeion. The speech of the deputee and future Prime Minister Sotirios Sotiropoulos was as follows:

> The government, since the year 1863 [. . .] published a resolution, through which it permitted the edification of the Olympics' establishment in Ludwig Square; but later, it was proved that neither was that place suitable nor had the state the right to cede it. [. . .] It was decided that we shouldn't diverge from the wish of the late Evangelis,[15] who desired to site the establishment as close to the ancient Stadium as possible. It was, thus, approved to erect that public establishment between the royal palace garden and the columns (of the temple) of the Olympian Zeus [. . .]. This area constitutes a part of the zone of the town and, in consequence, the edification of private buildings in it isn't permitted; [. . .] The committee of the Olympics, taking into consideration that it isn't about the edification of a simple establishment, but of an establishment of periodical exposition, which, because of its great means, is to take important dimensions, asked the government to define by law in

its favour all the uncovered area included within the above limits, the plots belonging to citizens not being excluded [. . .]. But the government, by extreme respect for the private property, didn't approve the committee's proposition, and with the project of law, which is going to be voted today, only the area belonging to the state is ceded [. . .]. All the occupied area is absolutely necessary to the exposition [. . .] as we won't be limited only to the Hall, but we will also erect several annexes and we must have the necessary spaciousness for the hippodrome, the competitions etc. It may also be considered necessary to form a garden around the Hall, for the production and multiplication of foreign plants and animals.

(*Μέγα Ελληνικόν Βιογραφικόν Λεξικόν Βοβολίνη*,
1960–1962, vol. 1, p. 409)

Very probably, the government's respect to private property was due to its incapacity to pay the necessary indemnifications. Finally, however, it was decided to expropriate the private plots too (Government Gazette, 5 December 1869).

Judging by the known examples, it can be expected that the research in the still not easily accessible archives of the time of King George I will reveal problems in the indemnification of the expropriated plots similar to those of King Otto's reign (regardless, there is at least one indemnification petition from that time for a plot occupied by the Royal Palace's gardens; G.S.A., 9 January 1865). Moreover, another persisting characteristic is the confusion about the jurisdictions of the different services and, consequently, about the obligations to indemnify the owners. A report of the 'financial curator' of Attica to the Ministry of the Interior mentions a dispute between the state and the committee of the Polytechnic about who owes the indemnification for the modification of the plots south of the institution (G.S.A., 7 March 1869). That intervention was done in order to insert in the city plan the plot offered by Helen Tositsa, because its limits were irregular and wouldn't permit the right insertion of the buildings' complex in it.

As a result, in order to avoid all those problems, the existence of public land, the law price of sale and donations were still decisive in the choice of the plots for public use. As with the Polytechnic, the solution to the much debated issue of the archaeological Museum's siting was given once again by Helen Tositsa, who donated to the state the necessary plot (Government Gazette, 13 April 1866), exactly next to the previous one. That donation led to the cancellation of a decree of 1865 (Government Gazette, 8 March 1865), which defined a site in Kerameikos (Government Gazette, 13 July 1866), elected on an ideological basis, as mentioned previously. However, apart from that, the plot belonged to the state, and it was close to the antiquities, which would serve the visitors (Theophilas, 1865, p. 4).

Another example is the concentration of hospitals in the capital's north-eastern perimeter. The salubrity of the area of Ambelokipi, in the north-east, where the city hadn't spread yet, was important in the choice of that place for the construction of almost all the capital's hospitals, which, moreover, were almost all built at that time. Nevertheless, it is questionable whether their edification in that specific location could have been materialised without the existence of the numerous plots of the Petraki monastery. That one, moreover, offered those plots gratis, when the hospitals were under Queen Olga's protection (Government Gazette, 24 August 1896, 30 March 1899, 26 April 1899, 10 November 1899, 19 November 1902, 7 November 1903, 10 February 1904, 9 July 1905). On the other hand, in case the monastery sold the plots (when those regarded the University), the choice of that area must again have been advantageous, since the plots out of the town centre were incomparably cheaper than the central ones. As the Municipal Council of Athens reports, the creation of the People's Garden in the initially predicted location would cost 6,000 drachmas, while opposite the future Polytechnic it would cost 100 drachmas – namely, 60 times less (G.S.A., City Plan, file 4). That huge difference in prices between central and remote plots intensified the aforementioned tendency that had already appeared under King Otto and led even more clearly to the 'elimination' of public functions from the capital's centre.

Finally, in case the necessary plot couldn't be ensured in any of the above ways, alternative solutions were sought, like under King Otto. Those usually meant again the sacrifice of the predicted free spaces – namely, squares, gardens, and so forth. That time the disappearance of the People's Garden was thus completed of the People's Garden. In 1872, it was decided to erect the City Hall in its last remaining part, on the western side of Athena Street. In a similar way and at that same time was also built the Municipal Foundling Hospital. That time the method was applied in the expense of Liberty Square, exactly in the same way the Mint had occupied a part of its symmetrical homonymous square. Likewise, later, the space defined for the garden of the Archaeological Museum fell victim of the need to extend the building. Finally, the Crown Prince Palace was a similar case. The area defined in 1889, when the building's plans were assigned to Ziller, served until then as the Royal Palace's vegetable garden (Biris, 1966–1967, p. 217). If it had been easy to acquire a plot, the sacrifice would have certainly been avoided. That demonstrates the change in that time's social frame. The monarchy, contrary to King Otto's time, avoided getting involved into disputes with citizens because of the royal residence. Moreover, the Royal Palace, the Royal Garden, the Royal Stables, and the Royal Pharmacy had been declared National Property in 1864 (Government Gazette, 11 April 1864). The different spirit of that time is visible everywhere.

The role of land availability 89

Notes

1 In the first years of King Otto's reign, the public services were staffed by a large number of Germans.
2 The name appears always in its Hellenised form.
3 Hill and his wife directed in Athens what was considered to be the best school for girls in the Hellenic world, still functioning today.
4 In the same file there are many more documents of similar content.
5 It isn't clarified what the court's 'factories' were.
6 A votive church for the Greek Nation's liberation, never realised.
7 However, the British historian isn't an impartial judge, being among the affected owners.
8 Hadji Ali Haseki was the voyvoda (governor) of Athens towards the end of Ottoman domination. In the late eighteenth century he built a wall to protect Athens from Albanian incursions.
9 Next to it there were plots owned by Stamatios Kleanthes, among which the one he sold to the Reverend Konstantinos Sargologos for the edification of the Catholic cathedral of Saint Dennis the Areopagite. Maybe the land was his and that was why he chose that location.
10 In the budget conserved in the Eye Hospital's archives, signed by the Bavarian architect Knecht (no first name is given), it is proposed to demolish twenty-three metres from the Civil Hospital's garden wall, which proves that the Eye Hospital was to be erected there.
11 In the Eye Hospital's archives, there are two manuscripts of a first 'regulation', the article no. 5 of which, finally omitted, mentions that cession.
12 Finlay writes that a French engineer had calculated that the cost of the excavations would exceed that of the excavations of Pompei.
13 It isn't known what was meant by 'two royal palaces'.
14 Documents dating from the years 1839 to 1843, accompanied by the respective plan.
15 Evangelis Zappas, one of the two cousins who financed the edification of the Zappeion Exhibition Hall.

Bibliography

Archives of the Catholic Archdiocese of Athens, 458, 461, correspondence of the chaplains to the bishop of Syros.
Biris, K. (1938–1940). *Αθηναϊκαί Μελέται*. Athens. Published by the author.
Biris, K. (1966–1967). *Αι Αθήναι*. Athens. Published by the author.
Burnouf, E.-L. (1887). La Grèce en 1886 – I. Son état matériel. *Revue des deux mondes*, 79, pp. 547–572.
Finlay, G. (1836). *The Hellenic Kingdom and the Greek Nation*. London: J. Murray.
Galatis, S. (1957). *Ιστορία της εν Αθήναις Φιλεκπαιδευτικής Εταιρίας*. Athens. Published by the author.
General State Archives (G.S.A.), City Plan, files 1–20; file 1, October 1834, January 1836, 8 May 1836, 24 November 1836, 7 December 1842, 30 June 1844, 7 October 1844; file 2, 11 April 1837, 24 March 1840, 5 February 1841, 27 June 1841, 12 January 1843, 15 April 1843, 11 April 1844, 23 November 1844, 24 January 1845, 11th May 1845, 5 October 1845, 14 September 1846, 17 November 1846; file 3, 8 February 1846, 16 December 1846, 8 April 1847, 30 May 1847, 22 August 1847;

file 4, 10 February 1848, 21 June 1848, 22 November 1848; file 5, 15 January 1851, 23 January 1851, 26 June 1851, 17 July 1851; file 6, 29 March 1852, 3 May 1852; file 7, 15 November 1852; file 10, 26 September 1833; file 13, 5 July 1862; file 15, 9 January 1865; file 17, 7 March 1869; file 3448.

G.S.A., Ottonian Record, M-Γ', file 107.

G.S.A., Ottonian Record, Ministry of Education, L, file 57, 22 August 1835, 29 May 1856; file 63, 30 April 1841.

G.S.A., Ottonian Record, Ministry of the Interior, file 213, 13 November 1835; file 214, 30 December 1838, 12 June 1843; file 215, 28 November 1853; file 221, 11 March 1833.

Government Gazette 79, 28 December 1836; 34, 30 July 1856; 14, 11 April 1864; 17, 8 March 1865; 28, 13 April 1866; 28, 13 July 1866; 51, 5 December 1869; 96, B, 24 August 1896; 62, A, 30 March 1899; 75, A, 26 April 1899; 242, A, 10 November 1899; 220, A, 19 November 1902; 260, A, 7 November 1903; 29, A, 10 February 1904; 121, A, 9 July 1905.

Kaftantzoglou, L. (9 August 1842). Esquisse d'un plan pour la ville d'Athènes (Letter, Constantinople, 5 August 1842). *Αιών*.

Kardamitsi-Adami, M., Papanikolaou-Christensen, A. (1994). Το Οφθαλμιατρείο Αθηνών, 1843–1993, Εκατόν πενήντα χρόνια από την ίδρυσή του. *Χρονικά αισθητικής*, 33, No.1, pp. 258–259.

Klenze, L. von (1838). *Aphoristische Bemerkungen gesammelt auf seiner Reise nach Griechenland*. Berlin: G. Reimer.

Maurer, G. L. von (1943–1947). *Ο ελληνικός λαός, εις τας σχέσεις του δημοσίου, εκκλησιαστικού και ιδιωτικού δικαίου, προ του Απελευθερωτικού αγώνος και μετ'αυτόν μέχρι της 31ης Ιουλίου 1834*. Athens.

Mendelssohn Bartholdy, K. (1876). *Ιστορία της Ελλάδος*. Athens. Published by the author.

Miliarakis, A. (1885). Αι προ πεντηκονταετίας μεγάλαι των Αθηνών οικίαι. *Εστία*, 19, pp. 23–27.

Stasinopoulos, E. (1973). *Ιστορία των Αθηνών*. Athens. Published by the author.

Stauffert, F. (1844). Die Anlage von Athen und der jetzige Zustand der Baukunst in Griechenland. *Allgemeine Bauzeitung, Ephemeriden*, 1, pp. 2–8, 2, pp. 17–25.

Theophilas, A. (1865). *Βραχύς τις έλεγχος της του αρχιτέκτονος κ.Λ.Καφταντζόγλου καλλιτεχνικής εξετάσεως των παρά του πρυτάνεως κ.Κ.Φρεαρίτου γενομένων έργων κατά την αποπεράτωσιν και ανακαίνισιν του Εθνικού Πανεπιστημίου*. Athens. Published by the author.

Αθηνά (12 August 1839).

Ήλιος (20 December 1858).

Μέγα Ελληνικόν Βιογραφικόν Λεξικόν Βοβολίνη (1960–1962). Athens: Βιομηχανική Επιθεώρησις.

Μεγάλη Ελληνική Εγκυκλοπαίδεια 'Πυρσός' (1927). Athens.

6 Functionalism in the creation of the new city

Functional principles in the time of King Otto

Parallel to the idealistic context of nineteenth-century Greece, there were also demonstrations of a very different wish: to apply the most recent functional principles of modern town planning, following the example of major European cities, and create a modern European capital, thus sealing the entry of Greece to the Western European family. That demand was especially supported by the most realistic protagonists of the creation of modern Athens, mainly the representatives of local authorities and, above all, the press. All these knew better that their city was very different from the idealistic image some foreign antiquity enthusiasts had of it. Those too wanted the modern monuments of Athens to be worthy of the ancient ones. But they didn't neglect the fact that there were parts of the city which, notwithstanding their historical value or their magnificent view to important ancient ruins and other famous sites, could be unsuitable in terms of rational town planning: they could be exposed to unhealthy winds or fumes from nearby swamps, subject to floods or simply too close to buildings of incompatible use, which would compromise the normal function of the projected construction; or, finally, any building sited there would be built above or among ancient ruins, which would mean the destruction of the latter.

Notwithstanding the subordination of the urban fabric to the antiquities, the Kleanthes and Schaubert project shows already an interest in functionality. In their plan, the civic buildings more frequently visited by citizens, like the Police, the Post Office, the Customs, and the Courts of Justice, are positioned in Piraeus Street, to facilitate their access by the merchants and businessmen, as the two architects themselves say in their memorandum (Russack, 1942, p. 192).

The plan's authors took into consideration the age-long location of the city's financial functions in the centre-west. Since ancient times, the main way into the city was from the south-west, the port of Piraeus, lying in that direction, being the city's main link to the outer world. That was due partly to the bad condition of terrestrial accesses and partly to the danger of brigands attacking travellers. Both those problems were more present than ever at the time of that plan's creation, so much so that the access from the south-west, through the port of Piraeus, was practically the only one.

Moreover, the memorandum informs us that 'in the city's oriental part, towards Ilissus and the Stadium, in the most calm and less noisy site, are to be found the establishments of science and education, the University, the Library, the Botanical Garden and the public schools'. They thus define two distinct functional axes, which coincide with today's Piraeus and Stadium Streets. In another part of the memorandum we read that 'the hospital, the slaughterhouses, the oil presses and the cemetery will be, as is the custom, out of the city' (Russack, 1942, pp. 192–193).

Nevertheless, it is obvious from the plan's intense symmetry that its authors ignored the fact that the Attica basin presents an inclination from the north-east to the south-west, and that most historic sites are situated in the south-west of the old city and not homogeneously distributed in it and around it.

Von Klenze's project seems to take more into account the Athenian landscape's particular morphology, adapting the initial plan's symmetry to it. However, von Klenze seems to ignore the location's functionality, positioning public edifices in a totally indicative way. Moreover, as von Gärtner notices, the site proposed by von Klenze for the construction of the Royal Palace was completely unsuitable because, among other reasons, of the ground's irregularity, which resulted in half the plot being on a slope (Hederer, 1976, p. 199). Despite the fact that the two colleagues were the favourite architects of King Ludwig, and thus rather rivals, the comment seems accurate. The irony is that von Klenze had made the same remark about the project of his predecessors, writing that, even if one executed the ground's arrangement predicted by the project, the western raw of ministerial buildings would be twenty feet lower than the eastern one (Klenze, 1838, pp. 435–436). We should add that the area of the ancient cemetery of Kerameikos chosen by him proved to be, as was only expected, full of ancient tombs, where innumerable antiquities were found, making that site perhaps the most unsuitable possible for building a royal palace.

The statesmen tended to be more practical than those more interested in idealistic principles, since they were the ones who had to deal with the practical issues arising from the city plans' application. Apart from that, the interest in functionality depended also on the architect, Kleanthes, for instance, having shown clearly by his projects and writings, that he was taking functionality seriously into account (Kleanthes, 1845).

A relatively precocious instance of the interest in functionality is the siting of the Eye Hospital. That was built in the direct neighbourhood of the University, with the purpose to serve the students of the Medicine School, to which it was besides subordinated in 1868 (Kydoniatis, 1985, p. 158; Markezinis, 1966, vol. 1, p. 283). The University's proximity is also underlined in 1836, in a report of the State Secretariat for the Interior on the Civil Hospital's location, because of the existence of the 'medical clinic' in the latter (G.S.A., 13 May 1836).

Similarly, it was also functional reasons that imposed the Ministries' placement in the Royal Palace's immediate neighbourhood. The politician Alexandros Rizos Ragavis had proposed that the government should acquire Dimitriou mansion (today's 'Grande Bretagne' hotel, in Constitution Square), opposite the Royal Palace, which in 1856 was put to sale. He also proposed the purchase of some other plots around the same square for the construction of the ministries, pointing out the practical advantages of that proximity (Ragavis, 1894–1930, vol. 2, p. 347).

Nevertheless, the functionality of a building also depends on the size of its plot. It was intended to build public edifices in spacious sites permitting a functional relationship with the urban fabric. This is obvious in both master plans but also results from a decree stipulating that public buildings had to be conveniently placed in the city in sites 'as open as possible' (Government Gazette, 27 May 1835). Already in 1834, someone writes to the Ministry Council such considerations about the Mint (G.S.A., Ottonian Record, Ministry of War, MB, file 331, 1834). Moreover, the aforementioned report of the Ministry of the Interior addressed to King Otto and referring to the choice of the plot for the construction of a building housing the Place Commandment, proposes the 'workshop plots' of the Kaisariani monastery in the intersection of Athena and Hermes Streets, because, among other reasons, of the streets' great width, and because the building would be 'isolated and surrounded by streets' (G.S.A., 25 February 1840).

The same wish to select the plots for the official buildings on account of the free space they would offer around them is expressed in 1844 by the aforementioned proposal made by a group of architects to erect buildings for the ministries and the State Audit Council on the plot opposite the northern side of the Royal Palace. They mention the plot's size and its great distance from every private house (G.S.A., 30 June 1844). The same plot's advantages are mentioned in other reports, some months afterward (G.S.A., 7 October 1844). However, the project was abandoned because of the financial incapacity of acquiring that large plot. That is why the property was finally divided in smaller plots and sold to rich citizens who built there their luxurious residences, today housing mainly embassies.

The site's salubrity is also a functional factor mentioned fairly often concerning public buildings' location, a factor that found its official consecration in the respective decree (Government Gazette, 28 December 1836). According to this, the location's salubrity had to be taken into consideration, an understandable wish, if one thinks of the hygienic conditions in the city of Athens at that time. As it had been observed with deception by all antiquity lovers, all famous rivers of ancient times, so closely related to the history and legends of Athens, had been degraded into rivulets or swamps. According to von Klenze, neither of the ancient rivers of Attica was reaching the sea anymore, but they all disappeared gradually at different parts of the basin (Klenze, 1838, p. 407). As a consequence, all low sites were humid and unhealthy (Klenze, 1838, p. 408).

In the case of the Royal Palace, the site next to the arc of Hadrian, where it was finally built by von Gärtner, was considered healthy, since it was situated high (*Αθηνά*, 12 February 1836, 7 March 1836; Klenze, 1838, p. 409), contrary to the place proposed by von Klenze (*Αθηνά*, 22 December 1834; Hederer, 1976, pp. 58, 199). Von Klenze thought nevertheless that the final location was threatened by Ilissus's floods, which carried away even houses (Klenze, 1838, p. 409). He also rejected the southern slope of Lycabettus, for he believed that its surface would be heated all day and would reflect the heat all day and all night long (Klenze, 1838, pp. 447–448).

Similarly, the healthy site of the Civil Hospital's location is mentioned in two documents (G.S.A., 7 May 1836, 13 May 1836). Furthermore, the Minister of Education writes about the Varvakeion Lyceum that 'a site [. . .] has been found, which, thanks to the agreeable, healthy and central location was judged to be the most convenient of all' (G.S.A., 29 May 1856). Finally, about the proposal to build the Academy in the area of Kerameikos (*Ήλιος*, 2 February 1857), along with the enthusiastic idealistic comments, it was said that the site was humid and therefore unhealthy, as well as not easily accessible (*Φιλόπατρις*, 12 January 1857).

The issue of salubrity wasn't, however, only a question of location, but also of orientation. As it had been observed, the winds dominating in Athens are these of north-northeast and south-southwest, following the direction of the Attica basin. According to von Klenze, the first were unhealthy because they brought snow and rain in winter, while in summer they froze the atmosphere abruptly. On the contrary, the winds of south-southwest were healthy, because they were hot in winter, arriving from hot regions, while in summer they cooled the atmosphere, since they cooled themselves passing above the sea (Klenze, 1838, pp. 405–406).

According to that observation, a decree of 1836 demanded 'a southern exposition' for public buildings (Government Gazette, 28 December 1836). In the case of the aforementioned plot north of the Royal Palace, proposed for the construction of the ministries, the advantageous orientation is underlined (G.S.A., 30 June 1844). Moreover, the Minister of the Interior proposed to the Ministry Council the construction of the Courts on the plot that Georgios Stavrou[1] intended to cede to the state,[2] among other reasons, because its location was healthy and it had a southern orientation (G.S.A., 10 February 1848). The fact that most public buildings, at least the most prestigious ones, are oriented rather towards the south-west may be a compromise with the idealistic demand for a view towards the archaeological sites lying in that direction.

There is finally an interesting instance where functionality has a moral nuance, at a time when, at least when it is a question of education subjects, moral criteria play a decisive part. This instance is to be found in the aforementioned report of the Minister of Education on the Varvakeion Lyceum's location (G.S.A., 29 May 1856). It contains an abstract of the report written by the committee charged with the Lyceum's construction and submitted to the Ministry in 1851. According to that, the committee 'having examined [. . .] the site [. . .] between the University and the Eye Hospital, found it utterly unsuitable, [. . .] because it isn't to any advantage to erect two big educational establishments close to each other' and considers that it is 'not at all in the interest of the education of the youth that the latter mixes itself incessantly with the students of the University' and that 'one avoids noises and disorder, which go along with the affluence of a great number of pupils'. Certainly, the finally resulting proximity of the Varvakeion Lyceum and the Municipal Market did anything but satisfy the committee's wish. The reasons for that unsuitable final choice, as well as for many others of a similar nature, were purely financial: the low cost of that plot, as the Minister's report informs us.

The situation under King George I: the intensified debate on functionality

Under King George I, despite the more realistic spirit, the need to take functionality into consideration in the creation of modern Athens still needed to be fought for. One of the most discussed cases is the siting of the Zappeion Exhibition Hall. The debate lasted a long time, because of the importance attributed to that building, supposed to advertise the technological progress of Greece. Kaftantzoglou finds the chosen location too 'narrow'

(Kaftantzoglou, 1880, p. 5) and says that, while the plans should have been made according to the location, they were on the contrary made before the building's plot was selected (Kaftantzoglou, 1880, p. 7). Also, Ragavis makes comments about the location's functionality:

> After several years have gone by, the site was selected, where the build-ing is actually under construction, behind the royal gardens, the origi-nal purpose of the building's later gradual expansion having evidently been abandoned, because there is no room behind it for other parallel perimeters.
>
> (*Μέγα Ελληνικόν Βιογραφικόν Λεξικόν Βοβολίνη*,
> 1960–1962, vol. 1, p. 396)

However, there is a practical side in the siting of public functions which seems to gain in importance: hygiene. The great progress of medi-cine towards the end of the century couldn't but affect greatly the Greek capital's development, as it happened all over the Western world. It is from the 1880s in particular that the question of hygiene is seriously treated in the city (*Αιών*, 5 August 1881, 11 August 1881; report of a medical council on the measures of hygiene in the city: *Αιών*, 3 Decem-ber 1881; decisions of the municipal council and the Police Direction on cleaning, *Αιών*, 30 December 1881); a commission was created, which was assigned 'health and embellishment' and lasted a year and a half (*Αιών*, 2 August 1883). With a report addressed to the Ministry of the Interior (G.S.A., City Plan, file 18, September 1871), the director of the Administrative Police of Athens and Piraeus forbids thus the creation of the Morgue and the Chemical Laboratory, judging them to be harmful to the neighbours' health, while they too had complained themselves to the same Ministry on that subject (G.S.A., 16 August 1871). Besides, as mentioned previously, the salubrity of the area of Ambelokipi, in the north-east of Athens, was an important factor in the choice of that place for the construction of almost all the capital's hospitals (Stavropoulos, 1985, p. 130). On the same subject there is also the decree 'concerning the creation of a commission with the aim to find a suitable plot in Athens for the construction of a hospital for contagious diseases'. That decree expresses the demand 'that it fills the requirements of hygiene' (Govern-ment Gazette, 23 January 1903, 7 November 1903).

However, also during that period, functional criteria with a moral nuance are still taken into consideration. It is again about an educational institution and more precisely the Arsakeion and its failed vicinity with the Courts of Justice. When, at the beginning of the year 1877, the government bought the plot next to the Royal Printing House, with the aim to build at last the Courts of Justice, the event upset the school's administration council. Its members predicted that the employees and the numerous visitors of the Courts would look from the new building's windows into the windows of the girls' school, and those coming to the Courts would harass the female teachers entering the school. The administration council, after taking the necessary steps, succeeded in stopping the works, although the foundations had already been dug (Galatis, 1957, vol. 2, chapter 1, pp. 18a–19).

In the end, however, the search of a suitable site either from an idealistic or from a practical viewpoint hadn't much more meaning in King George I's time than under King Otto. The final siting of the capital's public functions continued depending mostly on the availability of land. Consequently, realities put necessarily aside all efforts to plan the new capital according to specific principles, either rational or idealistic, leading to the subsequent random development.

Notes

1 The founder of the National Bank of Greece.
2 In Gherani, an area a little west of the top of the urban triangle.

Bibliography

Galatis, S. (1957). *Ιστορία της εν Αθήναις Φιλεκπαιδευτικής Εταιρίας*. Athens. Published by the author.
General State Archives (G.S.A.), City Plan, file 1, 30 June 1844, 7 October 1844; file 4, 10 February 1848; file 18, 16 August 1871; file 18, September 1871.
G.S.A., Ottonian Record, Ministry of Education, L, file 57, 29 May 1856.
G.S.A., Ottonian Record, Ministry of the Interior, file 188, 7 May 1836, 13 May 1836; file 208, 25 February 1840.
G.S.A., Ottonian Record, Ministry of War, MB, file 331, 1834.
Government Gazette 19, article 16, 27 May 1835; 79, 28 December 1836; 12, A, 23 January 1903; 260, 7 November 1903.
Hederer, O. (1976). *Friedrich von Gärtner, 1792–1847*. München: Prestel.
Kaftantzoglou, L. (1880). *Τα Ολύμπια εν Φαλήρω και το νυν μεταρρυθμιζόμενον Ζάππειον*. Athens. Published by the author.
Kleanthes, S. (1845). *Έκθεσις περί του εν Αθήναις ανεγερθησομένου καταστήματος της Φιλεκπαιδευτικής Εταιρείας*. Athens. Published by the author.
Klenze, L. von (1838). *Aphoristische Bemerkungen gesammelt auf seiner Reise nach Griechenland*. Berlin: G. Reimer.
Kydoniatis, S. (1985). *Αθήναι, παρελθόν και μέλλον*. Athens: Πνευματικό Κέντρο Δήμου Αθηναίων.
Markezinis, S. (1966). *Πολιτική Ιστορία της Νεωτέρας Ελλάδος 1828–1964*. Athens: Πάπυρος.
Ragavis, A. (1894–1930). *Απομνημονεύματα*. Athens. Published by the author.
Russack, H. H. (1942). *Deutsche Bauen in Athen*. Berlin: Wilhelm Limpert Verlag.

98   *Creation of the new city*

Stavropoulos, A. (1985). Η νοσοκομειακή και νοσηλευτική πολιτική στην Αθήνα τα πρώτα ογδόντα χρόνια της ως πρωτεύουσας. In: Y. Tsiomis, ed., *Αθήνα πρωτεύουσα πόλη*. Athens: Ministry of Culture, pp. 128–134.

Αθηνά (22 December 1834, 12 February 1836, 7 March 1836).

Αιών (3 December 1881, 30 December 1881, 2 August 1883).

Ήλιος (2 February 1857).

Μέγα Ελληνικόν Βιογραφικόν Λεξικόν Βοβολίνη (1960–1962). Athens: Βιομηχανική Επιθεώρησις.

Περί της δημοσίας υγείας (11 August 1881). *Αιών*.

Τα της υγείας των Αθηνών (5 August 1881). *Αιών*.

Φιλόπατρις (12 January 1857).

7 The role of official functions in the evolution of the city of Athens

The evolution of Athens under King Otto

The observation of the master plans made for the new city of Athens and their comparison with the finally realised plan reveals a strong contrast: on the one hand a desire for a homogeneous development, and on the other hand an unbalanced expansion of the city centre to the north-east, which became even more intense in the twentieth century. The uneven development is accompanied by the aforementioned uneven distribution of the city's official buildings, clearly concentrated in the same direction. This situation goes along with a respective distinction between 'privileged' and 'underprivileged' parts of the city, the former clustering around official buildings in the north-eastern quarters and the latter being situated to the west of the urban triangle.

As analysed previously, the buildings symbolising the entry of Greece in civilised Europe were planned out of the existing urban fabric, in the area predicted for the creation of the new city. However, the state was in no position to quickly realise the capital's expansion within its new frame and was even less quick to install all necessary elements of the urban fabric in it. Consequently, despite the efforts to create a capital of European standards, Athens under King Otto was characterised not only by a complete lack of a network of services (namely, streets, lighting, telecommunications, transports), but also by an absence of serious action to cover those needs. Contrary to Western European capitals, where the creation of the urban fabric was usually parallel to the realisation of public constructions, in the Greek capital public buildings preceded the other elements of the urban network (Raoul-Rochette, 1838, p. 185) and were constructed in practically desert areas. The lack of organised slaughterhouses, of a cleaning service and the existence of farms in the city's direct periphery, underlined the contrast with monumental buildings.

Moreover, as mentioned previously, the lack of public land within the area predicted for the new city led to the siting of official buildings at locations totally different from those predicted by the master plans. Therefore, since public constructions preceded the urban fabric, instead of the natural process of the city plan defining their siting, the opposite happened. In consequence, especially in the case of large buildings, the approved city plan had to be continuously modified, whether it had already approached and surrounded the public building or it was still at a distance from it. Only thus could the respective construction be connected with the urban fabric.

An early instance of that process is the Royal Palace. That building, on the one hand, because of its importance, particularly occupied the responsible architects with its insertion in the existing urban fabric, and on the other hand, because of its size, clearly influenced that fabric's form. In von Gärtner's plan, dating from 1836, the Royal Palace appears with its façade put directly on the building line of an avenue. That avenue would replace the peripheral street predicted by von Klenze's plan. Von Gärtner, modifying the plan at the city's eastern edge, was creating a square, which wasn't reaching the line of Stadium Street and Philhellenes Street, its extension to the South, because it was conserving next to them, on both sides of Hermes Street, two blocks destined to the ministries. The project also featured the Royal Garden, composed of two rectangles on both sides of the Palace and of a big hemicycle in the rear.

Von Gärtner planned the Royal Palace not in relation to the city and as a reference point of the whole composition, like Kleanthes and Schaubert did, but on the contrary as an autonomous ensemble at the city's periphery and in juxtaposition to its urban fabric. In his project, the Palace isn't even inserted in the landscape, since it ignores the topography, overlapping the ancient routes from the north-east, which disappear without reaching the city. On the contrary, both master plans predicted the connection of the new city to those ancient arteries.

Another construction that considerably influenced the city plan of Athens is the University. In 1836, for the siting of that building, the subject of arranging the plan of the north-eastern side of Athens was put again under discussion. The arrangement proposed to the Building Committee by Kleanthes and giving to the Boulevard its final form, somewhat different from that of the von Klenze plan, was approved in 1837.

That intervention, however, affected the arrangement von Gärtner had proposed for the Royal Palace, because the avenue he had created in front of the building depended on von Klenze's plan, which was now modified in that area. Therefore, the engineer charged with the Palace's edification, the German lieutenant Hoch, undertook to connect it with the Boulevard. He divided the surrounding area in two squares: the future Constitution Square in the lower part (west) and the actual Royal Palace square in the upper part (east). Bending almost symmetrically the Boulevard, he created

Queen Amalia Avenue. Moreover, in association to that and to Philhellenes Street, he defined the space for the edification of the Anglican church and, in general, the whole area's layout (Figure 2.2).

Hoch's plan was approved in 1837. The bends of the Boulevard created at its northern end, with the widening of the streets around Otto Square and perpendicular to Aeolus and Socrates Streets, led to today's end of University Street and, respectively, on the opposite side, to Saint Constantine Street. According to Hoch's plan, the Royal Palace Square would reach the line of Stadium and Philhellenes Streets. It was arranged and planted as a public garden immediately, because it mainly occupied a monastery property. Towards the end of 1837, or during the next year, since the monastery plot was extending even more to the west, with a new decree the square was widened to its today's surface, occupying also some private plots (Biris, 1933, p. 32; Biris, 1966–1967, pp. 68–69).

Even thus, however, the new city wasn't connected with the ancient routes at that location. Therefore, but also because there was no money for the expropriation of the whole area predicted by von Gärtner's project for the garden, Hoch composed another general plan, approved in 1839. According to that, the garden would extend only to one side, towards the south, in the extension of the Royal Palace's façade, at a length of three hundred metres approximately and a width of a hundred metres (see Figure 2.2). Toward the northern side, the Palace's precinct was put at a distance of only twenty-five metres from the building's lateral façade. In 1857, and according to that plan, a decree created the initial part of Kifisias Avenue, thirty metres wide and with lawns thirty metres large, but the temporary government after King Otto's dethronement limited the lawns' width to fifteen metres (G.S.A., 15 October 1862).

Anyway, that urban insertion stayed for a long time at the stage of project, since there is a plan of 1843, where the Royal Palace appears still with no connection with the urban fabric (G.S.A., City Plan, file 1). From the same year dates the plan of the French architect A. M. Chenavard (Chenavard, 1849), where there is still no connection of the Royal Palace with the city, but the avenue towards the north-east, predicted by the first two master plans, makes its first reappearance. However, its articulation with the city is still missing. It appears for the first time in the aforementioned plan of 1844, where the urban fabric tends towards its final form: the part of the Royal Garden blocking the ancient route has disappeared and the latter appears finally connected with the new city, under the name of Kifisias Street (Figure 1.3).

In 1836 was also made a modification of the city plan at the western side of the Market, between Socrates and Menander Streets, for the edification of the city's theatre, which was decided at the same time (Biris, 1966–1967,

p. 73). Moreover, there has been 'a modification of the alignment at the site of the theatre, which was built on a plot not destined to that purpose' (G.S.A., 30 October 1850).

Also in 1836 started the edification of the Civil Hospital, beyond the Boulevard, which constituted the city's north-eastern limit, meaning that the Hospital's building was out of the approved plan. According to the plan of the committee of 1847,[1] Hospital Street (today's Academy Street) was created at the north-eastern side of Athens, parallel to the Boulevard, in order to include the Civil Hospital and the illegal settlement of Proasteion (the name means Suburb, today's Neapolis; Biris, 1966–1967, p. 84). Therefore, the city's second extension to the north-east was done for the sake of one public building, like the first one.

The Military Hospital is a similar case. In 1845, the First Direction of the Military Engineers proposes to the Ministry of War the acquisition of the plots in front of the building, for the creation of a proportional square. Moreover, it proposes the extension of the city plan and its 'appropriate' connection with the respective modifications in the Hospital's surroundings (G.S.A., 14 June 1845), the latter lacking a connection with the urban fabric (Figure 7.1).

There are also other types of arrangements made for the sake of official buildings. In 1847, Andreas Metaxas, president of the Philekpaideutiki Society (which was directing the Arsakeion), asked for the 'architect of Athens' to be ordered to level the Boulevard, where the school was being built (G.S.A., 3 April 1847). Another modification of the city plan was proposed in 1857, with the unification of two blocks for the edification of the Municipal Theatre. That further changed the predicted layout for the People's Garden, which was continuously shrinking until it became Ludwig Square (G.S.A., 31 May 1857).

A later example is the Polytechnic. As mentioned previously, the plot offered by Helen Tositsa[2] for its edification was of a completely irregular form and out of that time's city plan. In order to make it suitable for its purpose, two actions were taken: its limits to another neighbouring plot were arranged and the Ministry of the Interior proceeded to the city plan's extension. The future Stournari Street was thus formed at the southern limit of an extended block with a front to Patision Street, where the Polytechnic's façade is today. The plan's extension was realised when the executors of Nikolaos Stournaris's[3] will asked for a construction permit for the Polytechnic (G.S.A., City Plan, file 13, August 1862, September 1862).

Finally, another type of intervention done for the insertion of public buildings was the opening of roads, since those edifices were often built in totally unshaped areas, with the Observatory being a characteristic instance (Government Gazette, 24 March 1859). However, even towards the end

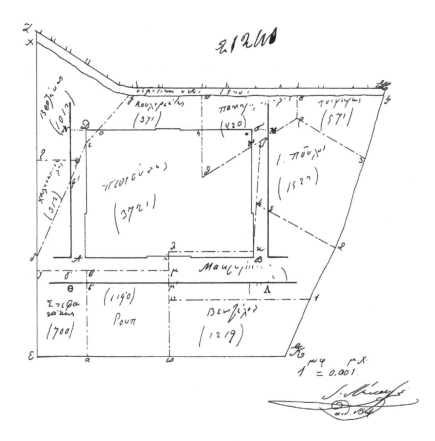

Figure 7.1 Drawing accompanying the document of 14 June 1845 and depicting the plot of the Military Hospital and those around it, whose purchase is proposed by the document

General State Archives, City Plan, file 5; re-drawn by the author

of King Otto's reign, up to the last year (1862), we have a plan presenting the University, then almost completed, still not connected with the urban fabric (G.S.A., City Plan, file 14). Even more impressive is an abstract of von Klenze's plan (G.S.A., City Plan, file 13), dating from the same year, with the buildings of the future Athenian Trilogy. It is noteworthy that the plan doesn't clarify the three buildings' connection with the city. That first appears in a plan of 1864–1865.[4]

However, it wasn't only the city plan's details that were directly influenced by the siting of public functions. Since the Royal Palace and the cultural public edifices were seen as symbols of the country's Europeanisation, they became a pole of attraction for those desiring to manifest their European orientation by building their dwellings, shops, and so on next to them. That had been predicted early by Kaftantzoglou. He writes that the Royal Palace should attract the inhabitants to build towards its side of the city. Moreover, he notes the need to define the locations of public constructions 'in the four directions of the city', so that it will be inhabited homogeneously (Kaftantzoglou, G.S.A., Ottonian Record, Ministry of the Interior, file 214). He expresses the same opinion when speaking of the area around Kerameikos, where von Klenze's plan had positioned the Royal Palace. He says that

> the area of the newly designed city around the aforementioned houses will remain empty for a long time, for, apart from their distance from the ancient city, the construction of the new Royal Palace is already diverging from there, it alone being able to attract inhabitants to that now remote and low place.
>
> (Kaftantzoglou, 1858, p. 13)

He mentions as an instance

> the formerly despicable location of Gherani,[5] where two years ago – i.e., in 1856 – the plots were sold for one and a half drachma per square pique, and today, after the edification of the Varvakeion Lyceum and some houses, the price has mounted to twelve, and it may mount to fifteen drachmas after the construction is completed.
>
> (Kaftantzoglou, 1858, p. 26)

The same happened at the location of Saint Sion, beyond the Boulevard. In 1836 the plot of the Civil Hospital was purchased by the Municipality of Athens for 0.16 drachmas per square pique. In 1847 the plot of the Eye Hospital was sold for 4 drachmas per square pique, while some months previously Michael Kallifronas had bought it from Kleanthes for 3 drachmas per square pique. The plot of the Catholic cathedral of Saint Dennis was sold by Kleanthes for 2.92 drachmas per square pique, while in 1856 Gregorios Papadopoulos[6] bought the plot of the Hellenic School for 3.45 drachmas per square pique (Kardamitsi-Adami, Papanikolaou-Christensen, 1993, p. 53). Undoubtedly, the decision to build there the Athenian Trilogy was decisive for that location's upgrading.

Kaftantzoglou observes a little later that 'the royal palace resembles a magnet. Like it drags the iron chips around it, likewise the palace will imperceptibly drag the new city to its surroundings' (Kaftantzoglou, 1842).

His aforementioned pessimist prediction about the limited future urban development of Athens was completely belied. On the contrary, his opinion about the influence of the Royal Palace and the other public buildings on that evolution was verified. The belief in the advantages of the Royal Palace's neighbourhood was expressed by the accumulation of private constructions around it. That tendency was particularly cultivated by the rich Greeks of the diaspora. Those, through their mass repatriation immediately after Independence and being the only ones disposing of the capital necessary to acquire large plots, gave with their choices the signal for the general tendency that dominated henceforward. The clearest indication of the criterion directing the choices of the upper class in their quest of a location for their mansions is the fact that, as long as the Royal Palace was supposed to be sited in the area of Kerameikos, the notables purchased massively plots along Piraeus Street, as Kaftantzoglou mentioned. However, as soon as the location of the royal residence was transferred to the diametrically opposite side, they hastened to abandon their initial installations and move around it.

Thus, the Royal Palace's displacement from the central position it occupied in the Kleanthes and Schaubert project initiated the overturn of the balance between the city's functions and the buildings related to them, as the subsequent evolution of Athens demonstrated. Since the official buildings were the expression in space par excellence of the state's authority and therefore of the dominating class's power, their positioning was directly linked to the location of the notables' residences in a two-way relationship. Therefore, from the moment the Royal Palace's position was final and, along with that, the position of the upper class residences as well, the distribution of the remaining official buildings within the urban fabric had been practically sealed (with other aforementioned factors taken into account). That was more so with those directly connected with the upper class, as an expression of its ideology and principles. Those buildings were the cultural ones, for the aforementioned reasons. Moreover, they were realised thanks to the donations made by the representatives of that class, who, as a result, had a say in the choice of their location, even when they didn't offer the plot as well. A characteristic instance is one of the first public buildings, which, as mentioned previously, started being constructed in 1835 as a theatre, according to von Klenze's city plan, to end up as the Mint. The fact that the first official building that it had attempted to create in application of the city plan was also the most representative of the emerging bourgeoisie and moreover would be erected in the square housing temporarily the royal residence could hardly be a coincidence.

The influence of the Royal Palace and of other public edifices on the city's evolution is attested in 1853 by the Minister of the Interior (G.S.A., 28 November 1853). He writes to King Otto that the transfer of the Royal Palace from the western part of the city [. . .] to the eastern part [. . .] and the tendency that the city is taking because of that transfer towards the north-eastern part, after the edification there of the University as well, dictate its extension – i.e., the extension of the city plan – towards that part.

Notably, in the highly ideological context of King Otto's reign, the University, among all official buildings, is chosen to be mentioned as a major factor of the city's evolution.

The same spirit is to be detected in the testimony that in 1850, Stadium Street, though far from the city centre and with few private constructions, was sufficiently frequented because of the area's public buildings. Those were the Ministries of the Interior and of Finance, the Printing House, the Mint, the Royal Stables, and 'above all'[7] the University, despite the existence of a stream along the street. Finally, Simon Sinas, when searching for a place to erect his residence, was initially interested in a plot opposite the Royal Palace. However, having found the price (192,500 drachmas) extravagant, he started considering the area of the Observatory, for he thought that, if the Academy was erected there, as it had been proposed (*Ήλιος*, 2 February 1857), the city would expand in that direction (Laios, 1972, p. 180).

Proposals for the dispersion of public buildings

The negative consequences of the uneven distribution of official constructions on the city's balanced development had been observed early. Therefore, the authorities expressed the intention to construct public buildings of any use in 'underprivileged' areas, in order to restore balance. That is indicated in 1848 by the aforementioned document of the Minister of the Interior, proposing the construction of the Courts of Justice on the plot Georgios Stavrou intended to cede to the state. He sustains that the government will thus reinforce the quarter of Gherani, limiting at the same time the city's tendency to expand to the East, because of the existence there of the Royal Palace, the University, and other 'establishments' (the University prevails again). The positioning of all official buildings to the East seems to him unprofitable, causing the destruction of those who built in the quarter where Stavrou's plot lies, according to the first city plan.[8] He says that, in order to satisfy the citizens complaining of the initial plan's modification, the strict justice demands that the public establishments, from which the value of the neighbouring private residences increases so much, aren't concentrated in a specific part of the city, causing the great gain of some and the obvious damage of most. Also from the architectural viewpoint, he believes that the public establishments, which contribute so much to the embellishment of big cities, must be dispersed, so that each quarter has something noteworthy for the visitor. As a proof of that principle he mentions ancient Athens and the European capitals (G.S.A., 10 February 1848).

The same plot must be the one mentioned in a memorandum of 1854. According to that, since the Royal Palace was erected in a location different from the initially defined one, the King decided to build the Theatre[9] in Gherani, 'in order to take care of that quarter'. Therefore, Schaubert and Stauffert, assigned to find the appropriate plot, proposed to Stavrou to cede for that purpose the plot he had there (its exact location isn't mentioned anywhere; G.S.A., City Plan, file 7).

In the end, the Theatre wasn't built in Gherani, but in Ludwig Square, as a Municipal Theatre. However, almost half a century later, the Royal Theatre was built in Gherani (Figure 7.2), but on a totally unsuitable plot, owned by Nikolaos Thon,[10] with a steep slope and not offering the slightest free space in front of it, for the movement of carriages and so forth. Despite also other factors contributing to that choice (*Η Αθήνα των ευεργετών*, 1997),[11] we couldn't exclude the survival of the same thoughts about the upgrading of the 'underprivileged' areas through the edification of official buildings. Moreover, the direct relation of that particular building with the royal family rendered it one of the city's most prestigious edifices. On the other hand, the insistence on placing specific uses in specific locations is noteworthy, since

Figure 7.2 The National, former Royal, Theatre
Photograph by the author

in Gherani the aforementioned plot was also chosen in 1838 for the construction of the theatre ran by the Italian Iosiph Kamilieri. We don't know
the exact relationship between that plot, the plot of Stavrou, and that where
the Royal Theatre was finally built. It is, however, noteworthy that all those
plots were in the same quarter.

The same idea inspired the proposal to construct the Varvakeion Lyceum
in the location finally selected. In his aforementioned report to King Otto
in 1856, the Minister of Education writes that 'the edification of the Varvakeion Lyceum there will also animate that part of the city, which up to
now seems to be abandoned' (G.S.A., 29 May 1856).

However, it wasn't only the authorities who occupied themselves with
the capital's regular expansion. The archaeologist Stefanos Koumanoudis
lamented the fact that the actual centre of life in the city, instead of coin-
ciding with the two major squares (i.e., that of the Palace and that of the
Mint), was to be found in the intersection of the two main commercial
arteries, Hermes and Aeolus Streets, close to the pre-revolutionary market area. As a measure against that 'antinomy', he proposed the construction of more public offices, clubs, and workshops around the two squares
(K., 1853, p. 442b).

As the last and, apparently, most ambitious effort made during King
Otto's reign to confront the problem, we could consider the aforementioned
proposal submitted in 1859 to the King by the Minister of the Interior about
the necessary plots for the edification of the *numerous* missing public edifices (G.S.A., 30 July 1859). A list of the buildings is given, along with the
proposed location of many of them 'according to the opinion of the competent Ministers'. Therefore, a central location is proposed for the Prefecture, the Direction of the Administrative Police, and the Post Office, while
locations 'in the four parts of the city' are proposed for the five 'buildings
of the Police sub-division'. The seven 'police stations' are positioned in
seven different parts of the city. For the three prisons, the Minister proposes
'an aerated and eccentric location'. The Customs are placed 'next to the
platforms of the railway' (still nonexistent), the Mint 'within the precinct
of the Royal Printing House', while the Revenue Office 'in the existing
Mint'. The Courts of Justice are sited next to the Varvakeion Lyceum and
two other schools 'in the city's northern side', while it is proposed to build
another school 'in Kifisias Street'.[12] Moreover, the Infantry barracks are
sited 'at the location of the Holy Trinity' (Aghia Triada), that of the Artillery 'on the slope of Lycabettus' and of the Cavalry 'next to the duchess's
house'.[13] Finally, the document predicts 'four partial' markets and a central
one. The same source reinforces the observation that practical principles

appear much more often in the case of public buildings other than those housing cultural functions.

That was probably the ultimate effort to apply a general urban design for the homogeneous distribution of the Athenian official buildings within the urban fabric, many years after the abandon of the first master plans, which predicted exactly that. It was, however, too late, as the subsequent evolution of the capital's city plan demonstrates.

The evolution of Athens after King Otto

What can be said is that the up to now little available information from the unpublished archival sources, which moreover cover only the first years of George I's reign, reveals a continuation of Athens' particularities. The urban development of the Greek capital continues being characterised by the state's exceptionally limited resources. A characteristic instance is a testimony of 1863 describing Ludwig Square as 'immense and desert; a waste plain with currents, mountains and gorges' (Lykoudis, 1922, p. 25).

Consequently, the fragmentary extensions of the city plan with the purpose to insert the plots lying out of it and destined to the edification of public buildings or to insert already constructed buildings continue. Thus, a decree stipulates the extension of the city plan 'with the purpose to erect the Didas-kaleion's building on the included area' (Government Gazette, 24 June 1876). Likewise, the city plan was extended in order to include the Annunciation Hospital (Evangelismos; Government Gazette, 21 June 1884 and 26 June 1886, A', abolished with Government Gazette, 1 August 1886, B').

Moreover, the modifications of the existing plan in order to insert public buildings continue. For the edification of the Academy, they changed the direction of Blind-Hospital Street (today's Sina Street; G.S.A., City Plan, file 14, 1864). Another instance is the Hatzikonsta Orphanage. In 1870 the Minister of the Interior informs the King that the Orphanage's administrative board bought a neighbouring plot with the purpose to extend the establishment and take care of more orphans. Therefore, they ask the abolition of the intermediate anonymous street, in order to achieve the unification (G.S.A., 15 July 1870), a petition that was approved, as the respective decrees reveal (Government Gazette, 8 October 1870, 28 May 1871). Moreover, the city plan was modified between the Polytechnic and the Archaeological Museum, after the donation of the Museum's plot (Government Gazette, 14 June 1879), as a continuation of the plan's extension to that direction, which had been done during King Otto's reign. With that were created the so-called Tositsa Street, between the Polytechnic and the Museum, as well as Asomaton Street behind the same establishments (apparently today's Bouboulinas Street). Moreover, when the extension of the Arsakeion was decided in 1900, the administration board asked from the municipality to widen Arsaki Street by three metres and to clean it. Finally, that was done only in the street's part included between the Printing House and University Street. The building line receded by 1.50 metre on either side and a space of 1.80 metre was left for a pavement (Galatis, 1957, vol. 3, chapter 1, p. 9).

The plan's modifications also include the creation of blocks (usually in the expense of squares) for the edification of public buildings. That intention is revealed by the decree 'Concerning the modification of the street planning chart of the city of Athens for the edification of a municipal establishment' (Government Gazette, 11 August 1872), which was, however, revoked (Government Gazette, 12 December 1872). The addition of a block to the city plan was also predicted by another decree related to the Foundling Hospital's edification (G.S.A., 15 August 1872; Government Gazette, 12 December 1872).

There are, however, cases where the modifications in the city plan were made with the purpose of creating axes of symmetry and visual relations. That is revealed by the decree by which the street connecting Theatre Square to Socrates Street is arranged in a way that its axis passes through the middle of the buildings of the Varvakeion and the Theatre (Government Gazette, 20 November 1869). The symbolical value of public buildings continues to play a major role in the city plan's layout and dictate it.

Notes

1 A plan made by a committee of architects, the first attempt to make a new master plan after those of Kleanthes and Schaubert and von Klenze, which took into account all the previous changes made on them. It was never approved.
2 The widow of the benefactor Michael Tositsas, who executed his wish to sponsor the Polytechnic.
3 Nephew of Michael Tositsas, who also wished to sponsor the Polytechnic.
4 That plan was started by the Direction of the Military Engineers and became the basic plan for the subsequent urban development of Athens.
5 An area a little at the west of the top of the urban triangle.
6 A scholar who founded the private Hellenic School, in Academy Street.
7 Quoted verbatim.
8 He means the city plan of Kleanthes and Schaubert.
9 It is obviously about the Royal Theatre, which was the initial aim of all related efforts.
10 Financial counsellor of King George I.
11 It is believed that the plot has been purchased under the owner's influence. Its price was scandalously high: 500.000 drachmes.
12 Today's Queen Sophia Avenue (Vasilissis Sophias).
13 He means the Duchess of Plaisance.

Bibliography

Biris, K. (1933). *Τα πρώτα σχέδια των Αθηνών*. Athens. Published by the author.

Biris, K. (1966–1967). *Αι Αθήναι*. Athens. Published by the author.

Chenavard, A. M. (1849). *Voyage en Grèce et dans le Levant fait en 1843–44 par A.M. Chevanard, Architecte, E.Rey Peintre, Professeurs à l'École des Beaux-Arts de Lyon, et J.M. Dalgabio architecte. Relation par A.M. Chenavard*. Lyon: Boitel.

Galatis, S. (1957). *Ιστορία της εν Αθήναις Φιλεκπαιδευτικής Εταιρίας*. Athens. Published by the author.

General State Archives (G.S.A.), City Plan, file 1; file 3, 3 April 1847; file 4, 10 February 1848; file 5, 14 June 1845; file 7; file 13, August 1862, September 1862, 15 October 1862; file 14; file 17, 15 July 1870; file 19, 15 August 1872.

G.S.A., Ottonian Record, Ministry of Education, L, file 57, 29 May 1856.

G.S.A., Ottonian Record, Ministry of the Interior, file 214, 31 May 1857, 30 July 1859; file 215, 30 October 1850, 28 November 1853.

Government Gazette 11, 24 March 1859; 47, 20 November 1869; 33, 8 October 1870; 19, 28 May 1871; 35, 11 August 1872; 49, 12 December 1872; 28, 24 June 1876; 35, 14 June 1879; 254, 21 June 1884; 168, 26 June 1886, A'; 208, 1 August 1886, Β'.

Κ. (1853). *Καθολικόν Πανόραμα των Αθηνών*. *Νέα Πανδώρα*, 67(3), pp. 440–445.

Kaftantzoglou, L. *Esquisse d'un plan pour la ville d'Athènes propre à remplacer le projet en exécution si mal conçu et impossible à recevoir jamais sa totale organisation*, G.S.A., Ottonian Record, Ministry of the Interior, file 214.

Kaftantzoglou, L. (9 August 1842). Esquisse d'un plan pour la ville d'Athènes (Letter, Constantinople, 5 August 1842). *Αιών*.

Kaftantzoglou, L. (1858). *Περί μεταρρυθμίσεως της πόλεως Αθηνών γνώμαι*. Athens: S. Pavlidis and Z. Gryparis.

Kardamitsi-Adami, M., Papanikolaou-Christensen, A. (1994). Το Οφθαλμιατρείο Αθηνών, 1843–1993, Εκατόν πενήντα χρόνια από την ίδρυσή του. *Χρονικά αισθητικής*, 33, No.1, pp. 258–259.

Laios, G. (1972). *Σίμων Σίνας*. Athens: Γραφείον Δημοσιευμάτων της Ακαδημίας Αθηνών.

Lykoudis E. (1922). Το κατάστημα της Εθν.Τραπέζης αμυνόμενον φρούριον (20 Ιουνίου 1863). In: *Σελίδες από τας νεωτέρας Αθήνας*. Athens: Eleftheroudakis, pp. 23–40.

Raoul-Rochette, D. (1838). Athènes sous le roi Othon, lettre adressée à Mr De Pouqueville. *Revue des deux mondes*, 16(2), pp. 179–192.

Η Αθήνα των ευεργετών (1997). *Exposition*. Athens: Cultural Centre of the Municipality of Athens.

Ήλιος (2 February 1857).

8 Public space and monumental architecture

From the grandiose plans of a
European metropolis to a peripheral
capital between East and West

Athens from the Ottoman domination to independence

The relationship of public space with official architecture in Athens isn't
the usual one of a European capital, but rather a mixture of it with strong
influences from the city's long Ottoman past. Note that we have to bear in
mind, however, that Athens, like many other towns of the Ottoman Empire,
wasn't created ex nihilo, but was an adaptation of a pre-existing town to
the requirements of Ottoman administration and society, and therefore in a
way not an Ottoman, but an 'Ottomanized' Byzantine town (Pinon, 2008,
pp. 144, 147). The scarcity of cul-de-sacs in Athens is already a feature of
non-Ottoman character, according to Pinon's analysis (Pinon, 2008, p. 150).
Unlike in most other European countries, the Western notion of public space
was practically unknown in Greece before independence. The observation
of the plan of Athens, which, in its core, remained essentially the same from
the high Middle Ages up to the 1820s (Figure 8.1), reveals an urban organisation that reminds considerably of the medieval cities of Western Europe.
Among other common features, public space is very restricted in both cases.
In medieval Western European cities, the main reason for the scarcity of
public space was the squeeze of the population within the walls. On the
contrary, Athens, after the departure of the Florentine dukes Acciaiuoli in
1458 and the surrender of the town to the Ottomans, had no need for walls
(Pinon, 2008, p. 152). The town had thus henceforward the possibility of a
free development beyond its old limits. Theoretically, there was no material obstacle to the creation of extended open spaces. There was, however,
another obstacle, that was much stronger.

As is well known, in oriental societies, such as the Ottoman one was,
privacy was and still is a particularly strong notion. In Athens, although the
great majority of the population during Ottoman domination was Christian,
the non-Muslim inhabitants had adopted many of their rulers' habits, including that of restricted public life – although for different reasons[1] – which
became inexistent when it came to women. That led to little interest in the

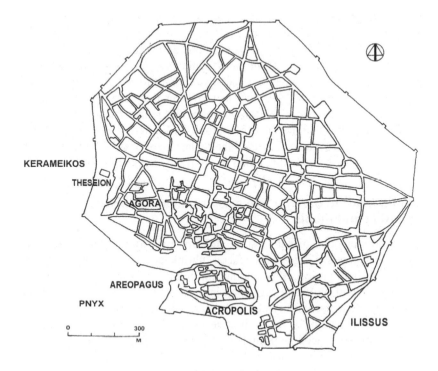

Figure 8.1 The town of Athens at the moment it became capital of Greece in 1834, with the medieval street network surrounded by the eighteenth-century walls

Drawn by the author, according to several plans of that time, with the addition of location names

arrangement of urban space, which was limited to markets, surrounded by the local governor's residence, churches, mosques, and finally baths, the principal areas of social contact. In the Ottoman towns, space was defined and delineated more by the different uses – daily market, weekly market, and so forth – than by the buildings themselves (Bastea, 2000, p. 98). The similarity of that lifestyle with that of the Byzantine period facilitated the adoption of those social models. The Christianization of the Greeks had given them a totally different perception of space than that of their pagan ancestors. Ancient Greeks, at least men, spent almost all their day outdoors and, the most important, even religious ceremonies took place out of the temples. On the contrary, the Christian religion, with ceremonies taking place inside dark and suggestive rooms, gave an introvert character to their lives. That character survived, through Ottoman domination, up to the day of independence (Fatsea, 2000, pp. 89–90, 92).

Therefore, the revival of the values of classical antiquity – including its perception of space – that swept Europe since the Renaissance didn't even touch most of the Greek territory, apart from regions ruled by the Venetians, almost exclusively islands. The ostentatious and theatrical arrangement of squares and gardens, with statues and fountains, typical of the Renaissance and the Baroque, was something unknown to the part of Greece that formed the first independent Greek state. The provinces that kept in touch with the developments in Western Europe – namely, the Ionian Islands and Crete – didn't form part of that first state. Therefore, the Western image it was desired to give to modern Athens included the replacement of the oriental minimal public space by the imposing urban space of the Greek-Roman heritage.

Public space in the first two master plans of Athens: ambition and utopia

From the viewpoint of public space, the first two master plans have some common features. Despite the general 'shrinkage' of urban space by von Klenze, in both projects this is either formed by large squares surrounded by monumental buildings organised in groups, mainly according to their destination, but also with symbolical criteria, or by a central building form-ing the gravity point of the respective urban space, or even both. In the first case public space is surrounded by monumental constructions, while in the second one public space surrounds official architecture. The groups of buildings of the first case would have common typological and formal fea-tures. Moreover, these complexes are characterised by symmetry between one another, as well as in their distribution within the city plan. Finally, the presence of extended gardens in both projects should be noted.

At the time von Klenze was modifying the plan of Athens, von Quast had a somewhat different vision. Instead of a city plan with several homo-geneously spread squares, he was imagining one main urban space, at the foot of the Acropolis, around which all public buildings would be placed. The model for his vision, as he himself writes, was Saint Marc's Square in Venice, perhaps the most impressive in the world (Quast, 1834, p. 32). As will be demonstrated, this latter view would prove to be the most utopian for the Greek capital.

Public space in the subsequent local city plans: the gradual domination of reality

Perhaps the greatest difference between the initial plans and the finally realised ones is the difference of their urban spaces and their architectural surroundings. However, the same desire to create organised public spaces framed by European-style architecture is apparent even in those various local plans. The earliest and one of the most characteristic expressions of that desire is represented by the Markets of the first two master plans, as well as by the proposition made by the Italian businessman Francesco Feraldi (G.S.A., 14 August 1834).

Feraldi made his remarks on von Klenze's project (G.S.A., 27 October 1834) and deposited his own proposal, before the capital's transfer (Figure 8.2). That market would have nothing to envy from Western European buildings of similar function. The complex would include forty-eight shops and thirty-two apartments in two floors, built 'in the European way', as it is described, and a fountain, surrounded by trees (G.S.A., 14 August 1834). The plans depict a complex – more Renaissance than neo-classical – surrounding a rectangular square, arranged with flowerbeds and water. There would be a ground floor and three more storeys. The shops would be behind an arched colonnade running around the whole ground floor, while arcs were predicted in two of the upper storeys. It is the model of merchant squares encountered in Mediterranean countries, especially Italy and Spain, but also in the old merchant Flemish towns. These squares are almost always the central ones and the heart of commercial and other activities.

Here appears the desire to create a space that will constitute a bourgeois representation centre. However, it is doubtful whether the Athenian upper class of these early years could claim that denomination, although they tried to follow the lifestyle of the Western European bourgeoisie. That intention ignores not only the Athenian social structure, but even the way commerce was exercised in that Balkan city and reflects a different way of life, that of the bourgeoisie of a Western European metropolis.

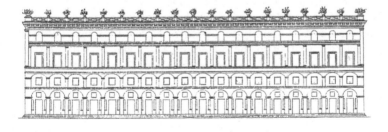

Figure 8.2 The proposal of Francesco Feraldi for a market in Athens, façade
General State Archives, Ottonian Record, Ministry of the Interior, file 78

A note on Feraldi's plans, commenting in a negative way on the changes imposed by the government is very illuminating on the reflexion of the latter's ideology on the buildings' form. The note observes that the project's commercial spirit was overlooked. There was no longer the demand for a market, nor a fountain, nor shops, and the complex was transferred to the town's periphery, where nothing could give an impulse to commerce. The note concludes that the project was transformed into a case of luxury instead of public facilities of 'indispensable importance', equally advantageous to the state, the city of Athens, and the contractor (G.S.A., 12 November 1834). Thus, even a clearly utilitarian building was treated as an element of decoration, just a part of the desired European-style scenery. A similar fate awaited many other projects trying to make Greece enter the European family.

In the Royal Palace, which followed immediately, Lange's project expresses the same intention to create urban scenery. Repeating the spirit of the two master plans, the architect placed on both sides of the Royal Palace Square two two-storey Ministry buildings presenting similarities with the royal residence (Kokkou, 1983, pp. 136–137). The same connection between the Royal Palace and the Ministries was also predicted by the finally chosen project by von Gärtner, which was realised only as far as the Royal Palace itself was concerned.

There seemed to be a general intention to connect in space the buildings expressing power – namely, the royal residence and the Ministries – thus creating an imposing complex. Several documents demonstrate that this intention persisted at least during the whole reign of King Otto. In one of them, the Ministry of the Interior asks Kaftantzoglou to make the plans for a building housing several Ministries and proposes their positioning on the plot lying north of the Royal Palace (G.S.A., 21 July 1844). In another document written by a minister (of the Interior?) and addressed to the Ministry of Finance (G.S.A., 5 October 1845), the same plot is considered advantageous because of its vicinity to the Royal Palace. Likewise, the Minister of the Interior, writing to the prefect of Attica and Boeotia, reports the choice of the two blocks lying across the Royal Palace for the purpose of constructing the Ministries (G.S.A., 15 July 1848). The same information is given to the Ministry of the Interior by a citizen reporting that the block across the Royal Palace, between Hermes and Cathedral Street (Mitropoleos), is destined to the public services (G.S.A., 26 May 1851). Finally, the Ministry of Foreign Affairs, writing to the Ministry of the Interior about the location of its offices, which has to be 'one of the most exquisite of the city', proposes a plot lying at the square in front of the Royal Palace (G.S.A., 15 September 1859). However, financial reasons never permitted the realisation of those plans.

The realised projects: cultural ensembles

The most interesting case in the formation of the capital's urban space is that of the Athenian Trilogy, which survived all modifications proposed for von Klenze's plan. Moreover, the desire to have a homogeneous ensemble housing the capital's cultural institutions was expressed even prior to the government's transfer to Athens. A decree of that time orders clearly that the general aspect and disposition of the complex formed by the Library, the Academy, the University, and the Theatre should remain unchanged (G.S.A., 30 September 1834). Additionally, the long process of the first three buildings' construction hasn't affected their general form (Ganz, 1972), a perhaps unique case in the monumental architecture of Athens, especially since those buildings were among the most expensive. The positioning of the Athenian Trilogy according to von Klenze's project, its relationship with the urban fabric, its connection with the across lying Mint Square through an axial street, and the relationship between the buildings themselves were applied with only slight modifications. Thus they formed one of the Greek capital's major urban spaces. Even the Theatre, the fourth of those buildings, had started being built exactly where that project predicted it, on the plot where the Mint was finally constructed.

However, the cultural complex was seen, perhaps more than any other, as pure scenery, without any interest in functional requirements concerning each building's interior, or the whole building itself. It isn't a coincidence that, although the building of the Academy was finished in 1888, the Academy as an institution was only founded in 1926, as mentioned previously, which means that the most expensive building of Athens (*Μέγα Ελληνικόν Βιογραφικόν Λεξικόν Βοβολίνη*, 1960–1962, vol. 1, p. 470)[2] remained useless for thirty-eight years. The difference with other urban ensembles is that in this case we have much more information. Many plans of the Trilogy buildings were prepared, without the destination of each one of them being final. The siting of the Academy south of the University was decided after many discussions, although already in 1850 that area is reserved for the 'Academy of Fine Arts' (G.S.A., 11 February 1850). After the location of that building was defined, that of the other one north of the University (today's National Library) was self-evident – in order to maintain the symmetry of the complex – but its destination wasn't. When Theophil Hansen started preparing the Academy's plans in 1858, King Otto gave him the order to make also the plans for the building on the other side of the University, as a Library or a Museum (Niemann, Feldegg, 1893, p. 29; Biris, 1966–1967, p. 214), without more precision than that. A painting made by the Danish architect in 1859 features his proposition for the Trilogy, presenting the northern one of the three buildings as a Museum, a proposition repeated in a plan of 1862 (Figure 8.3). The plans of this Museum don't differ substantially from Hansen's much later plans, when it had been decided that the building in question would be the National Library, which proves that its destination didn't matter particularly. The decree stipulating that in the square of Otto's University the Academy will be erected at its eastern side and another public building at its western side (Government Gazette, 10 June 1859) gives a clear image of that way of thinking. That ambitious project wasn't destined to be completed prior to the advent of the twentieth century, when classicism, even in Greece, was marching to its sunset.

Towards the end of King Otto's reign, in 1860, an unsigned document proposes an even bigger complex than the Trilogy, including a building combining the Polytechnic with the Museum, behind the University, at the Civil Hospital's place (*Αθηνά*, 4 May 1860). However, it wasn't even attempted to realise that project, because of the immense funds it would need. Finally, apart from the higher cultural institutions, there was a thought of concentrating all the capital's schools in one complex, built gradually

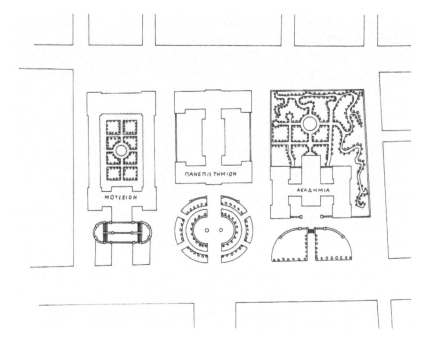

Figure 8.3 The proposal for the Athenian Trilogy dated 15 November 1862, including a Museum instead of the National Library

General State Archives, City Plan, file 13; re-drawn by the author

(G.S.A., 25 April 1836). Von Klenze's project seems to express that thought, with his enormous school building in Saviour Square – today's Concord Square. However, the form of that public space wouldn't encourage the creation of an urban ensemble integrated in the city's life. This is proved by today's Concord Square, which has been innumerable times the object of arrangements trying to give it that character, but always in vain. That was mainly because of the lack of communication between the central open space and the buildings surrounding it, due to the circular road separating them, modified only recently. The same disposition was predicted for the cultural complex of Kleanthes and Schaubert project, around today's Constitution Square. Anyway, there have been no serious efforts to realise the project of Concord Square, which remained just a vision, like most projects concerning that time's Athens. The case of the Athenian Trilogy was destined to remain unique.

The treatment of public space at the end of the century: crystallisation

Under King George I, the arrangement of urban space in Athens and its connection with public architecture has a difference from Athens under King Otto: it has to be planned in an already built environment. Moreover, it is more realistic, in the generally more practical spirit of the new dynasty.

The public space of the Athenian Trilogy occupies mostly the thought of those responsible for the planning of the new city of Athens. Apart from the dominating thought of making the third building a museum, there was also the idea of building there a chemical laboratory, an idea sealed by a decision of the University's council. Ziller made the plans, adapted to the style of the Trilogy's other two buildings (Skarpia-Heupel, 1976, p. 271; Kardamitsi-Adami, Papanikolaou-Christensen, 1997, p. 83). The final decision was taken with a great delay, since it was published in the Government Gazette only in 1886 (Government Gazette, 20 August 1886). The respective article says that the plot was defined as the location of a public building with a decree of 1859.

Another monumental architectural unity of that time, creating an important urban space, was formed by the Polytechnic and the Archaeological Museum. That had already been proposed at the end of King Otto's reign, but much more to the South than the realised complex. The difference with the Athenian Trilogy is that no such combination was predicted by the master plans. The latter didn't even predict the city's expansion to that area. The reason for the realised combination was purely financial, reflecting the changes in mentality. According to the donation contract of the plot for the Archaeological Museum, Helen Tositsa wanted to complete the offer of the Polytechnic's plot 'in order to concentrate in the same part of the city these two institutions necessary to the fine arts' (Kokkou, 1977, p. 231). In that way, another cultural unity was created.

The citizens' choice: the intimate public space outweighs the monumental ones

While under King Otto the interest focused on the arrangement of the urban space related to the Royal Palace and the Athenian Trilogy (the already presented extract of the City Plan is a very rare example of proposition for the arrangement of public space) – namely, the political and the cultural centre – under King George I the interest shifts towards the arrangement of the urban space related to other types of buildings.

An ensemble dating exclusively from that period was in Ludwig Square (Government Gazette, 1 November 1865, 11 August 1872). It was composed by the City Hall, the Municipal Theatre, the 'Grand Hôtel d'Athènes' (from 1900 Central Post Office), the capital's most luxurious hotel, and from 1900 also the premises of the National Bank. These four buildings composed one of the main urban complexes of Athens up to the Municipal Theatre's demolition, in 1940. Interestingly, the previous architectural ensemble wasn't predicted by the city plan, and three of its four buildings were the outcome of private initiative. As mentioned previously, the National Bank is the result of a successful unification of two private residences, giving the impression of having been conceived as one building. The Municipal Theatre was financed by Andreas Syngros, a wealthy citizen who installed shops and his private bank in the building's ground floor, imposing a change of plans for that purpose.

This public space, created with no prior planning, proved to be the most successful as a pole of attraction of the citizens, as that time's literature reveals. It was perhaps the only architectural complex surrounding an urban open space, thus resembling the non-realised ensembles of the master plans in Piraeus Street. Thus it permitted the citizens to feel they were 'in' it, contrary to the others, which had a linear positioning, thus keeping a distance from the people. An additional factor of homogeneity was the fact that three of the four buildings (precisely those built with private funds) were planned by the same architect, Ziller, who was the favourite architect of the Athenian upper class and whose characteristic is the mixture of neo-classical and Renaissance architectural elements. The only one differing in style was the austere Doric City Hall designed by Kalkos, which was the only purely public one from the beginning; and that was hidden by the Municipal Theatre just a few years after its construction, letting the other three dominate the square.[3] Moreover, all four buildings were the major symbols of the increasing power of the upper class in the Greek capital: they symbolised respectively their civic rights, cultural interests, and financial power. Differently from them, the more monumental cultural ensembles like the Athenian Trilogy and the complex of the Polytechnic and the Archaeological Museum were rather symbols of a more restricted intellectual elite. Therefore, the more intimate and less monumental Ludwig Square proved that the 'success' of public space in Athens wasn't in the hands of the designers, but was decided by the inhabitants, with very different criteria from those motivating the capital's official planning. The authorities recognised that evolution, since they attempted to integrate that unpredicted complex into the city plan through an aforementioned decree. According to it, the street connecting Theatre Square with Socrates Street was arranged in a way that 'its axis would pass through the middle of the buildings of the Varvakeion and the Theatre' (Government Gazette, 20 November 1869).

However, apart from the square's scale, form, and functions, its location was also decisive in its role in the city life. Due to the city's slow expansion, the centres of the city life were the new urban creations, but only within the limits of the old town (Ludwig Square and the intersection of Hermes and Aeolus Streets), while other much more imposing public spaces, such as those connected with the Athenian Trilogy and the complex of the Polytechnic and the Archaeological Museum, remained out of the city's most active zone. That situation survived until well in the twentieth century and has contributed to the subsequent decline of those parts of the city. On the other hand, the success of specific urban spaces was accompanied by arbitrary interventions made by their users and independent from the designers' aims, a practise that approached them to the respective spaces of the Ottoman town they were supposed to erase and replace. The Municipal Theatre and the neighbouring Varvakeion Lyceum, with its own homonymous square, focal points of the axis uniting the ancient nucleus with the modern European city, lost most of their public space, predicted by the official plans, in favour of rough and arbitrary – as well as illegal – constructions housing commercial activities and reminding intensely of the respective constructions of the pre-revolutionary town's bazaar (Figure 8.4). Those constructions were de facto cancelling any effort to create a European public space and making an intense contrast between the 'modern' monumental neo-classical buildings and their 'pre-modern' surroundings. The oriental perception of space, rooted for so many centuries in the small Ottoman town, wouldn't willingly recede in front of its European equivalent, but would survive until today (Bastea, 2000, pp. 105, 131–139; Fatsea, 2000, p. 273), as is proved by the images offered by focal points of the old town, such as Monastiraki Square, commercial heart of the ancient nucleus, and starting point of the axis uniting the ancient with the nineteenth-century city, at the intersection of Hermes and Athena Streets (Figure 8.5).

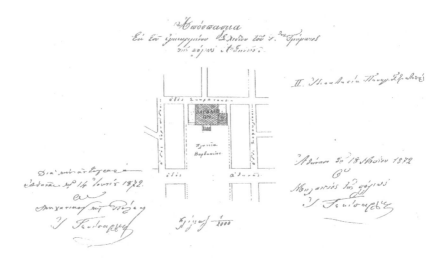

Figure 8.4 The Varvakeion Lyceum in an extract of the city plan dated 18 May 1872. The plot accompanies a document dated 14 June 1872, where the owner of the lot lying to the building's right proposes to sell it to the school as a schoolyard

General State Archives, City Plan, file 19, re-drawn by the author

Figure 8.5 The Tzistaraki mosque, from Monastiraki Square

Photograph by the author

The scale of new Athens: intentions and final development

The public architecture initially planned for Athens after Independence is characterised by a monumentality that seems excessive for a city that was supposed to have 50,000 inhabitants and for the Greek state's financial capacities. In that time's literature a lot is said about those buildings' scale in relation to the equivalent buildings of big centres of classicism, which constituted the models for Athens. The graphic comparison performed here will endeavour to investigate to what extent those opinions were accurate.

The desire for monumentality in the Kleanthes and Schaubert project was already noticed by the most pragmatic (or, according to others, by the most short-sighted). One of them was Carl Mendelssohn-Bartholdy, who writes about the first plan of Athens:

> The two Athenian architects wanted to build the future capital in colossal dimensions, to erect buildings destined to annihilate the greatest monuments of both hemispheres and to construct streets so broad, that the houses along the streets would appear like summer cottages to those standing in the middle. They assured the Regency council that destiny had in store for them to found the most beautiful and most famous city on Earth.
>
> (Mendelssohn Bartholdy, 1876, vol. 2, p. 704)

We must point out that the two architects had conscience of that contradiction, which they justify saying that the public buildings they put on their plan have only an indicative value and that the government would have to adapt their number and size to the capital's population. They add that the project would demand half a century for its application and that it corresponded to future realities (Papageorgiou-Venetas, 1994, p. 36). Additionally, in a meeting on 27 June 1834 about the plan of Athens, they repeated those remarks, adding that the plan didn't contain even half of the buildings that the government would probably need (Papageorgiou-Venetas, 1994, p. 102). Besides, when Kleanthes and Schaubert received the order to make the plan of Athens, it hadn't been clarified to them if it was about the future capital or a simple provincial town and what financial means would be available for its construction (Russack, 1942, pp. 187–188). That choice would certainly influence the plan's form, as is revealed by the record of a session of the Municipal Council. According to this, the government's transfer to Athens would demand a much greater plan than in the case that town wouldn't become the capital (G.S.A., 5 October 1837).

The contrast between the initial architectural plans and the financial capacities of the Greek state is vividly described in a letter sent to von Schinkel by his friend the prince Hermann Ludwig Heinrich von Pückler-Muskau. In that letter, the prince reports to the architect on the luck of the latter's project for the Royal Palace on the Acropolis: 'There is such poverty here, that nobody is capable of putting into function a road towards Mount Pentelicus and that is why the columns of the Royal Palace's entrance will be built with bricks'. The architect's complete ignorance of the new Greek state's financial situation is evident in his letter addressed to the Crown Prince of Bayern Maximilian in 1834. In it, he writes that his project is of a very medium size, adapted to the country's scale (Papageorgiou-Venetas, 1994, p. 131), while in fact it was exactly the opposite. The Royal Palace on the Acropolis was competing with the biggest palaces of Europe. Therefore, the project was very probably rejected not only for reasons of respect towards the antiquities of the Acropolis, as is generally accepted, but also because the state's finances wouldn't permit its realisation. However, even the finally built Royal Palace, after the abandon of von Klenze's plans, too, although much smaller than the previous projects, was enormous for the Greek standards, and according to all opinions expressed upon it, it exceeds the scale of the so praised landscape of Attica.

Another characteristic instance of the gap between projects and real conditions is the contemporary case of the University. For that institution, a project had been submitted by Kaftantzoglou. That project concerned a complex for 2,000 students, which demonstrates how unrealistic it was for a city with no more than 10,000 inhabitants. But Kaftantzoglou didn't admit it, attributing his project's rejection to prejudice (Kaftantzoglou, 1865, p. 15).

However, although the finally applied project by Christian Hansen was of a much more rational scale, About calls the building of the University, along with the Royal Palace, a 'monument', while the same man calls the Arsakeion building 'huge' (About, 1854, pp. 244, 257). Also, the historian Constantine Paparrigopoulos describes the Arsakeion as a 'colossal building' (*Πανδώρα*, 15 September 1851). That reveals that those buildings, despite the abridgments, appeared even to the citizens of big European countries as exceptionally monumental for the Greek standards.

A somewhat later testimony on the subject of monumentality concerns Lange's project for the Saviour's church in Otto Square. That would demand 5,000,000 drachmas for its execution, a colossal sum for that time (Stauffert, 1844). Also, Boulanger's project for the Municipal Theatre could be considered as another case of unrealistic luxury.

There were, certainly, cases where the financial incapacity of Greece was taken into consideration, but the project was made on the basis of a future amelioration of the situation and of the needs that would arise then. Such a case appears at the end of King Otto's reign with the Polytechnic. Thus, in 1859, the executors of Stournaris's will gave Kaftantzoglou the order to make the project, expressing their desire to build in Athens 'a splendid Polytechnic'. They also suggest to the architect to have in view for that purpose 'not only the Nation's present state, but also the progress it is expected to make in the future'. That is why they ask him to submit the more appropriate and splendid project for the Polytechnic, worthy of the wishes of Stournaris and his uncle Michael Tositsas (who also made a donation), and 'of the glory of our ancestral art' (Biris, 1956, p. 204). Also Theophil Hansen thought that Kaftantzoglou's project not only fulfilled the needs indicated by the programme, but also that with its splendour, it would serve as an appropriate home of the Greek arts, which barbarity – it is meant of Ottoman domination – had chased away from Greece (*Αιών*, 17 May 1861). According to an anonymous article (*Αιών*, 2 May 1870), the Polytechnic would be built 'in honour of Athena Ergani,[4] namely, for the reinforcement and development of the common and fine arts in modern Greece'. That was, besides, Kaftantzoglou's purpose, as he expressed it from the post of the institution's director (Kaftantzoglou, 1851, p. 13). But unfortunately, like in many other cases, the demands of the initial conception in scale and luxury exceeded by far the available funds.

Nevertheless, the incapacity of realising the grandiose projects for those buildings didn't discourage their inspirers. Despite the financial difficulties, they continued to insist on the preparation of majestic projects, with the hope that one day it would be possible to fulfil them. The opinion of Stournaris on the Polytechnic is characteristic: the initial sponsor of that institution made clear that he didn't decide to make his donation because he considered the old building insufficient in size or of a badly organised interior, but because he thought that its appearance was too humble compared with its high destination. And the desire he expressed in his will wasn't simply the edification of a new building for the Polytechnic, but of a 'splendid' Polytechnic. According to his will, if the sum didn't suffice to build a splendid building with all the necessary equipment, then the capital should be deposited for a few years in the National Bank, in order to increase with the interest. Tositsas seems to be of the same opinion. He doubled the sum for the edification of a 'splendid Polytechnic', as he too asks in his will (Biris, 1956, p. 225). Those were the wishes Kaftantzoglou's project had to serve, and that is why we mustn't be surprised by his conception's excessive monumentality compared with the limits of the available funds. There was always the hope that other benefactors would appear, who would permit the fulfilment of that majestic project. That hope, at least in the Polytechnic's case, was realised in its greatest part.

However, the viewpoint of postponing the edification of a public build-ing, if it couldn't be magnificent enough, wasn't unanimously accepted. In 1862 the newspaper 'Aιών' wrote on the subject of the Archaeological Museum:

> Giving up ridiculous demands and vain demonstrations, let's not waste our time studying its plans, because, despite all the study we will make, the building of our Museum cannot achieve the fame of the Poikile Stoa, neither be considered as an architectural monument. Today we need four solid and safe walls, some well illuminated and wide rooms, in order to place the relics of our ancestral antiquity, still barbarously dispersed.

That opinion was diametrically opposed to the viewpoint of the members of the Academy of Munich, who rejected all the projects of the interna-tional architectural contest launched in 1858 for the building of the National Archaeological Museum, with the purpose of 'saving' Athens from a build-ing unworthy of it.

The case of that contest demonstrates that the opinions on the monu-mentality of the Athenian public buildings weren't objective, but depended directly on the existence or absence of the necessary donations. The National Archaeological Museum is perhaps the only building for which detailed instructions on its monumentality were given, instructions quite contradic-tory. Thus, according to the decree 'About a project of the Museum of the Antiquities' (Government Gazette, 31 July 1858), a Museum of Antiquities was about to be built 'worthy of their glory'. The decree launched at the same time the architectural contest for the preparation of the plans, which had to follow the general instructions. A little later came the decree under the title 'Instructions on the Construction of an Archaeological Museum' (Government Gazette, 14 August 1858). That decree mentions the need to build 'an appropriate monument' to keep the antiquities. The same decree stipulates that a building destined to include the splendid works of the master artists of the antiquity must not be unworthy of them from the artis-tic viewpoint. However, because of the financial conditions in Greece, its beauty must derive more from the plans' artistic harmony than from the luxurious execution. The decree proceeds inviting architects all over the world, those who desire and consider it an artistic need to build a decorous Museum in Athens, 'that mother of fine arts', to make and hand in their project. The contest had been launched immediately after Dimitrios Ver-nardakis's donation, which wasn't, however, as large as that of the dona-tors of the Polytechnic and the Academy or the National Library. Thus, reactions here were different. The projects of the architects exposed in

Athens were so majestic, that they created the impression that their execution 'demands the riches of Croesus or the personal work of the Athenians at the time of Pericles to build the Parthenon' (Biris, 1966–1967, p. 211). It is characteristic that the 'judgement' (the evaluation of the projects participating in the contest) of the Academy of Munich said about one of those projects (no 14): 'The generally majestic character and its per se agreeable appearance don't characterise an Athenian museum and would suit more an international city, such as Paris, and the building of an industrial exposition' (Kokkou, 1977, p. 221).

Nevertheless, contrary to the initial intentions and efforts for the construction of monumental public buildings, in the final application that monumentality, wherever it existed, was usually expressed in any other way than scale. After the Royal Palace, the scale of official buildings was significantly limited and the only building designed under King Otto, even if executed later, in a real monumental scale, is the Polytechnic. The main, perhaps, marking difference between the public edifices of Athens and those of the great European capitals is that the Athenian buildings, in their final form, are characterised by a diminution of their dimensions and especially their surface. That diminution may partially result from the opinion expressed by many people – namely, that the man-centred scale of the attic landscape demanded a respective adaptation of the scale of the edifices that would be built, like the ancient Greeks had understood long ago. Nevertheless, it must be attributed mainly to the financial limitations and to the lack of public land in the city, which limited the available surface. The Kleanthes and Schaubert project is a characteristic expression of the effort to create a capital in European dimensions. On the contrary, von Klenze's project, especially as applied, expresses the city's adaptation to the landscape's scale, but also to the existing circumstances. The final public buildings of Athens, in case they were financed by benefactors, acquired the sought-after monumentality through their materials and their fine elaboration, with the Academy in the summit. Contrary to these, those who didn't have that luck either were never constructed, or became not only small, but also of poor construction quality.

Testimony of the graphic research

The information given by sources is completed by the graphic comparison of some Athenian buildings with some of their European equivalents. The buildings selected for that comparison aren't random. They have been chosen according to the following criteria: they had to house the same function and date approximately from the same time, in order to permit comparison. The examples have been taken from the cities related to the architects who were the protagonists of the creation of neo-classical Athens. Therefore, they belong to German-speaking Europe: it is Munich (city of the Kings Ludwig and Otto and of all the architects related to them), Berlin (city of von Schinkel and his pupils Kleanthes and Schaubert), and Vienna (where the greatest part of Theophil Hansen's activity took place). Not by coincidence, the finally constructed buildings, which, for practical reasons, constitute the main examples, are precisely those representing the rise of the Athenian upper class and its desire to imitate the bourgeoisie of the countries that were the models for Greece (again, for the same reasons, mainly the German-speaking countries).

The first example is the City Hall of Athens, compared with those of Paris, Berlin, Munich, and Vienna (Figure 8.6). Paris was added next to the German-speaking cities, because its City Hall was constructed at the same time and is one of the French capital's very few public buildings permitting a comparison with the selected Athenian examples, giving interesting results. Thus, it becomes evident that the Athenian building is a miniature in comparison with its northern equivalents.

The next example is the Parliament of Athens (today's National Historical Museum), which is compared with those of Vienna and Berlin, but also with the respective buildings of the Kleanthes and Schaubert project and the von Klenze project (Figure 8.7). Also here the Athenian building is a miniature in comparison with its northern equivalents. Moreover, the comparison with the Parliament of the Kleanthes and Schaubert project and the Senate of the von Klenze project demonstrates that, although the buildings of the general city plans of Athens were much bigger than the finally realised one, the

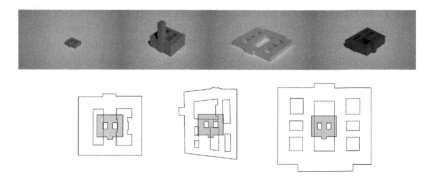

Figure 8.6 Comparison of the City Hall of Athens with those of Berlin, Munich, and
          Vienna in outline and volume

Drawn by Maria Raptopoulou, Aineias Tsouklas, and Despoina Xepapadaki, with supervision
by the author

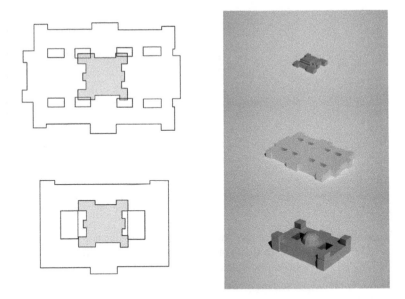

Figure 8.7 Comparison of the Parliament of Athens with those of Vienna and Berlin in outline and volume

Drawn by Maria Raptopoulou, Aineias Tsouklas, and Despoina Xepapadaki, with supervision by the author

aforementioned conviction that they were of a size similar to the examples of the great European metropolises seems exaggerated. In fact, they were of an intermediate size.

The next example depicts a similar comparison of the Municipal Theatre of Athens and the Royal Theatre of Athens with the Opera of Paris, the Opera of Vienna, the Burgtheater of Vienna, the Opera of Munich, and the Opera of Berlin, but also with the theatre of the von Klenze project (Figure 8.8). Paris has again been added next to the German-speaking cities, because its Opera dates from the same time and is the most emblematic building of such use in the whole nineteenth-century Europe, serving as model for numerous theatres. Also in this case, the same remarks on scale can be expressed in relation to the North European examples and to the von Klenze project. The Bavarian architect's theatre is again somewhere between the examples of the great European metropolises and the finally realised buildings in Athens.

An instance of a different nature has been introduced because of the particular interest of its conclusions (Figure 8.9). It is a comparison of

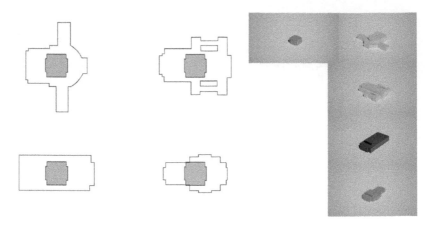

Figure 8.8 Comparison of the Municipal Theatre of Athens with the Burgtheater of Vienna, the Opera of Vienna, the Opera of Munich, and the Opera of Berlin in outline and volume

Drawn by Maria Raptopoulou, Aineias Tsouklas, and Despoina Xepapadaki, with supervision by the author

Figure 8.9 Comparison of the outlines of the schools projected and realised in Athens in the course of the nineteenth century: School complex of the von Klenze project, First and Second Primary School for Boys, initial building of the Arsakeion School for Girls, Papadopoulos Lyceum, Varvakeion Lyceum, Commercial School, Marasleion School, new wing of the Arsakeion School for Girls

Drawn by the author

the outlines of the schools designed and realised in Athens in the nineteenth century: school complex of the von Klenze project, First and Second Primary Schools for Boys, initial building of the Arsakeion, Hellenic School, Varvakeion Lyceum, Commercial School, Marasleion School, and the new wing of the Arsakeion. The comparison demonstrates that schools have initially followed the same course, from large scale projects to very modest realisations, but in the long term the evolution was towards an always bigger scale. That exception is a very eloquent demonstration of the particular importance of educational buildings, which managed to overcome the general lack of the means to realise the grandiose projects for Athens.

The last example is a comparison between the 'Trilogy' of cultural edifices of the Kleanthes and Schaubert project, the 'Tetralogy' of the von Klenze project and the 'Tetralogy' of Vienna (Parliament, City Hall, University and Burgtheater; Figure 8.10). The final Athenian complex

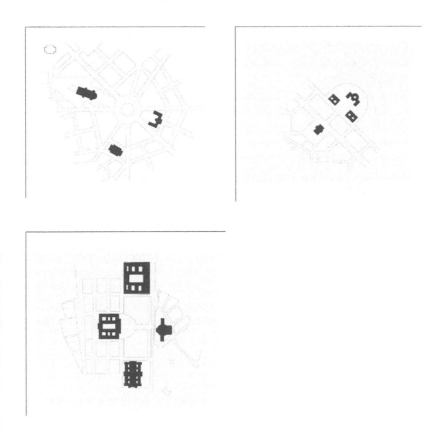

Figure 8.10 The 'Trilogy' of the Kleanthes and Schaubert project, the 'Tetralogy' of the von Klenze project, and the 'Tetralogy' of Vienna

Drawn by Maria Raptopoulou, Aineias Tsouklas, and Despoina Xepapadaki, with supervision by the author

started being formed in 1859, when the construction of the Academy, the second of the three buildings, started. It was just at the time the Ringstrasse's plan in Vienna was ratified. The Ringstrasse presents many similarities with the general form of the Boulevard, in the way it surrounds the old city, opposing to it several majestic palaces facing it – the very different scale taken, of course, into consideration. Again, the difference in scale between the finally realised Athenian Trilogy and the Viennese complex is impressive. Moreover, the non-realised projects are again of a scale between the two, and not really as unrealistically majestic as was sustained by contemporary critiques. The previous comparison is particularly interesting, for one of the buildings of the Viennese Tetralogy (the Parliament) and two of the buildings of the Athenian Trilogy (the Academy and the National Library) were designed by Theophil Hansen. The comparison between them demonstrates clearly the fundamental difference between Athens and its models, giving to the Greek capital its unique character.

Thus, the official buildings predicted in the first master plans of Athens were much larger than those finally built, but the claim that they were as large as those of big European metropolises proves to be exaggerated. It is, nevertheless, noteworthy that the diminution of dimensions didn't necessarily lead to a respective abstraction of the constructive and decorative details. Thus, the Athenian buildings – especially the Academy – became often 'miniatures' of their European prototypes. This constitutes perhaps the main reason of their charm and the aesthetic superiority of some of them over the imposing North European buildings. The latter, with their volume, diverge from the equilibrium that characterised classical art, from which they were supposed to be inspired. The apparently more humble Greek examples, often out of necessity, prove to be more faithful to the principles that the whole European classicism was trying to follow. The final result reflects perfectly the financial, but also the ideological realities of nineteenth-century Greece, thus becoming an interesting and original subject of research.

Conclusions

The facts exposed by the present book reveal a great divergence between intentions and actual possibilities in the creation of nineteenth-century Athens. The almost complete inexistence of public land in the capital of the newly founded Greek state, along with the lack of funds and organisation, overturned entirely all projects, which were based on totally idealistic foundations, ignoring the country's financial and social realities. Additionally, pre-modern characteristics of the time of Ottoman domination, incompatible with Western standards of urban planning and architecture, survived and interfered with these efforts. On the other hand, the disproportionate ideological burden of some buildings affected excessively the capital's normal development. Consequently, all projects aiming at the rational and organised creation of a monumental new capital of European standards that would worthily supplant the humble Ottoman town, expressed by the original city plans, had to be abandoned and replaced by solutions of necessity, according to the circumstances of the given moment. The new state had undertaken tasks totally disproportionate to its real capacities, and its capital city was expected to reflect aspirations to a role that was in complete contrast to its real potential. The ideological burden of Athens was based entirely on circumstances of thousands of years ago and bore no relation to nineteenth-century realities. It is impressive how much all neo-classicists insisted on overlooking what was obvious and tried obstinately to transform nineteenth-century Athens into the object of their visions. Unfortunately, the most sincere and enthusiastic efforts of Greek and foreign lovers of ancient Greece would never be able to overcome such prosaic realities. As a consequence, although all the architects, archaeologists, scholars, and representatives of the authorities who participated in one way or another in the creation of post-revolutionary Athens wanted to apply in their propositions, all the contemporary European ideas on architecture and urbanism, the newly founded capital had to take a significantly more trivial form, very different than the idealistic image especially foreigners had of what they saw as a modern revival of the most glorious city of antiquity.

Notes

1 The non-Muslims had to avoid the ostentation of any signs of opulence, in order to protect their fortunes from their rulers' cupidity.
2 Simon Sinas paid for the building of the Academy the sum of 3.360.000 drachmas.
3 The City Hall was completed in 1872, while the Municipal Theatre was finished in 1888.
4 Of labour.

Bibliography

About, E. (1854). *La Grèce contemporaine*. Paris: Hachette.
Bastea, E. (2000). *The Creation of Modern Athens: Planning the Myth*. Cambridge: Cambridge University Press.
Biris, K. (1956). *Η ιστορία του Εθνικού Μετσοβίου Πολυτεχνείου*. Athens. Published by the author.
Biris, K. (1966–1967). *Αι Αθήναι*. Athens. Published by the author.
Fatsea, I. (2000). *Monumentality and its shadows: A quest for modern Greek architectural discourse in nineteenth-century Athens (1834–1862)*. PhD. MIT.

134 *Creation of the new city*

Ganz, J. (1972). Theophil Hansen 'hellenische' Bauten in Athen und Wien. *Österreichische Zeitschrift für Kunst und Denkmalpflege*, 26, pp. 67–81.

General State Archives (G.S.A.), City Plan, file 1, 5 October 1837, 21 July 1844; file 2, 5 October 1845; file 4, 15 July 1848; file 5, 26 May 1851; file 7, 11 February 1850.

G.S.A., Ottonian Record, Ministry of Education, L, file 57, 25 April 1836.

G.S.A., Ottonian Record, Ministry of the Interior, file 78, 14 August 1834, 27 October 1834, 12 November 1834; file 214, 15 September 1859; file 219, article 16, 30 September 1834.

Government Gazette 30, 31 July 1858; 34, 14 August 1858; 24, 10 June 1859; 47, 20 November 1869; 50, 1 November 1865; 35, 11 August 1872; 225, A, 20 August 1886.

Kaftantzoglou, L. (1851). *Λόγος εκφωνηθείς κατά την επέτειον τελετήν του Βασιλικού Πολυτεχνείου (τη 7 Οκτωβρίου 1851) επί της κατά το έβδομον καλλιτεχνικόν έτος εκθέσεως των διαγωνισμών*. Athens. Published by the author.

Kaftantzoglou, L. (1865). *Καλλιτεχνική εξέτασις των κατά την αποπεράτωσιν και ανακαίνισιν του Εθνικού Πανεπιστημίου έργων του πρώην πρυτάνεως Κωνσταντίνου Φρεαρίτου*. Athens. Published by the author.

Kardamitsi-Adami, M., Papanikolaou-Christensen, A. (1997). *Ernst Ziller, Αναμνήσεις (Περικοπαί-Σημειώματα υπό κ.Ι.Τσίλλερ-Δήμα)*. Athens: Libro.

Kokkou, A. (1977). *Η μέριμνα για τις αρχαιότητες στην Ελλάδα και τα πρώτα μουσεία*. Athens: Ερμής.

Kokkou, A. (1983). *Σχέδια αθηναϊκών κτιρίων. Προτάσεις που δεν εφαρμόστηκαν*. In: *Νεοκλασική πόλη και αρχιτεκτονική*. Edited by the Workshop of History of Architecture of the Department of Architecture of the Aristotle University of Thessaloniki, Greece: Aristotle University of Thessaloniki, pp. 135–144.

Mendelssohn Bartholdy, K. (1876). *Ιστορία της Ελλάδος*. Athens. Published by the author.

Niemann, G., Feldegg, F. von (1893). *Theophilos Hansen und seine Werke*. Wien: A. Schroll & Co.

Papageorgiou-Venetas, A. (1994). *Hauptstadt – Athen: ein Stadtgedanke des Klassizismus*. München: Deutscher Kunstverlag.

Pinon, P. (2008). The Ottoman Cities of the Balkans. In: S. Jayyusi, R. Holod, A. Petrucciolli, A. Raymond, eds., *The City in the Islamic World*. Leiden: Brill, pp. 143–158.

Quast, A. F. von (1834). *Mittheilungen über Alt und Neu Athen*. Berlin: George Gropius.

Russack, H. H. (1942). *Deutsche Bauen in Athen*. Berlin: Wilhelm Limpert Verlag.

Skarpia-Heupel, X. (1976). *Η μορφολογία του γερμανικού κλασικισμού (1789–1848) και η δημιουργική αφομοίωσή του από την ελληνική αρχιτεκτονική (1833–1897)*. PhD. Aristotle University of Thessaloniki.

Stauffert, F. (1844). Die Anlage von Athen und der jetzige Zustand der Baukunst in Griechenland. *Allgemeine Bauzeitung, Ephemeriden*, 1, pp. 2–8, 2, pp. 17–25.

Αθηνά (4 May 1860).

Αιών (17 May 1861, 2 May 1870).

Πανδώρα (15 September 1851).

Index

Milton Keynes UK
Ingram Content Group UK Ltd.
UKHW020322111024
449327UK00041B/2568

9 780367 670504